LIVING
THE YOGA LIFE

LIVING THE YOGA LIFE

PERSPECTIVES ON YOGA

SWAMI NIRMALANANDA GIRI
(ABBOT GEORGE BURKE)

LIGHT of the SPIRIT
PRESS
CEDAR CREST, NEW MEXICO

Published by
Light of the Spirit Press
lightofthespiritpress.com

Light of the Spirit Monastery
P. O. Box 1370
Cedar Crest, New Mexico 87008
www.OCOY.org

ISBN-13: 978-1-955046-07-7

Library of Congress Control Number: 2021943719

Bisac categories:
OCC010000 BODY, MIND & SPIRIT / Mindfulness & Meditation
YAN024090 YOUNG ADULT NONFICTION / Health & Daily Living
/ Mindfulness & Meditation

First edition July 2021

The photo on the cover was taken in the "Badlands" of the Anza-Borrego
desert in Southern California.

05142024

CONTENTS

By persevering effort and mastery, the totally
purified yogi, perfected through many births,
reaches the Supreme Goal.
The yogi is superior to ascetics, and considered
superior to jnanis and superior to those
engaged in Vedic rituals.
Therefore be a yogi.

(Bhagavad Gita 6:45-46)

INTRODUCTION

This is a compilation of random thoughts I put down quite some time ago that were completely without any order. Unlike *Satsang With the Abbot*, it is now somewhat arranged according to subjects. I hope it will be useful to those who read it.

This is not a book about the technique of yoga, but about the Yoga Life which makes the successful practice of yoga possible. Yoga is not just a practice or a philosophy; it is an entire way of life. And by yoga I mean the quest for liberation of the spirit, for Yoga is an eternal science intended to reveal and manifest the Eternal.

Consider a tree. The bark is not the tree; the leaves are not the tree; the branches are not the tree; nor are the roots the tree. But taken all together, that is a tree. If a single one of these elements is missing, then the tree will die. It is the same with yoga: nothing can be missing.

In various places mention is made of Soham Yoga. I recommend that you consult my books, *Soham Yoga: The Yoga of the Self* and *Light of Soham*.

Swami Nirmalananda Giri
(Abbot George Burke) .

CLIMBING THE LADDER
OF CONSCIOUSNESS

As the human being moves up the ladder of evolution, the center of his consciousness moves into successively higher bodies. Those of the lowest evolutionary status are aware only of their physical entity and live as though that alone were real. Simple survival and physical maintenance are their sole drives. It is these people who demand that their religion promise them earthly benefits, an opulent earth-type afterlife, and in some religions: the eventual resurrection of the body and its possession by them eternally.

In the next step of evolution the individual begins to identify intensely with his feelings, especially his emotions, and gauges all things by his emotional reaction to them. This person demands that his religion be a devotional one of inspiration and "love" that will reunite him with his "loved ones" in "the sweet by and by" where he will be everlastingly "happy."

On the next rung of the evolutionary ladder, the human being becomes identified with and absorbed in the senses, reaching out for more and novel sensory experiences. He demands that his religion be one of beautiful and impressive worship, and one which will take him to heaven where he will hear beautiful music, seek beautiful scenes, and eat of the fruits of paradise.

Stepping up to the next rung, the human being discovers the wonder of his intellect. Therefore he will demand of his religion (if he does not think he is "beyond religion" by virtue of his intellectual brilliance) that it explain everything to him through an elaborate and sophisticated system of philosophy and theology and make all mysteries known so that there is nothing he does not "understand." He will like it even better

1

if it imparts to him the knowledge of "mysteries" that those outside the religion do not understand, thus making him superior to them. Although physical, emotional, and sensory conditions may still greatly affect him, he has grown somewhat tired of them. But now he has this new toy, the whole new dimension of the intelligent mind, the ability to bring into his scope of perception ideas of things he never dreamed of in previous lives. And so he becomes like a bird that has been caged so long he only wants to fly and fly and fly in the realms of the intellect. Just as a person who has almost died of thirst tends to drink too much, or someone who has been starving tends to eat too much, in the same way the intellectual man ends up with mental indigestion.

Finally spiritual intuition arises in him, and it dawns on him that playing with all those ideas has not really produced any change or gotten him anywhere. He realizes that he can think and think about water, discuss water, learn its chemical formula and read books on water, but all that does not give him a single drop of the real thing.

So in time he comes to realize that abstractions are not enough. But most of the great teachers in the world have spoken in abstractions—at least publicly or through scriptures—on a very high and exclusively intellectual level.

Although the writings of great masters of wisdom might speak of what attainments are possible through the evolution of the human consciousness and urge people to move on higher to these states, the "how" has almost always in time been lost because people have preferred to hear the ideals rather than learn the process for their actualization. We keep a description of the goal, but we lose the map, so we cannot find the goal.

It is very inspiring to read such things as how the goal of the spirit is to be like the radiant drop of dew which drops into and merges in the infinite Ocean of Being. But how do we get to that Ocean of Being? It is thrilling to hear that he who knows the Immortal Being becomes himself immortal. But how will we accomplish that immortalizing knowing?

There must come a time when we leave the advertising aside and get busy obtaining the product.

And that is when Yoga begins, for Paramhansa Yogananda often said: "Yoga is the beginning of the end."

Sanatana Dharma, Sanatana Yoga

When you get into an auto, turn on the ignition, press the accelerator, and guide the forward-moving vehicle by means of the steering-wheel, you are acting on a number of premises. The same is true of yoga. Yoga is not just a mechanical practice; it presupposes the vast body of metaphysical principles known as Sanatana Dharma, the Eternal Dharma, that is the basis of all true religion. Intelligent practice of yoga is not possible without knowing and adhering to those principles.

The system of practical methodology we call yoga was originated and perfected in India by great sages, every one of which was an adherent of the Eternal Dharma, which in turn was incalculably enriched by the subsequent teaching of the master yogis who were enlightened through the yoga system. Both yoga and the philosophy on which it is based—or rather, which stimulated the discovery and development of yoga—are truth in the purest form, exactly like mathematics. Therefore it is not amiss to speak of Sanatana Dharma and Sanatana Yoga—Eternal Dharma (Philosophy) and Eternal Yoga.

Sanatana Dharma is the presentation of the principles of existence itself—of the ultimate Facts of Life and nothing more, cultural or religious. Euclid was Greek, but Euclidian Geometry has no tint of Greek culture, philosophy, or religion. In the same way Sanatana Dharma should never be equated with what is known as modern "Hinduism," the religion that is rooted in Sanatana Dharma but has developed into an elaborate system of beliefs and practices that are in many cases purely cultural and subjective—so much so that it can be said to conceal Sanatana Dharma more than reveal it. People can spend an entire lifetime as "Hindus" and never know Sanatana Dharma except in the most obscure and ineffectual manner.

What, then is Sanatana Dharma? Shankara put it this way: "I shall tell you in half a sloka what has been written in millions of books: Brahman is real. The world is illusory. The jiva is nothing other than Brahman." Obviously these root facts imply a world of principles which a human being needs to know in order to realize the potential that is a living seed within every sentient being. Yoga–philosophy and practice–is that world. Sanatana Dharma and Sanatana Yoga are really the same thing. That which goes outside them is an obscuration not a clarification, a hindrance rather than a help.

Yoga and Dharma are realities, not speculations or conclusions. They are discoveries of universal, unalterable principles that are verifiable by each individual. Through the ages each yogi has found for himself that they are true. They are not revelations given by an arbitrary deity or a representative of such a deity. They require no faith or bowing of the head to any authority. They are verifiable facts, requiring nothing more than correct practice coupled with intelligent perception. No matter how many yogis there may be, Yoga and Dharma are always purely individual–in fact nothing can spoil Yoga and Dharma more than "groupism" or "movements." The yogi is always an individual, always a whole, never a part. And so is a Sanatana Dharmi yogi

Dharma and Yoga are the supreme sciences, independent of all else. It is essential that our philosophy and practice be purely an expression of eternal verities. Authentic Dharma and Yoga have nothing to do with "East" or "West" and should have no connotation of them. Again, they are like Euclidian Geometry. The seers that discovered them were from what we call "the East," but they are universal and neither Eastern nor Western.

THE ATMAN/SELF

The fundamental reality of each one of us is our own eternal Self. From that Self all things have come. The world is the thought of God, held in the mind of God. And our personal world is the same, held in both the mind of God and ourselves. The Divine Dreamer is dreaming of universes and creation cycles without number, and we in him are dreaming our countless lives as we move upward to conscious union with and within him. This being so, every one of our incarnations originates within us and is an expression of our will, just as we create worlds every night in dream and populate them with our mental projections. Yoga is the means of awakening from our dream state and living truly and consciously within God as gods.

All kinds of ways have been sought to put an end to immersion in the ocean of samsara. But there is only one true way: awakening into the Self. For at the core of our Self is God, the Self of our Self, since we are a part of God and draw our eternal existence from God. That is why the German mystic Angelus Silesius said that if he ceased to exist, God would also cease to exist. We are inseparable from God, for there is only ONE. Therefore our meditation should be directed inwardly to the jivatman, within which we shall realize the Paramatman. First is Self-realization, and then God-realization follows automatically.

As the boat is in the water but is not the water, so the Atman-Self is not part of samsara, but is only in samsara temporarily. Just as the boat originates outside the water and can be taken from the water, in the same way the Atman seems to come from Brahman into samsara and eventually return to Brahman, since Brahman is the essence of its being. But only when the eternal nature of the Self is revealed does that become evident and the Self becomes freed from the experience of samsara.

The Self is untouched by actions or laws. But the not-self is touched by nothing else. So we must decide whether we will live in the samsara of the not-self or in the freedom of the Self. If we decide for freedom then we will have to purify the not-self and transmute our consciousness into that of the Self alone.

The Self is not a material entity, nor is it really ever a part of relative existence, though it experiences the illusion of relative existence. The Self is the Experiencer, the Witness, and never is an object of observation, for it is the Observer. The Self is consciousness for whom all else is an object while it is the eternal subject.

The entire world-experience is experience of the most superficial aspect of a person, the outer appearance. Our life in this world is only a life of externals, even our mental states being external to our witnessing Self. Therefore our evaluation of this life should be according to its minimal significance, and we must seek the reality which it hides: the Self and the Supreme Self.

The world "around" us is really within us. That is, our sense experiences are nothing more than neurological interpretations conveyed to and interpreted by our brains. Certainly, something is "out there" but that which we consider external reality is really only our internal imaging of it. The cosmos is a dream of Ishwara, of God, and we, our Selfs, are dreaming inside that dream. Therefore, to know the world as it is we must know the Self.

The Self never acts and never determines anything. Therefore positive and negative exist only in relative existence, never in the spirit which transcends relativity. We should never think that evil acts make us evil or that good acts make us good. Our true nature, the Spirit-Self, cannot be affected in any way by action because the Self exists beyond the realm of action and reaction.

The Atman-Self cannot be changed in any manner whatsoever. Therefore the Gita says: "This Self by weapons is cut not; this Self by fire is burnt not; this Self by water is wet not; and this Self is by wind dried not. This Self cannot be cut, burnt, wetted, nor dried. This primeval Self is eternal, all-pervading, and immovable. Unmanifest, unthinkable, this Self is called unchangeable" (2:23-25).

Our Self never changes, but it seems to undergo change because the mind projects the illusory images of change on the screen of our consciousness and we mistakenly identify with them. It is all a dream in which we have vivid experiences, but when we awaken into the consciousness of our Self we will know they were only dreams, that from the highest perspective nothing at all has really happened. It is all the play of maya, of illusion/delusion.

Our Spirit-Self is trapped in the cage of the gross and subtle bodies and identifies with them and believes that whatever happens to the cage happens to them. This is why we think we act and think that we reap the consequences of actions. "Do not say: 'God gave us this delusion.' You dream you are the doer, you dream that action is done, you dream that action bears fruit. It is your ignorance, it is the world's delusion that gives you these dreams" (Bhagavad Gita 5:14; Prabhavananda translation).

The wise fix their attention and purpose on the Self that is their true essence, their true heart. They do not mistake the container for the contents, and they purify and transmute through yoga the container in order to reveal and manifest the contents. The outer is little, but the inner is great.

The truly awakened realize the need to live in Spirit-Self awareness and the necessity of ordering their life according to what hinders and what reveals that awareness. This is much higher than mere good and bad, virtuous and evil, as viewed by the wandering, ever-changing mind. The essence of all things, the reality behind mere appearance, is the focus of their mind and life. They penetrate into immortality and leave death behind.

The wealth of the yogi is the knowledge/possession of his own Self, the God within him. This is the secret treasure he has been carrying within from the moment he entered into relativity and began evolving in the universe, climbing the ladder of evolution, striving upward to possess Divine Consciousness.

The Self is stable, the material is ever-changing, so those who are intent on the Self are firm in mind, and those who are immersed in externals are unstable and unreliable.

My friend, Saguna Hejmadi, a cousin of Swami ("Papa") Ramdas of Anandashram, was once at the Anandamayi Ashram in New Delhi (Kalkaji) when Ma Anandamayi was there. Somehow an ignoramus standing nearby learned that she did a great deal of meditation. "Why are you wasting your time with all that?" the man asked. "Women cannot attain liberation; only men can attain liberation." Mistakenly she began arguing with the man, who bolstered his assertions with many scriptural quotes. In the midst of this altercation, Anandamayi Ma came walking through the room. "MA!" called out Saguna, "Is it true that women cannot attain liberation?"

Still walking on, Ma nodded and answered: "That is true. Women cannot attain liberation."

Saguna stood there completely thunderstruck as the man chuckled and chortled at his "triumph."

After standing and stewing for nearly half an hour, Saguna saw Ma returning. Ma came right up to her, said: "And men do not attain liberation either!" and walked on and out of the room.

Then Saguna understand: only those who transcend body identity and "live in the spirit" can attain liberation.

Since the Self is in all things, nothing can be disregarded, including other people. We must not just value the Self in us, we must extend that respect to the Self in others. All around us we see people sunk in ignorance and many in moral degradation. Just as a person can see a leper and shudder and turn away from the sight, in the same way we may inwardly shudder and turn away from those darkened and deformed by ignorance and evil, but what we are seeing is just a veneer. Beneath that appearance is a pure, perfect and divine Self, just as much as in Krishna, Buddha, or Jesus. When we see such persons we must send them vibrations of kindness and good will, inwardly acknowledging their true value. Sometimes kind words and deeds are needed, also, but the inner blessing is the most important. Let me give you an example.

Luther McKinney, a friend of mine, came from the standard background of unawareness that grips the world. But in time he became a yogi, intensely dedicated to the search for God-realization. His little meditation room (really a kind of storage area accessed through a tiny door you had to crawl through) was one of the holiest places I have ever entered, even though it was in the midst of Harlem, surrounded by all kinds of social and spiritual ills.

Luther was very close to Dr. Lewis, Yogananda's first American disciple. Just a few years after becoming a yogi, Dr. Lewis told him, "Luther,

you have purified your heart, and from now on you will purify others."
Luther doubted Doctorji's words, but they were nonetheless proven true.

Luther was a guard in the New York City subway, complete with a gun, but Luther was an angel of peace. Once two drunk women, holding on to each other, staggered over to him and began to speak with him in the rambling manner of drunks. Luther conversed with them for some minutes, and then they shambled on. This was repeated several times. Then one day only one of the women came shuffling up alone and demanded: "What did you do to my friend?" When Luther asked her to explain, she told him: "As long as I have known her, Evelyn has been an alcoholic. But now she is completely cured and never touches a drop. And she tells everyone that you cured her!"

Luther was as amazed as she was, but Dr. Lewis, who had by that time left his body, would not have been. And knowing Luther, neither was I when I learned about it. Through Luther God's Light had healed that soul. And we should do our best to become and do the same.

The Self is that which draws us upward into our Source, the Supreme Self. Behind the seeming life of the body is the real life that is the Spirit-Self. One is the machine and the other is the worker of the machine. We have to get them both in perspective. Then alone will we have real peace.

BHAKTI AND JNANA

True bhakti–devotion–in its ultimate nature is conscious, deliberate union with the Self; and therefore with God the Supreme Self.

Bhakti has one purpose: union with God in which all semblance of separation between God and the individual spirit is dispelled and a unity of being and identity is attained. Not that the individual becomes the Absolute, but that total union of the individual with the Absolute is realized in the yogi's consciousness.

What is true bhakti? It is like the oil in a lamp without which there would be no light. It is the inner power that moves the yogi forward, intent on his goal. Unfortunately bhakti is usually considered to be emotion directed to God, especially as love. But bhakti means dedication to the search for God. It is Ishwarapranidhana, the offering of the life to God, which Patanjali says is the way to superconsciousness (Yoga Sutras 2:45).

Shankara simplified and clarified it greatly when he said that bhakti is seeking God and jnana is finding God.

Bhakti and jnana purify the heart. But bhakti is not emotion, and jnana is not intellectuality. Instead, they are dispositions of mind and heart, a psychological frame of reference within which the entire life is lived. Sri Ramakrishna revealed their ultimate essence. He said that bhakti was the attitude (bhava): "God is the Master and I am His servant." Jnana, he said, was the attitude: "God alone is real; all else is unreal."

What begins as an attitude, a kind of intuitive conviction, ripens into direct realization. The person no longer "feels" or "thinks" those principles, but knows them and embodies them.

True jnana in its essence is the atmic experience which authentic yoga produces directly. This is vijnana, the transcendental knowing beyond intellectual knowing. Unfortunately in India and elsewhere there is constant propaganda about how bhakti is the easy path and the best "for this Kali Yuga" and similar ideas. But anyone who reads the Gita with intelligence can see that genuine bhakti and jnana are interdependent, each fostering the other. Pious dummies do not find God. Sri Ramakrishna used to say: "Be a devotee, but why a fool?"

True bhakti is always centered in intelligence, in the buddhi. The Gita tells us: "Among the virtuous, four kinds seek me: the distressed, the seekers of knowledge, the seekers of wealth and the wise. Of them, the wise man, ever united, devoted to the One, is pre-eminent. Exceedingly dear am I to the man of wisdom, and he is dear to me. All these indeed are exalted, but I see the man of wisdom as my very Self. He, with mind steadfast, abides in me, the Supreme Goal" (7:16-18). The true devotee seeks God because he knows it is his nature and purpose to do so, that God alone is his goal.

In the sixth chapter of *Raja Yoga*, Vivekananda wrote about false and harmful pseudo-bhakti: "All over the world there have been dancing and jumping and howling sects, who spread like infection when they begin to sing and dance and preach; they also are a sort of hypnotists. They exercise a singular control for the time being over sensitive persons, alas! often, in the long run, to degenerate whole races. Ay, it is healthier for the individual or the race to remain wicked than be made apparently good by such morbid extraneous control. One's heart sinks to think of the amount of injury done to humanity by such irresponsible yet well-meaning religious fanatics. They little know that the minds which attain to sudden spiritual upheaval under their suggestions, with music and prayers, are simply making themselves passive, morbid, and power-less, and opening themselves to any other suggestion, be it ever so evil. Little do these ignorant, deluded persons dream that whilst they are congratulating themselves upon their miraculous power to transform human hearts, which power they think was poured upon them by some Being above the clouds, they are sowing the seeds of future decay, of crime, of lunacy, and of death. Therefore, beware of everything that takes away your freedom. Know that it is dangerous, and avoid it by all the means in your power."

Vivekananda knew what he was talking about because Bengal, his native land, was gripped by the false bhakti of the "dancing and jumping and howling sects," especially Gaudia Vaishnavism (the Hare Krishna movement in the West), and still is to a great extent.

His fellow countryman, Paramhansa Yogananda, said: "No one country or religion has an exclusive franchise on ignorance. In the West they say: 'O sweet Holy Ghost!' and in India they say: 'Hare Krishna!'"

I remember walking down a street in Brindaban one evening with an authentic Vaishnava devotee. Suddenly around the corner there careened what appeared like a bunch of drunks expelled from a bar, but they carried banners and holy imagery. Their singing underscored the impression of drunkenness as they straggled along. But then their leader caught sight of me. Westerners mean money to such people and maybe even sponsoring of a world tour. So the leader called them to a halt, and as they started running into one another, he began shouting: "Sing louder! Sing louder! Dance! Dance!" There is no way I can describe the chaos that followed, but my friend was delighted and began laughing so hard he nearly fell over. When the leader saw that, he began shouting again for louder singing and faster dancing. Apparently he thought it was working. Anyhow, my friend said: "Swamiji, let's get out of here before

I fall down and they claim to convert me!" So we sped away with them watching us, wondering what had gone wrong.

Real, God-centered bhakti moves upward in us and manifests as awakened consciousness, not emotion and display. Swami Sivananda used to say: "Bhakti begins with two and ends with One."

BRAHMAN

Satchidananda–Existence-Knowledge-Bliss Absolute–is the fundamental term for Brahman, as it defines Brahman as nearly as is possible for human language. Sat is the Real (or Reality); Chit is Consciousness; and Ananda is Bliss. The totality of Reality, Consciousness, and Bliss is Brahman, and since Brahman is the essence of our being, those three aspects also comprise our true Self. The Supreme Reality is personal in response to those who are drawing near to It. For It is both immanent and transcendent in nature. As we relate to It, so It relates to us.

Brahman is the Sole Substance of all things–all the worlds and whatever is within them. Simple!

Brahman is beyond all measuring. Infinity is not just being immeasurably big, it transcends all measure and is neither small nor large.

Brahman, the Paramatman, is the source of all in cosmic life, and the individual Self, the jivatman, as part of Brahman is the source of its personal life sphere.

Everything is a potential within Brahman. When these potentials manifest we have creation, and when they are withdrawn it is dissolution, but all the time they are nothing but Brahman. Nothing could exist if it was not eternally present within Brahman in potential form.

All things should be known in their essence, at their point of origin, otherwise their external forms will delude us as to their true nature. It is necessary to see all things in their true nature as Brahman alone. This is why non-dual philosophers in the West have referred to Brahman as the "Ground" of our being and of all that exists. At all times Brahman and Brahman alone is the essence of all things.

It is often said: "The jiva [the individual spirit] is Shiva [the Supreme Spirit]." Although writings such as the Puranas present Shiva as a matted-haired ascetic riding around the Himalayas on a bull, in the ancient texts Shiva is always a title of Brahman the Absolute, and refers to the non-dual Reality. This is especially true in the spiritual writings of South India, including the teachings of Sri Ramana Maharshi. It is those who are established in advaitic bliss that are the true Shaivites.

The visible and the invisible are Brahman. "For in him we live, and move, and have our being" (Acts 17:28). We live in Brahman every moment, but usually do not realize that and think we are separated from him. We are seeing Brahman at every moment of our life, but we do not realize that, either. Only through yoga can that be changed and our awareness expanded to include his immediate presence in our lives.

All elements or components of the universe have a single root principle in common to all: The Supreme (Para) Brahman Itself. All things have not just come from Brahman, they are Brahman in extension.

We are like a tree. We have many "roots," many sources of our life, including karmas, samskaras and desires from previous lives. But to the wise, only the "mother root" is of primary importance. And that is Brahman Itself which is the root of all beings—*is* all Being. Our life involvement must be with Brahman above all else. Further, our life's focus and purpose must be the realization of Brahman, and thereby the realization of our Self.

Since Brahman is absolute unity, the experience of unity is a sign we are approaching the Brahman nature. The experience of oneness which we must come to be established in is a totally interior experience. If we think we see oneness outside of ourselves it is not a delusion, but it is not the attainment of Brahmanirvana, either. True Brahmanhood is the awareness of unity within ourself.

Our life and breath (for "prana" means both) are Brahman in manifestation. The fact that we live and breathe is evidence that we are ever one with that Reality: we embody It. This fact is the foundation of all dharma. Within the context of this truth all aspects of our life should be considered. We should never let the illusions of relative existence cause us to forget our true nature, nor should we ever lose the optimism it ensures. Our identity with divinity is the prime principle of true religion.

Brahmananda, the bliss of communion with Brahman, is beyond expression. Immersion in that ananda is jivanmukti: liberation in this life. "Not by might, nor by power, but by my spirit, saith the Lord of hosts" (Zechariah 4:6).

The prevailing idea that we need only escape from physical embodiment, or pass out in some kind of "samadhi" to experience Brahman, is absolutely not true. Continually in the Bhagavad Gita we see that the illumined yogi sees Brahman right here and now. It does not require some kind of abstraction or loss of perception of material objects. This is why the Isha Upanishad opens with the words: "All this, whatever moves in this moving world, is enveloped by God [Isha]." That is, we should be seeing Brahman at all times and all other things only secondarily. We do not need to rid ourselves of the world, we need to bring the perception of Spirit into our experience as a constant factor. Only such persons are really liberated.

The individual spirit enters into the direct knowing of itself and Brahman when its consciousness (chit) unites with its own reality: the Self. Only through meditation does this come about. Satchidananda is both an experience and the Self.

The pinnacle of yoga is when our consciousness (chit) unites permanently with the Supreme Consciousness (Sat). When that occurs, the result is Bliss (Ananda), the bliss of Brahman (Brahmananda), the supreme bliss (Paramananda), the bliss of Existence-Knowledge-Bliss (Satchidananda), the bliss of Yoga, of Divine Union (Yogananda).

All things rise from the universal consciousness, from Brahman in the form of Mulaprakriti, the primal, causal matter. All difference springs from there as the many forms or bodies make their appearance. Therefore the wise seek to center their awareness at all times in the eternal, the permanent: Brahman. When we directly perceive the indwelling Parampurusha, Brahman, in all things, then we are liberated.

Just as Brahman is Sat (Reality/Existence), Chit (Consciousness) and Ananda (Bliss), so also is the individual person, but in him the three divine qualities are separated. When the yogi unites the three and becomes a perfect reflection of the infinite Satchidananda, then he has attained yoga: union.

When a yogi has truly become one with Brahman in the absolute, nirguna sense there can be no return to the former ways when he was centered in saguna consciousness. He may speak to others who are in that state to encourage them to seek higher realization, and even use their terminology, but he is always established in the supreme state.

Someone asked Shankara, like Pilate to Jesus: "What is truth [satya]?" Shankara replied: "There is no such thing as truth. There is only the True

[Sat]." Truth is never a string of words or an idea, however lofty. Truth is the True, the Real: Brahman. Therefore if we do not know Brahman, we are dwelling in untruth, in unreality: delusion–maya.

Brahmajnana is the only shelter from the delusion of maya. All kinds of "faith" and religiosity accomplish absolutely nothing. Consciousness (chitta) is the one requisite, for Brahman is Consciousness, as is our Self. "Unmanifest, unthinkable [is] this Self" (Bhagavad Gita 2:25). As Krishna told Arjuna, we must become yoga siddhas, perfect yogis.

The only cure for samsara is the Absolute: Brahman, the Supreme Consciousness. The mantra of Brahman is the consciousness expressed by Tat Twam Asi–Thou Art That. This is the So'ham Bhava, the consciousness: I Am That. That is why in the oldest upanishad, the Isha Upanishad, the sixteenth verse concludes: *Yo sav asau purushah; so'ham asmi.* "I am that Purusha [Spirit-Self]: I am So'ham." In the next oldest Upanishad, the Brihadaranyaka Upanishad, we are told: "In the beginning this [world] was only the Self [Atman], in the shape of a person. Looking around he saw nothing else than the Self. He first said, 'I am Soham'" (1:4:1). Thus, Soham is the "first speaking" of the Absolute Itself: the expression of the knowledge and knowing of the Self. We, too, are Soham. (See *Soham Yoga, the Yoga of the Self.*)

Soham Bhava is the inmost consciousness, the innate and eternal Self of all things. Soham Bhava is the essence of each jivatman and the Paramatman, and is the sole factor that which makes them one. *So'ham asmi*–I am that I am–is exactly what God told Moses was his Name (Exodus 3:14), and that is the same as his Consciousness.

Duality is the cause of suffering. It produces suffering and maintains it in a seemingly unbreakable cycle. The only solution for it is the realization of the sole reality: Brahman which is the Self.

When we realize the Infinite, the finite ceases to exist for us, for what we previously thought was the finite was really the Infinite, but we were blinded to the truth of It.

The Unconditioned Consciousness that manifests as all things and in which all things rest is the Chidakasha. At the heart of all things is Consciousness, and at the heart of Consciousness is the Chidakasha that is Brahman Itself.

It is commonly thought that shakti or prakriti is completely separate from the Self, that when liberation is attained the various bodies, which are all formed of energies (shakti), drop away and are dissolved, leaving only the pure Atman. But just as Mahashakti or Mulaprakriti is an emanation from Brahman and is Brahman in extension, so also are our bodies, which are not shed but resolved back into our Self at liberation. Sri Ramana Maharshi indicated this when he said that the mind eventually merges into the Self as the Self.

When we realize that all this is part of the cosmic dream, it is not at all puzzling or contradictory. It is the same with creation and dissolution. The creation emerges from Brahman at the beginning of a creation cycle and merges back into Brahman at the cycle's end.

The bliss of Brahman *is* Brahman: Satchidananda. A person who is in Brahmananda is a true God-bearer. In his presence people are in the presence of God. The wise seek out such people to draw near to God, not to adore them and act like fans of rock stars. There is no "scene" around the genuinely enlightened. Just God consciousness.

ISHWARA

Ishwara, the Lord, is Brahman within creation as its guide and evolver. Though Brahman and Ishwara are one, Brahman is transcendental Reality and Ishwara is immanent Reality. Brahman is beyond all relative existence, and Ishwara pervades all relative existence. Brahman is impersonal and Ishwara is personal. All these differences are in our mind. Unity is the only Reality, but for us this duality exists in a very pragmatic manner.

God–Ishwara–dreams the cosmic dream and we dream our own finite lives within that dream. The dream arises from God and the Self, yet the dream is neither God nor the Self. This is so important to realize, that in the Bhagavad Gita Krishna says: "All this world is pervaded by me in my unmanifest aspect. All beings dwell within me, but I do not dwell within them. And yet beings do not dwell within me: behold my Divine Yoga. Sustaining beings and yet not dwelling in them, I myself cause all beings to come into manifestation. As mighty winds move everywhere, yet always dwell in the ether, know that even so do all beings dwell within me. At the end of a kalpa, all beings merge into my Prakriti: at the beginning of another kalpa, I myself send them forth. Resting on my Prakriti, I send forth again and again this entire multitude of beings, helpless under Prakriti's power. And these acts do not bind me, sitting as one apart, indifferent and unattached in these actions. With me as overseer Prakriti produces both the animate and the inanimate; because of this the world revolves" (Bhagavad Gita 9:4-10).

All things have their origin in God, yet must at all times be distinguished from God. Everything is God and no thing is God. This is not contradictory, but only the yogi will be able to grasp it and eventually experience it for himself.

BREATH

The breath is the very basis for our existence. Breath is the power of birth and death, the determiner of all that occurs to us in this world. Even more: it is the basis of our sadhana.

Breath and life are identical. When there is breath there is life, and when there is no breath, there is death. In Sanskrit a single word—prana—is used for both breath and life. Breath is the prime trait of all sentient beings. It is an absolute.

It is good to keep in mind when reading translations from Sanskrit or Sanskrit-based languages that "breath" is a translation of "prana." Sometimes prana means the physical breath, sometimes it means the subtle internal energy, and at other times it means both. So we should carefully consider this when studying any text in which "prana" or "breath" occur.

The breath is intimately connected to our consciousness, to our Atman-Self, the word "Atman" coming from the root *at* which means "to breathe." So the Atman is the breather. This is why breath is always a part of authentic yoga meditation practice. The breath is a reflection of our state of consciousness at all times. It is a kind of spiritual weather gauge.

The breath rises from the Self, so the Self is the seat (sthan) of the breath. That is why we observe the breath in meditation. It arises from the chidakasha, from the internal paramananda (supreme bliss), the paramashanti (supreme peace). The inmost, subtle breath makes the subtle sounds of the atma-mantra "Soham" by its very movement.

The psychological effects of the breath can be perceived especially in yoga practice. There is no doubt that yogis of prolonged practice breathe differently from non-yogis—not just during meditation, but also outside meditation. Yogananda insisted that the quality of a yogi could be gauged by his breathing, and I have found it to be so. My breathing changed fundamentally—not intentionally, but purely automatically—very soon after I began practicing yoga meditation.

Through the breath the inner life is opened and becomes accessible to us.

Artificial and strenuous breathing exercises are not authentic yoga, but are in the realm of physical culture called Hatha Yoga. Although they can in time produce some minor psychic abilities, they are are really no more than illusions that have no real substance, and therefore no real benefit. Such things eventually evaporate, leaving behind nothing but emptiness and a wasted life. This is true of a great deal of "yoga."

There is an inner and outer breath. The outer breath moves the lungs as it flows in and out. The inner breath moves inside in a movement that approximates inhalation and exhalation, but there is no movement of the lungs. Rather, it moves completely independently on its own. The diligent yogi experiences this for himself. There is no need to cultivate or practice it, it arises spontaneously and all the yogi need do is observe it.

As long as the breath is an external matter involving drawing in air from outside through the nose and holding it in the lungs, etc., it is not pranayama. Only when the breath becomes a fully internal process, a movement of the inner pranic forces through the subtle nadis, is it pranayama. Until then it is no more than Hatha Yoga breathing. We should not spend years on gross breathing in the hope of suspending the breath or "conquering the breathless state" in some unspecified future.

Breathlessness certainly can occur, but the really important condition is that of the internalization of breathing.

Awareness of the internal breath can only be accomplished by right meditation. And it is not some future thing, but should be achieved by the yogi after only a short time of practice. It is, though, impossible for those who have not become purified by following all the observances of yama and niyama. Patanjali would not have made them the first step of Yoga if that were not so. Only the refinement produced by their observance makes the internal pranayama (and passing even beyond that) possible. The external breath is a small river, and the internal breath is the sea which we must cross to the Other Shore of the union of jivatman and Paramatman.

Various passages in the yoga upanishads underline the absolute necessity of the breath for the maintenance of life. The Sanskrit word prana means both "breath" and "life." As the body ages, the breath, both the physical action of the lungs and the function of the prana, begins to lessen until death occurs. Thus breath is the index of the body's health and strength. The body cannot function as it should if the breath is in any way inhibited. This is why the yogis put so much emphasis on the breath.

Cultivation of the breath is fundamental to yoga practice and indicates that the transforming power of yoga is working. Shivashakti, the awakened personal power of the yogi, accomplishes all things, but primary in value is the spontaneous rising of the pranas into the Sahasrara chakra. This is where everything lasting takes place.

Yogis realize that the breath is not a mere physical function, necessary though it is for the maintenance of life in the body. Rather, it is a manifestation of the prana which is the substance of the living universe itself. Vivekananda has explained that if we want to get hold of our inner being, the antakharana, the subtle energy mechanism upon which our manifested existence depends, we must work with the breath.

In *Raja Yoga*, he says this in the second chapter: "Breath is like the fly-wheel of this machine, the body. In a big engine you find the fly-wheel first moving, and that motion is conveyed to finer and finer machinery until the most delicate and finest mechanism in the machine is in motion. The breath is that fly-wheel, supplying and regulating the motive power to everything in this body.

"There was once a minister to a great king. He fell into disgrace. The king, as a punishment, ordered him to be shut up in the top of a very high tower. This was done, and the minister was left there to perish. He had a faithful wife, however, who came to the tower at night and called to her husband at the top to know what she could do to help him. He told her to return to the tower the following night and bring with her a long rope, some stout twine, pack thread, silken thread, a beetle, and a little honey. Wondering much, the good wife obeyed her husband, and brought him the desired articles. The husband directed her to attach the silken thread firmly to the beetle, then to smear its horns with a drop of honey, and to set it free on the wall of the tower, with its head pointing upwards. She obeyed all these instructions, and the beetle started on its long journey. Smelling the honey ahead it slowly crept onwards, in the hope of reaching the honey, until at last it reached the top of the tower, when the minister grasped the beetle, and got possession of the silken thread. He told his wife to tie the other end to the pack thread, and after he had drawn up the pack thread, he repeated the process with the stout twine, and lastly with the rope. Then the rest was easy. The minister descended from the tower by means of the rope, and made his escape. In this body of ours the breath motion is the 'silken thread;' by laying hold of and learning to control it we grasp the pack thread of the nerve currents, and from these the stout twine of our thoughts, and lastly the rope of Prana, controlling which we reach freedom."

This is why Paramhansa Nityananda said: "Those who do not concentrate on breath have no aim, no state, no intelligence and no fulfillment." By "no aim" he is speaking about sadhana. What is the aim of yoga? Union with Brahman. And how do we go about that union? By sadhana which is in accord with that aim. And that sadhana according to him is Raja Yoga, the yoga of the breath, of the universal life force, the prana. Anandamayi Ma said: "Nothing can be achieved without cultivation of the breath."

Yes, I know that in contemporary India there is a cacophony of yogis peddling their wares that range over a huge territory intellectually and emotionally. But Raja Yoga truly is the royal (raja) way, according to the Upanishads, Bhagavad Gita and Yoga Sutras; it is the way they all point us toward.

The state of consciousness which is necessary for perfect realization of the Self, is that which is naturally produced by *authentic* Raja Yoga, by *authentic* pranayama. The intelligence of the awakened intellect (buddhi) is also a direct product of pranayama. The practice of yoga produces the realization that is its fulfillment. And this fulfillment is experienced all the way along in the practice. Just as an acorn germinates, grows and becomes a great oak tree, the raja yogi experiences the inner germination and growth that is the unfolding of consciousness, the same consciousness that expands to infinity in its last stages. So as Emily Dickinson said: "Instead of getting to heaven at last, I'm going all along!" That is, the pinpoint of light that is the beginning experience of the raja yogi develops into the revelation of the full sun that is the Divine Self. So the ultimate experience is ours in seed form right from the start.

Liberation of the spirit is the liberation of the breath from downward polarization to upward polarization. Right away in his practice the yogi should become aware that through his breath the subtle prana is being steadily moved upwards. This leads in time to the yogic state known as urdhvareta, in which the pranas always predominantly flow upward into the Sahasrara chakra (corresponding to the brain) where liberation is experienced and the senses are transcended. This is peace.

INDIA AND SANATANA DHARMA

Sanatana Dharma is often called Manava Dharma, and it is usually thought that this expression means the Dharma expounded by Manu. But it also means Human Dharma, the path by which an aspirant can become a true human being, one who is fulfilling the very purpose of existence: the passage from humanity to divinity. This is why so few yogis, especially in the West, succeed. They try to scramble up the ladder to divinity before they are even genuine human beings. Only those who follow the principles of Sanatana Dharma, especially the yama-niyama observances, have any chance of achieving humanity.

It is often very difficult for someone from the West who has very strong samskaras for both yoga and India to force themselves to take a very real look at contemporary Hinduism and honestly see what is foolish and what is wise. When I reached India I jumped in and a swam like a duck that had never seen a puddle, much less the marvelous ocean that is India. It was a love match. But after some years I had to brush the stars out of my eyes and take a real, honest and uncompromising look at everything I so loved and accepted and reveled in. It took a while for me to get the *ajnanatimira*, the glaucoma of ignorance, out of my system. But at last I did, and I found that I loved India and its wisdom even more. But I had to distinguish between treasure and trash, and keep on doing so.

THE IMPORTANCE OF INDEPENDENCE

There are two pieces of good advice to the yogi.

First, be self-sufficient; understand that all the resources of the spirit are in you and delve deep within and bring forth these divine potentials and actualize them in your life and consciousness. The yogi must be "a world unto himself" in the sense of perfect self-sufficiency and independence.

Second, understand that all that is outside is primarily inside. So you must develop the inner eye to truly see, understand and deal with all things. The inner life must be understood and experienced as the genuine life. "He whose happiness is within, whose delight is within, whose illumination is within: that yogi, identical in being with Brahman, attains Brahmanirvana" (Bhagavad Gita 5:24).

Everything must be tested in our own life laboratory. Our experience must be taken into account, along with straightforward good sense. This is a cardinal principle of spiritual life, and it is as much ignored as it is necessary. Everyone cites some kind of authority and accepts that, when the only real authority is our own knowing. Certainly we should study the teachings of the wise, but our purpose should be to further our own search for the revelation of truth. Truth must be realized by each individual. No one can impart enlightenment to us, we must gain it ourselves. There are no exceptions. A thing can only really be true when it is part of our own knowing, our own experience. This is one of the glories of yoga: it enables each person to know for himself what is true and real. Nothing need be proven to the yogi, it only needs to be experienced by him.

We must hold on to our ideals and pursue them without caring what others think of us when we are "selfish" and "anti-social" by refusing to waste our time with their idle-minded way of life that by its nature can lead nowhere. And we should not waste our time attempting to explain or justify ourselves. Jesus said: "Give not that which is holy unto the dogs, neither cast ye your pearls before swine, lest they trample them under their feet, and turn again and rend you" (Matthew 7:6). This is the plain truth, and following Jesus' counsel will save us from very real trouble.

Neither dharma nor adharma are understood by those who muddle through life together, copying one another mindlessly and running with the herd. These are the people obsessed with "community" and "relationship." The yogi must break loose and strike out on his own if he is to be a real person on any level. It is good if he can find other (real) yogis to associate with, but never just to run with a herd.

Few things terrify "normal" people more than original thought or original action. I knew a very intelligent and creative man whom a colleague tried to insult by saying to him: "You are an 'original.'" An original is always worth more than a copy, even in the yoga world. One of the first steps in the yoga life is the decision to live entirely by one's principles. "A law unto himself" is a good description of a yogi in relation to society. The more an organism evolves, the more complex and the more individual it becomes. That is also true of an evolving consciousness. "To thine own self be true" is profound wisdom.

Children, absorbed in their toys and romping around, cannot conceive that there is anything more enjoyable or satisfying. That is why they often bring toys to adults and cannot understand when they are not interested in playing with them as they are. As they grow older, they themselves become totally disinterested in such things, seeing nothing interesting in the diversions of childhood. Quite the opposite: they see them as silly and pointless. The same thing will happen for those who grow beyond ordinary consciousness and seek ever higher levels of awareness. They will find "normal" interests boring, foolish, or even harmful. Having left behind the obvious, they have begun to live in realms unthought of by those living around them heedlessly.

I often think of my maternal grandmother's house. Across the street was a rich family of F. Scott Fitzgerald type drunks. Next to them was the town gossip who wandered the streets several hours a day, relaying the latest news (but never malicious or derogatory). To the west was the house of the town grouch, to the east was the house of the town librarian, a real lady. On the north side lived a mother and daughter whose interest in life was the mental destruction of "poor little Willie," the daughter's only child. (They succeeded. Considered mentally incompetent but not dangerous, he inherited the house, lives on welfare, and roams the town all night, looking in the windows at a family life he never had.) But when I walked into my grandmother's house I was always flooded with the vibrations of healing and holiness. It was a different dimension altogether. No one guessed such a treasure was there: a great healer and spiritual clairvoyant who kept her gifts a secret to everyone but me. There was hardly a household in that town without someone she had healed in silence and anonymity. She had long ago left behind the ways of "normal" people. Everyone who knew her considered her virtuous and even angelic, but did not realize at all the greater world in which she moved every day. My sharing of that world was the great blessing of my life, superseded only when I came into the orbit of the great saints of India after her departure from this world.

It is the innate nature of a plant that determines what it produces. Growth is the manifestation-demonstration of what is the inner character of the plant. So it is with human beings. Even if a large number of people have the same environment, yet they will differ in their character and development. True life is from the inside out, not the outside in. In school they tried to brainwash me into accepting a lot of foolish ideas, one of which was that environment had a greater influence than heredity. I never believed it for a moment–and still do not. Although environment is very important, that, too, is determined by our karma and our samskara: our real heredity. But for a successful life we must live according to our inner character, our swabhava, and work according to our swadharma. To do this intelligently we must have experience of our inner being through meditation.

THE INTELLIGENT PATH

In the beginning of spiritual life we would be helpless without the counsel of scriptures and worthy teachers, but we must never think that anything we learn from them is true wisdom. We gain true wisdom only through our own experience. A yogi should not be overconfident, but he must never lack positive confidence in himself, for after all, do we not hold Tat Twam Asi–That Thou Art–as a foundational principle? (Chandogya Upanishad 6.8.7-6.16.3.) Prudence is always good, but unsureness and hesitation can be deadly for us. Therefore we must not pass our whole life believing something because someone else said it. We must use our intelligence and good judgment, even from the beginning.

There is a tremendous amount of nonsense in popular Hindu religion and contemporary yoga, some of it actually harmful. Unless we use our reason and intuition we will end up in a dead end, going around and around in circles, being nothing and getting nowhere, yet damaging ourselves. Just look at the population of the "yoga world" and draw your own conclusions. (For more about this see my book *Dwelling in the Mirror*.)

Once a man wrote to me lamenting that thirty-six years of practicing "the highest yoga known to man" had done nothing for him. Because he was so hypnotized by the mythological claims about his guru and the yoga, and also so fearful of "leaving the path" through "disloyalty to the guru," there was really no way out for him, though plain good sense and trust in his own experience (or lack thereof) could have freed him to seek and find real yoga. So his incarnation was wasted by staying with a worthless practice given him by worthless teachers.

It is important that we pass from believing to genuine knowing. The jnana which Shankara insists is essential for liberation is the result of each yogi's experience. It cannot be borrowed from another.

There is simply no place in spiritual life for ignorance on any level. The idea of the naive or childlike yogi is pure bunkum. Yogis are never cunning or calculating, but they are always intelligent and aware–that is what buddhi yoga is all about.

The yogi's treasure is prajna, illumined consciousness, most commonly known as buddhi, the principle of intelligence. True yogic experience affects and is stored in the buddhi, not in the emotions or the body, except as reflections or side-effects.

Yoga is always a matter of intelligence, which is why Yogananda said that stupid people cannot find God. The aspiring yogi should take care to refine and increase his intelligence, and therefore his skill and responsibility in living his life.

Fake devotion is the antithesis of spiritual intelligence, as is the absurd attempt to be "childlike" and be without thought and will as a form of "trust" or "surrender." The Gita says it right: "Therefore, stand up resolved to fight" (2:37).

The ancient Greeks said the single factor that made a human being truly human was the power of logos: word. And by that they meant the ability to think. It is the same in Indian philosophy. He who truly thinks is a true human being. Those who do not think are really animals, instinctual rather than rational. I am confident we have all encountered quite a number of "humanimals" in our lives.

This does not imply that a human being is necessarily intellectual, but that all true human beings are intelligent. Therefore it is imperative that the aspiring yogi cultivate his intelligence as part of his sadhana.

Many yoga cults browbeat anyone who dares to read anything but their publications and fume and fuss about those with inquiring minds who love to learn and develop their knowledge. I know because I started out in one. One leader of a branch center of that yoga cult had an entire personal library when she joined the cult. But when I met her she had only six books left, all publications of the cult. Love of ignorance is a hallmark of such deluded unyogis.

THE INTERNAL LIFE

Because through countless incarnations we have been thinking of ourselves as being born and dying and passing from body to body, we are utterly absorbed in the relative universe which we view through the bodily faculties. Therefore, no matter how spiritual we may think ourselves to be, or how metaphysically we think and speak of ourselves and the world around us, we are completely materialistic, but unaware of that. Continually we must make ourselves face the truth that we are uncreated beings, just as God is Uncreated Being. Whatever we experience that is not uncreated is therefore illusion and ignorance.

When our present externalized consciousness is completely changed into internal consciousness, "not agitated in misfortunes, freed from desire for pleasures, from whom passion, fear and anger have departed, steady in thought" (Bhagavad Gita 2:56), then all fears based on mistaken identity with externals are at an end.

We tend to think of ourselves as small and the universe as large. The universe, the macrocosm, is seen outside of us, and only the tiniest bit at a time. But the microcosm, the original of which the entire creation is but a reflection, is seen within ourselves. So finitude is seen outside and infinitude is seen inside. This is our true nature, and it must be cultivated continually.

We usually think of the macrocosm as being the same as the universe/creation, but the macrocosm is the Transcendental Absolute or Brahman. So we can go beyond creation by turning inward through yoga. And inside us is the Transcendent Reality. Everything is there, and "where your treasure is, there will your heart be also" (Matthew 6:21).

There are two kinds of people: those who are in the world and those in whom the world is contained. The second are those who have internalized their experience of the world and "digested" it. They always look within, because the inward look alone will reveal the truth of things since that is where the Self dwells in union with the Supreme Self, God. Therefore in a prophetic description of the Virgin Mary, David (who later was born as Jesus) wrote: "The king's daughter is all glorious within" (Psalms 45:13), because she was a perfected "interior soul," having for lifetimes lived and evolved completely within in the kingdom of God.

Since we are a point of consciousness in the Ocean of Consciousness that is Brahman, we naturally think that we must look outward and move out of ourself to encounter God. But it is the opposite. We must increasingly turn inward, because God is the very core of our existence. The Bhagavad Gita speaks of Brahman as "seated in the heart of all" (13:17), and the Self as "seated in the body" (13:32), and "abiding in the heart of all beings" (10:20). Therefore the yogi must be habitually in-turned.

The yogi comes to know that the real life is interior and hidden by the exterior. Just as the shell hides the nut, so the physical body hides the antahkarana, the inner mechanism that really keeps the yogi alive.

Life in this world is a tapestry of tides or cycles: ebb and flow, rising and falling. And these movements are to be found in some extent even in the life of the yogi. Not that the yogi is unstable, but change is in the nature of things. Therefore we should be ever vigilant regarding our interior life and development and ready to immediately apply that which we know will increase and stabilize our basic state of consciousness.

In the Gita Krishna says the yogi spends his time catching hold of the wandering mind and bringing it back to where it belongs. And he does this over and over. "Whenever the unsteady mind, moving here and there, wanders off, he should subdue and hold it back and direct it to the Self's control.... Without doubt the mind is hard to control and restless; but through practice (abhyasa) and dispassion (vairagya) it is governed. I agree that yoga is difficult to attain by him whose lower self is uncontrolled; but by him whose lower self is controlled by striving by right means, it is possible to attain it" (6:26, 35-36). The Buddhist term "cultivation" for this process is perfect. An artificial garden will stay the same and need no upkeep whatever. But a real, living and growing garden will need perpetual care. So it is with us. Yoga is not for the lazy and careless.

It is a common human failing to think that external situations or events are going to produce a change in us, but they cannot because they are only effects, not causes. In India I have seen very many people wearing orange and living utterly bored and aimless lives, cynical and dreary of mind and heart. This is because they had the foolish, theatrical idea that they would go through a ceremony, be given a new name and clothed in gerua, and like a rocket they would fly to the infinite and become one of India's leading yogis. Visions of ashrams, crowds of adoring devotees, and (of course) world tours that would result in streams of moneyed Americans coming to their ashrams in reverent adoration, danced in their heads. But of course no such occurred. And they should be glad it did not, for then they would be crocks and cult leaders.

Without a foundation there is no need to raise walls, for they will fall down, as do the yogis that have no foundation to their sadhana. We must ensure that all aspects of our life are causes: that which will bring about change in the form of evolution of consciousness. Then we will move onward to the Goal, empowered by life-giving elements such as discipline, purification and constant japa and meditation.

The Bhagavad Gita, speaking of true wisdom, jnana, says: "By this you shall come to see all creation in your Self and then in me" (4:35). Everything is contained in the inner world, and we must come to see and experience that inner world. Yogis can actually see the universe within themselves rather than outside.

The ability to perceive is more important to the individual being than anything else. Consciousness is the very substance of spirit and Spirit. Therefore the wise yogi considers that his state of consciousness alone matters and he keeps intent on that, ignoring the ego-circus of phenomena that captivates deluded human beings.

The yogi understands that all his external experience is really internal; that the thing that matters is its effect on his mind: does it help him to the goal or hinder him? The very fact that he has such a perspective ensures that his life will not be wasted in the manner of most people. Others are addicted to the world, and every little breeze or current claims and absorbs their attention. As a result, in every life they make little or no spiritual progress. And it does not really matter to them. Every distraction along the way keeps them entertained and unaware that life is draining away from them over and over.

The yoga adept sees with both the two physical eyes and the single, spiritual eye, but he knows that what is seen by the inner, spiritual eye is real and to be valued above all. Therefore he gives most of his attention to the inner sight while not neglecting the outer sight and the world it reveals.

The wise know they cannot describe or define anything by external perceptions, but they must gauge every thing by what their inner sight, their higher intuition, reveals about it. They truly do live within, even though they clearly see that which is without as well as that which is within.

The inner world is much vaster than the outer world, and the yogi who has transmuted his inner world is the master of all he surveys. Therefore: "He whose happiness is within, whose delight is within, whose illumination is within: that yogi, identical in being with Brahman, attains Brahmanirvana" (Bhagavad Gita 5:24).

Writing this, I am reminded of a prime example: Sri Yogeshwar Brahmachari. I saw him several times at spiritual conferences in India. Sri Ramakrishna used to say that a yogi's eyes often have an inward look "like the eyes of the mother bird hatching her eggs. Her entire mind is fixed on the eggs," so her eyes have an indrawn expression. It was the same with him. He would sit on a platform for hours without any movement whatsoever. Usually he had his eyes closed, but when they were open they had exactly this indrawn expression. It was the same when he was walking about. Even when he spoke, that inward-turned look remained somewhat.

The inward vision reveals the difference between the Real and the unreal. The master yogi "sees true" at all times. This is both viveka and vairagya.

JAPA AND SOUND (SHABDA)

We know the opening of Saint John's Gospel: "In the beginning was the Word and the Word was with God and the Word was God." That, however is only a paraphrase of the Vedic verse: *Prajapati vai idam agra asit. Tasya vak dvitiya asit.* "In the beginning was Prajapati [God the Creator], and with him was the Word [Vak]" (Krishna Yajurveda, Kathaka Samhita, 12.5, 27.1; Krishna Yajurveda, Kathakapisthala Samhita, 42.1; Jaiminiya Brahmana II, Samaveda, 2244). This shows that the true, original Christianity is deeply rooted in the philosophy and yoga of India–actually *is* the philosophy and yoga of India.

The world is generated (manifested) from/by sound: shabda or vak. Sound is the foundation of all relative existence. Everything is Sound. Sound is the foundation of all evolving life, and therefore the foundation of yoga itself.

Every element (bhuta) has a sensory experience that is common or "native" to it. Earth (prithvi) has smell; water (apa) has taste; fire (agni) has sight; air (vayu) has touch; and ether (akasha) has sound (shabda). The power of sound alone has both an active and passive aspect. Akasha possesses the power to both generate sound and to hear it. Furthermore, akasha alone is pure; all the other elements have admixtures of one another, including akasha.

Even more, the elements predominate in each one of our five bodies. Earth predominates in the annamaya kosha, the physical body. Water predominates in the pranamaya kosha, the pranic body. Fire predominates in the manomaya kosha, the body that is the sensory mind. Air predominates in the jnanamaya kosha, the body of the intellect. Ether predominates in the anandamaya kosha, the body of the will.

Since ether is the ruler of the elements, and it has two powers, will and sound, yoga is based on sound produced by the yogi's will and in which he becomes absorbed in meditation. This is an important principle to keep in mind because many aspirants throughout the ages have wasted their lives practicing methods not based on these two powers of ether, and therefore became wanderers, and often self-distracters and self-deluders.

All living things produce sound, and the Sanskrit language is a verbal reproduction of the sound patterns that are the sonic blueprint of all objects, conditions, and mental states (bhavas). Shabda is life, the primal sound-impulse at the heart of all manifesting things, physical, mental, and spiritual.

Although there is a great deal of interest in gimmicks and tricks in yoga and endless expositions of "shakti" and suchlike, the yogi really has one all-absorbing interest: sound (shabda). He begins with sound and ends with sound, and his involvement in sound is what carries him along the path and ensures his success and prevents his going astray. Those who do not follow this path will almost surely go astray and wander afar.

The atma and akasha are inseparable. From akasha arises shabda, divine sound which leads us to atma-bhava and then to atma-chaitanya: the Self. Then the jiva will be revealed as Shiva.

The chitta is the mind-intellect (manas-budhhi) complex. If the sensory, ego-oriented mind dominates the chitta, then it becomes soiled by the distraction, confusion and delusion that is inescapable in that condition. But if the buddhi dominates the chitta and maintains its ascendency, then it becomes purified and becomes chidakasha, the ether of space. In that akasha atmic consciousness arises automatically and reigns. That is why the last sutra of the Brahma Sutras says that enlightenment is attained through sound. Sound arises in akasha, and sound and consciousness are inseparable.

In India I once had a conversation with the disciple of a very great master, whom I eventually met. He said to me that even though his teacher had instructed him in a very complex and sophisticated yoga practice, he knew many villagers, most of them illiterate, whose simple japa and meditation practice had produced the same yogic mastery and perfection of consciousness that the complicated system did. This is logical, because liberation is an attribute of the Self, not of any yoga method. He told me of several simple village yogis who, though in good health, foretold their leaving the body, which they did by a conscious act of will at the specified time. The proof of the pudding will always be in the eating.

Why, then, did the master teach the complex practice? The disciple told me that he had just come from a gathering of disciples with the master. In a conversation the master explained that people like them with a Westernized university education had their minds shaped by it and always wanted "scientific" rationales for everything, even yoga. So what he taught them suited their complicated minds, especially since laboratory testing and a subsequent paper read at a prestigious conference of neurologists in Europe had proved the viability of the practice and made a big (but only temporary) stir. Most Indian yogis not only have no use for such an approach, they consider it pointless. Therefore the ancient, simple and direct traditional methods suit them and they attain realization from their practice.

Internally we must always be immersed in the Divine through japa and meditation, which become the two illumined eyes through we shall see ourselves, others and the world. That is jnana. When the mind is immersed in the Self, desires are gone like the illusions they were. Then bliss and liberation are ours.

We are living in maya, which is both a condition and a power of illusion. Maya causes us to see duality and multiplicity even though unity and oneness is the truth. Because of this our mind is fragmented and scattered, a conglomerate of confusion and contradiction. But the more unified the mind is through yoga practice, the more powerful its focus of attention becomes. And since everything is really Mind, whatever we focus our mind on will become affected, even transformed. This is why both Vyasa and Shankara, commenting on the Yoga Sutras, tell us that meditation is a continuous stream of identical thoughts. This is the secret of mantra. When the mind becomes united through continuous repetition of Soham which is an embodiment of Atmabhava—the consciousness of the Self—then the Consciousness that is the Self, is revealed and our awareness becomes established in that Self through prolonged and continuous practice. The mind is then revealed as the Self, as Satchidananda Itself, and therefore Paramananda: Supreme Joy.

One of the most important events of my spiritual life was the discovery of a tiny book by M. P. Pandit, a disciple of Sri Aurobindo, called *Japa*. When I read it I knew I had found the way to spiritual transformation. I bought several copies of the book and gave them to my friends who were struggling to be yogis. By the wisdom we found in *Japa* we no longer struggled but applied and discovered the benefit for ourselves.

Here is the essence of *Japa* for you to read:

JAPA

The tradition of Japa in India dates back to the ancient times of the Rishis of the Veda. "Knowing, speak His name," enjoins Dirghatamas (Rig Veda 1.156.3). "Of all the Yajnas [offerings or sacrifices] I am the Japa Yajna," declares Lord Sri Krishna to

Arjuna (Bhagavad Gita 10.2). "Japa yields the fruit of all other Yajnas," states the *Tantrasara*.

What is Japa? What is its rationale? What is its process? Japa is the repetition of a Mantra, a potent syllable or syllables, a word or a combination of words, done with the object of realizing the truth embodied in the Mantra. The object may be mundane like the achievement of certain states of affluence, health, power; or it may be spiritual, say, the attainment of God in any or many of His aspects. In either case the Mantra which is chosen for Japa has the necessary power within it and by constant repetition under proper conditions the power can be evoked into operation to effectuate the purpose. The vibrations set up each time the Mantra is repeated go to create, in the subtler atmosphere, the conditions that induce the fulfillment of the object in view. The Divine Name, for instance, has the potency to stamp and mould the consciousness which repeats it into the nature of the Divinity for which the Name stands and prepare it for the reception of the gathering Revelation of the Godhead.

At the basis of the Science of Japa is the ancient perception of sages all over the world that Creation proceeds from Sound. The universe has issued out of *Nada Brahman*, Brahman as Sound. Each sound has a form, a subtle form which may not be visible to the physical eye. Equally each form in the creation has its own sound-equivalent, the sound which preceded its formation on the subtler planes of existence. When this particular sound is reproduced—even in its transcription on the human level in terms of our speech—*vaikhari* as it is called—it sets in current the very vibrations which brought and therefore can bring that entity into being. Thus the Rishis perceived the sound-bodies of the Devatas, Deities, in their spiritual vision and [clair]audience and they instituted them as Mantras, as terms of Call to the respective Deities. When a Mantra is uttered effectively it sets in motion vibrations that evoke the corresponding Deity into the atmosphere where it is uttered. This in brief is the principle underlying the Mantra and Japa Yoga. That sound has form is a truth which is being confirmed today by Science starting from the opposite end.

Now this perception of the inherent power of sound, *shabda*, was applied with remarkable success by Indian adepts in Yoga who have reduced their knowledge and experience to an exact Science. The tradition continues to this day and is kept alive by its votaries.

...When repeated for a long time, the Mantra goes on creating vibrations which press upon the layers of the inner consciousness till one day there comes a sudden opening and the Truth ensouled in the Mantra reveals itself.

JAPA WITH THE BREATH

The Upanishads say right from the beginning that sound and breath are the two fundamental spiritual powers of the human being, and are to be united to accomplish the destiny of the human being: liberation. Japa and meditation consisting of joining mantra to the breath joins the buddhi and manas, and then unites them with the Paramatman.

The breath is the helm of meditation, and it moves us onward to the goal when mantra is joined to it.

The shabda (sound) which arises in the akasha during yoga sadhana is also the Mahaprana, the undifferentiated, intelligent cosmic life-force that becomes the five pranas. All things contain the Mahaprana and are manifestations of the Mahaprana. Mahaprana is the dynamic aspect of universal Consciousness; the superconscious Divine Life in all things.

In the lesser levels of the individual and the cosmos, prana moves as the force of life, but in the higher levels Mahaprana moves as the unalloyed Divine Life, which includes Divine Sound that is embodied in mantra. Because of this, repetition of a mantra both lifts the yogi up to and invokes the Mahaprana, enabling the yogi to truly live the Divine Life.

There are two kinds of sound: ahata (shabda) and anahata (nada). Ahata occurs in nature, is material sound even when subtle, but anahata is Divine Sound (Divya Shabda) and is spiritual, conveying spiritual opening and insight. Only the proficient yogi whose perceptions have been refined can hear these true sounds (Sat Nada) during his practice, for mantra sadhana opens the yogi to the inflow of Mahaprana and increases the inflow the longer it is practiced.

For this reason mantra japa is itself pranayama, especially when the mantra is joined to the breath.

Shabda and kundalini are essentially the same in the yogi. Through joining mantra to the breath (which is the true and highest pranayama) the kundalini is activated and through that activation the mantra comes to its fruition in moksha. Japa and the breath must never become separated. This creates the resolve and aspiration that is the highest bhakti and leads to mukti itself.

The only way to fix our attention on the buddhi, to center our consciousness *in* the buddhi, is through sound and breath centered in the sahasrara. Then our consciousness can merge into the heart-space, the chidakasha, in which pure consciousness alone exists, the consciousness which is our true Self as well as the Supreme Self.

JNANA

Jnana consists of one thing only: Self-knowledge—not in the sense of philosophy about the Self, but as direct experience *of* the Self *as* the Self. And that is experience of Unity.

Jnana is not a set of ideas or even of insights, but a condition of the buddhi itself, the state of enlightenment even in its beginning stages. So a jnani is not a philosopher but a yogi whose inner eye is opened and steadily developing.

We must not mistake intellectuality and philosophizing for jnana, as is commonly done. Perfect jnana is Self-realization: liberation here and now.

Intelligence (buddhi) and knowledge (jnana) are divine powers inherent in us. They are the highest levels of our being which in their totally purified (vishuddha) state actually "touch" Brahman and act as a conduit through which the divine life descends and transforms us. Eventually they themselves merge into Brahman and are revealed as Brahman.

Jnana is the fruition of a purified mind and life.

Jnana is not something the buddhi pursues or perceives, but it is a *condition* of the buddhi. It is a process of direct communication between the Highest and the buddhi without intermediary. It is very easy for intellectually keen people to assume that the perceptions of their buddhi are jnana when they are merely formulations of the buddhi rather than spiritual intuitions. Insight can be either natural or supernatural, and the lesser certainly is often mistaken for the greater.

There is a mystical state in which buddhi and jnana are one. That jnana is not something seen or experienced by the buddhi, but which is known in a direct manner: an action of divine realization. And it can be described.

THE JNANI

When the darkness of ignorance has been transformed into the light of knowledge, then we are jnanis. It is liking extracting gold from ore. Until then it is just rock, but when it has been smelted, the shining metal appears. In the same way, tapasya in the form of meditation extracts the wisdom of the Self from the unrefined ore of our former ignorance.

When needed, the jnani can function perfectly in the world in an extremely practical manner, even accomplishing astonishing things for the benefit of others. He can, if he will, communicate with even the ignorant on a level they can comprehend. On occasion he is seen to be brilliant beyond human genius, and possessed of vast worldly knowledge without ever studying anything.

A perfect jnani does nor regard anyone as truly, essentially, ignorant, for ignorance is itself a false appearance, part of the ignorance/wisdom duality (dwandwa). Since the jnani "sees true," he perceives the true nature of all who meet him. His response is one of respect, love, and compassion for their unawareness of their eternal, immortal Self. That is why Sivananda usually addressed his correspondents as "Divine Immortal Self" and closed with the words: "Thine own Self." This was not a pose or an exercise in positive thinking. He spoke as he *saw*. This was why he could inspire so many to achieve so much in the realm of spirit. He saw and believed absolutely in our divinity, in our perfection. In some wonderful way this was communicated to us and we began to share in his vision. What joy we had! No one felt he was a sinner or unworthy.

Depression and discouragement were not possible in his presence; just the opposite.

A jnani cares nothing about being sophisticated and worldly-wise, aware that "the wisdom of this world is foolishness with God" (I Corinthians 3:19). In the motion picture, *The Adventures of Baron Munchausen*, when the Baron is told by a snitty little bureaucrat that he has a very poor grasp on reality, the Baron replies: "As for what you call reality, I am glad to say I have no grasp of it at all."

In her poem, "The Preacher," Emily Dickinson had this to say about a "liberal divine" of her day:

> He preached upon "Breadth" till it argued him narrow–
> The Broad are too broad to define.
> And of "Truth" until it proclaimed him a Liar–
> The Truth never flaunted a Sign–
>
> Simplicity fled from his counterfeit presence
> As Gold the Pyrites would shun–
> What confusion would cover the innocent Jesus
> To meet so enabled a Man!

Dwelling in unity, the jnani knows that duality is only a dream, and he lives accordingly, ignoring differences and often doing impossible things because he does not "know" they cannot be done.

KARMA AND KARMA YOGA

Knowing the eternal law is an absolute necessity for the attainment of freedom in the spirit. For it is the law that produces or prevents all things. The three great components of the eternal law are: karma, reincarnation and the evolution of consciousness. If we can get a thorough grasp of these three we will understand and accomplish everything. For it is these three that together are the Eternal Religion, the Sanatana Dharma of India.

The knowledge of cause and effect is an absolute necessity if we are going to understand anything about our life. Those that do not understand about karma and rebirth have no idea why they are here and how they should live.

All the religiosity in the world cannot substitute for practical spiritual knowledge. Consider how the "one lifers" lay all the blame for human suffering and misery at God's door rather than rightly attributing it to human action (karma). So they claim that all this mess is "God's will" supposedly "for a reason."

Buddha stated the essence in the Four Aryan Truths: There is suffering. There is a cause of suffering. Suffering can end. There is a way to end suffering. The power behind all four of these statements is insight into the Law of Karma. Otherwise we keep whirling and suffering.

It is our karma that brings us here and takes us away, until enlightenment frees us and we leave of our own liberated will.

We must know good, evil, right and wrong, for obviously they exist. And there are definite principles in getting through the maze of this world. There is no place for the ego-myths of "your truth" and "my truth."

Things are good, evil, right and wrong because of their karmic reactions on us. Patanjali, in enumerating the principles of yogic behavior explains carefully to us what the good, even miraculous, results will be if we are perfect in yama-niyama. We certainly do need to know them. If we follow these sacred laws, peace and realization must come to us. There is no doubt or exception.

If the nature of karma, the law of cause and effect, is not understood, then only confusion and even hypocrisy will be the result. It is karma which drags us back into rebirth over and over again, blocking us from attaining the degree of evolution needed to enable us to pass into a higher world at death and progress onward to perfection, rising from world to world until relativity itself is transcended. And every human being should aspire to that.

The creation is a living entity which responds to the will and action of sentient beings, especially human beings. It can be used by them to accomplish much, but its real purpose is their evolution.

The cosmos is "available" to everyone to the same degree to be used by them according to their intention. The difference in use and response is purely a matter of their mind, which is one aspect of why Sri Ramakrishna would often say: "The mind is everything." Limitations do not exist in the outer world, but in the personal, inner world of each person's mind.

Prakriti is neutral, it is our own mind and will that determine how it reacts to us. For here is the great secret: karma is not a mere "force" and certainly not "destiny," but karma is embodied in our mind and will conditioned by past actions. Karma creates karma, so to say. Karma comes from our mind, conditions our mind, and determines the kind of karma it will produce in the future. This is a corollary to the principle that seer, seen, and seeing are the same thing: the mind. So also, then, are action, actor, and acting. All is mind, as Mary Baker Eddy said to the derision of nearly everyone at that time.

Paramhansa Nityananda said: "Everything comes out from within; not from without." This is one of the most important principles we can know. Those whose inner eyes are blinded by continual immersion in material experience think that everything comes from outside. And some people's lives do seem to be a barrage of things just hurled at them. But that is because they do not recognize karma as the force behind all phenomena, and if they do, they think of karma as an outside power that hits them at random.

When thinking cosmically, materialistic people think that in the beginning was matter from which somehow consciousness arose. To them material existence comes first and only later does consciousness develop. This is absolutely backwards. Matter and material existence proceed from consciousness, not the other way round. First there is spirit, and then there occurs a series of expansions of consciousness that, the further they are away from the originating impulse, appear as grosser and grosser states of existence. But matter is not the seed of the cosmos, consciousness is. When we realize the implications of these two views and the effects they have on spiritual inquiry, we see how important it is to hold the right view: that of the East.

Many think of karma as a kind of cosmic force that operates upon all, that human beings are helplessly subject to karmic retribution/reaction. Karma is often a bugaboo they use to frighten childish aspirants. But if the seeds of jnana are operative in them they will come to realize that karma is completely within the mind of each one of us, that karma is the mind in operation, and that we are moment by moment creating our inner and outer environment.

Thought is the most powerful tool of the human being and creates the most powerful form of karma, especially in the form of samskaras and vasanas that determine our life path from life to life. This is why Jesus said that evil mental desire and intention are themselves real deeds. "Ye have heard that it was said by them of old time, Thou shalt not commit adultery: but I say unto you, That whosoever looketh on a woman to lust after her hath committed adultery with her already in his heart" (Matthew 5:27-28). Thinking evil but not doing evil overtly does not make a person good, because thinking is doing and every evil thought is an evil deed. We often excuse ourselves because we do not realize (or accept) that this is the truth.

We may say that another person is the cause of our being good or evil, but that is not true. Rather, it is our attunement to that person which evokes either good or evil from within us. In other words, it is our thoughts and attention to that person which causes us to begin vibrating to their subtle levels. We do not absorb good or evil from them, but we reproduce in ourselves their qualities by an act of highly subtle will. Furthermore, their qualities evoke the same qualities buried in our subconscious, so they surface and will eventually manifest in our outer life. This is why we should avoid as much as possible all ignorant, negatively oriented, undisciplined, irreligious and outright evil people. The wise yogi may have to work with them, but he goes home, closes his door and is alone with God. And when he becomes really good, those people will avoid him.

One of the most important teachings of Buddha was the fact that the character of our karma is determined by the disposition and intention of our mind when we act. So the fruits of our actions will be according to our inner purpose when we did those actions.

Everything, without exception, material, or immaterial, arises from a cause, and is a revelation of that cause. Because of this, everything has a meaning. Those who believe in karma should carefully analyze their life situation in order to understand what kind of actions from the past are coming to fruition now and to see what their minds were like in that past. The real lesson to be learned is that just as the present is created by the past, the future is created by the present, sometimes combined with elements from the past. Before, we were unaware that we were creating the future, but now we do know, and can take complete charge of our destiny. The best thing, of course, is to "fry" the karmic seeds through yoga sadhana.

Cause is the impulse to manifestation and the effect is the cause itself come into manifestation. This implies that if God is the cause of anything, then that thing itself is God. Therefore all that exists or occurs is essentially a revelation of God. Everything is gained when God is realized. This was the principle Jesus had in mind when he said: "Seek ye first the kingdom of God, and his righteousness; and all these things shall be added unto you" (Matthew 6:33).

Since all our problems are really inward, only seeming to be outside us, they can be dissolved by the cultivation of interior consciousness, the awareness of our true nature. The process of awakening is simple and direct: the practice of yoga meditation.

All comes from God, but in response to our thoughts and actions. So God is the giver of all, but we alone determine the nature of the gifts. That is karma in a nutshell.

This is fundamental truth: we create our future totally—no one else. This is why karma must be grasped fully and kept in mind at all times in order to have a right understanding of where we are, what we are, and why we are.

In the film *The Third Man* Harry Lime points out that in centuries of terrible political turmoil and plague Italy produced some of the greatest literature, music, and art of Western civilization, whereas Switzerland during that time was free of all conflict and tribulation and produced nothing but the cuckoo clock. Adversity is a matter of karma, and karma is not for mere enduring, but for our learning. So if we avoid the adversity we will deprive ourselves of the learning we need. And in time the karma will catch up with us, anyway.

If medicine tastes bad, we may think it is poison, but often it is the cure for our illness, without which we might die. In the same way, those who have set their feet on the path to liberation must realize that any obstacles or troubles they might encounter are really aids to their success in spiritual life. If they carefully ponder them they will see the lessons to be learned and the way to pass through them and be benefitted by them. It is delusion that makes us afraid of them and feel helpless before them. If we face them in the context of dharma and yoga will will see them very differently and respond to them courageously and effectively.

"Hell" is the suffering of samsara, physical or astral. Our prayer should be that we may be led toward God and attain the cessation of all the suffering caused by ignorance. Sometimes, though, we have to be led into the swamp to learn that it is a dangerous place and to be avoided in the future. Some children are sensible enough to believe it when they are told an object is hot, but some have to touch it and get burned to learn for themselves. Fortunately, both learn.

It has been my observation that misfortune can have two effects. It can cause the unfortunate to fold back in on themselves in self-pity, making them blind to the reality and worth of everyone but themselves. Such persons are supremely incompassionate and seldom if ever give a thought about others. However, misfortune enables some people to understand and sympathize with the pain of others and motivates them to extend help and comfort to those around them.

We must be like this second type. When something happens to us we should be aware that countless others are undergoing the same thing, that they are fellow-sufferers to be cared for and consoled. And when we awaken to the fact that Self-realization should be our prime concern, we should consider the same of others and do what we can to help them journey along with us from the unreal to the Real, from darkness to Light, from death to Immortality.

Notice I say help, not force or impose. We must always respect the will of others, and realize that until they awaken to the same understanding as ours, they cannot travel the way we are going. Until then our consideration and care should be given in the context of their present level of understanding.

It is foolish to provoke difficulties, but it can be equally foolish to do everything we can to avoid them. The more wind pushes against a tree the more its roots go deeper and get stronger. I think we have all seen spoiled children who were completely unprepared for real life by their parent's pampering and indulgence. We must not do the same with ourself.

It is karma and the level of evolution that determines the birth of all beings. Not only that, the soul is attracted by those who are like it in karma, samskara and basic character. Yogananda said that when a man and woman engage in sexual relations an astral light emanates from their base (muladhara) chakras. Highly evolved people emit bright light, whereas those of low development emit a dim and murky light. Souls waiting to be born are attracted by that light, but unless the light is completely harmonious with them, they turn back and only those that are compatible with the light will come near and try to enter and be conceived. No matter how rebellious a child may be in relation to his parents, if there was not a powerful affinity with them (even if it is bad karma and enmity carried over from past lives) he could never have become their child.

All the evil and good that comes to us comes from ourselves: from the karma we created in the past. So we alone harm and we alone help ourselves. What about "grace"? Karma is grace, as is everything.

People pray and good comes to them. Praying is the karmic seed and receiving the good is the fruition of the seed. Just to turn to God and holy people for help is powerful karma. Without good karma people do not even think of God in time of trouble. That is why the American country singer, Roy Acuff, wrote in his song "Wreck on the Highway:"

> Who did you say it was brother?
> > Who was it fell by the way?
> When whiskey and blood run together,
> > Did you hear anyone pray?

> I didn't hear nobody pray, dear brother,
> > I didn't hear nobody pray.
> I heard the crash on the highway
> > But I didn't hear nobody pray.

> When I heard the crash on the highway
> > I knew what it was from the start.
> I went to the scene of destruction
> > And a picture was stamped on my heart.

There was whiskey and blood all together
    Mixed with glass where they lay.
Death played her hand in destruction,
    But I didn't hear nobody pray.

I wish I could change this sad story
    That I am now telling you,
But there is no way I can change it,
    For somebody's life is now through.

Their soul has been called by the Master.
    They died in a crash on the way.
And I heard the groans of the dying,
    But I didn't hear nobody pray.

I didn't hear nobody pray, dear brother,
    I didn't hear nobody pray.
I heard the crash on the highway,
    But I didn't hear nobody pray.

Being solely the action and reaction of the gross and subtle bodies, karma has nothing to do with the Self. It is only a force of gross and subtle materiality. The ego-mind can certainly say "my karma," but to the Self karma does not exist except as a dream.

Yogananda's most advanced disciple, Sister Gyanamata, once wrote to Virginia Wright (Ananda Mata): "Your own will always come to you. Indeed, you can have nothing but your own." That is karma. There are no "just lucky" people, nor are there "just unlucky" people. The present of each one of us is a creation of our own actions in the past, either in this life or in past lives. It is also a creation of past inaction, as well. We reap what we sow; and we do not reap what we do not sow. Our entire life in all its aspects is a result of just one thing: us. Looking in the mirror of life shows us our own face. That is its purpose. The wise learn, the heedless do not.

Whatever we encounter is a projection of our own mind in the form of karma. When we experience kindness from others it is our own kindness being returned to us. When we experience the opposite, it is also our own karmic voice echoing back to us. The "face" of our outer life is the face of our inner life and mind. Whatever comes to us is our own, actually *is* us. We should never forget this when we are tempted to retaliate. Through the law of karmic return we are doing to ourselves that which we dislike. That is why, when two disciples came to Yogananda with complaints about each other, the Master simply said: "Change yourselves."

KARMA YOGA

The Gita continually tells us to follow the path of karma yoga, which is Right Doing, and at the same time to realize: "I am doing nothing." Who can do this but the yogi whose buddhi can penetrate beyond the appearance of this world to the reality of things—including himself?

As its root, action is an "act" of the buddhi, the seat of the will. Karma yoga, then, is also purely intellectual. Even though carried out in external action, it is primarily an internal affair.

Sri Ramakrishna said that meditation and yoga practices are all part of Karma Yoga. The Gita insists that Right Action is the path to freedom.

When the intellect and the intuition are in direct contact with the Self, then no actions create karma. The Gita describes the perfect karma yogi, saying: "Offering actions to Brahman, having abandoned attachment, he acts untainted by evil as a lotus leaf is not wetted by water. Karma yogis perform action only with the body, mind, intellect, or the senses, forsaking attachment, performing action for self-purification. He who is steadfast, having abandoned action's fruit, attains lasting peace" (Bhagavad Gita 5:10-12).

If we "fry" karmic seeds in the fire of intense spiritual discipline (tapasya) they will not be able to manifest in the future. This is the safest way to deal with karma.

Deluded people often if not usually get cause and effect reversed, and think that an effect is a cause. For example, there are those that think that if they act like they are a certain kind of person then they will be that kind of person. Wrong. As Swami Sivananda said: *Be* Good. *Do* Good. Just acting without really being something is valueless.

KUNDALINI

Kundalini is power (energy), but it is predominately conscious-ness. It is not the energy which forms the external world, but the primal power from which that creative energy emanates. This is very important, because awakening of kundalini is primarily the awakening of consciousness. There are all kinds of pathological manifestations of bodily energies that are mistaken for kundalini, and the yogi must be aware of this fact.

Kundalini is awakened and oriented upward by pranayama since prana/breath is a permutation of kundalini. The pranayama recom-mended by yoga siddhas for this is Soham Pranayama, the mental intoning of *So* when inhaling and *Ham* (pronounced "hum") when exhaling with the mouth closed. (See *Soham Yoga, The Yoga of the Self*.)

Although we usually speak of our awakening kundalini, it is really kundalini that awakens us. And when that awakening is complete it is liberation (moksha).

Because of all sorts of books on the subject, we think of the action of kundalini as a kind of cataclysmic shaking, a psychic typhoon, but that is a neurological aberration, a herald of abnormal and even psychotic states in the individual. The true action of kundalini is the awakening of the perception of spirit-consciousness in the individ-ual. When kundalini becomes operative in the Sahasrara—for that is where it is, not in the Muladhara—ultimate consciousness awakens in the yogi.

Nearly all descriptions of kundalini are totally physical and neurological, and therefore pathological and delusional. Kundalini is Primal Consciousness, and its workings take place in the most subtle manner. It is not cataclysmic, it is transformative in the most direct and practical manner. Therefore only those whose buddhi is both purified and refined can have any true experience of kundalini and experience the changes its ascent and awakening of the subtle bodies produces.

LIBERATION

Our descent into this relative world is temporary because the world itself is temporary, only a momentary appearance. Ascending out of this relative world back into the higher worlds from which we came is permanent in its effects, the main one being never to return to this fever dream we think is real life.

When we realize that we are finite dreamers in the Dream of the Infinite Dreamer, then we need not worry about all the things we encounter in this world. We should have only one concern: awakening from the dream into the being of the Dreamer.

Sanatana Dharma alone tells us that the supreme attainment is inherent in us. It is not some artificial state or even something that is given to us by God. It is our essential nature. There is nothing else so important to us. Attaining liberation is simply "finding" ourself, realizing what and who we really are. Therefore the search for liberation is an inner search. Jivanmukti is found only in each person's Self. Looking for salvation outside ourselves can only fail. We must look within, and that is only possible through yoga. Supposed mystical experiences that come from any source but the Self are of no lasting value. We must not mistake the psychic for the spiritual, something which most religions do.

Death is the cause of birth, for the Gita says: "Of the born, death is certain; of the dead, birth is certain" (2:27). So the only way not to be born is not to die—to undergo the process of death helplessly—but to easily and intentionally slip out of the body in full consciousness, not really "dying" at all.

The true state of Unity is not the blank unconsciousness that is touted as the non-dual (advaitic) state by the ignorant or deluded. In the real state there is total awareness of all aspects of consciousness, not just the highest level. Cosmic consciousness means exactly that: awareness of everything, including the mere appearances mistaken for realities. It is not an experience, but a mode of seeing: "most secret knowledge combined with realization, which having known you shall be free from evil" (Bhagavad Gita 9:1).

Being always centered in the Self and absolutely stabilized in con-sciousness, a liberated man already lives outside of time and perceives that he really goes nowhere—not "here" or "there." He merely responds to the external conditions, but has no inward preference at all. That is because he sees the universe and all in it as Brahman: his own Self. Unity alone occupies his awareness.

The practical result of true non-dual consciousness is seeing the whole universe is Brahman, the inner Self of all sentient beings. Brahman is the real "yogi," for It unites all within Itself. The individual yogi may employ various practices, but it is only the Being of Satchidananda experienced in meditation that brings about the revelation of the eternal union that is the truth of us all.

The purpose of becoming one with the Absolute is to live in joy, in a kind of joyful play (lila), aware that it is all the dream of the Supreme Bliss. During my first trip to India I met a little French girl who, though knowing nothing of Indian religion, had had a vision of Krishna soon after arriving there. Her parents told me that a group of pandits assem-bled and questioned her regarding the vision. She had seen Krishna as an adult, and her vision matched exactly and in detail the traditional scriptural description of Krishna. They were naturally quite amazed. One of the pandits asked her if she would like to see Krishna again.

When she said yes, he asked her what she would do if Krishna came to her again. "Why, I will dance with him!" she replied. She certainly had gotten the idea.

In the nirvikalpa state the consciousness becomes thoroughly oriented toward the ananda at the core of our being. That is why Krishna says: "He whose happiness is within, whose delight is within, whose illumination is within: that yogi, identical in being with Brahman, attains Brahmanirvana" (Bhagavad Gita 5:24).

The experience-identity or bhava of duality—and therefore separation—is hell. The bhava of absolute unity—a real experiencing, not an intellectual conviction—is itself liberation (moksha). To be united with Brahman is not heaven, for heaven is just the other end of the hell-heaven duality (dwandwa). Brahmajnana transcends hell and heaven, and is absolute liberation from all such dualities.

IT IS ALL UP TO US

"Blessed are they which do hunger and thirst after righteousness: for they shall be filled" (Matthew 5:6). The yogi must truly hunger and thirst for purification and liberation. He must realize that all else is death, so attaining perfection in yoga is literally a matter of life and death.

When I was a beginning yogi who had moved halfway across the country to seriously study yoga, I found myself with others who had come hundreds and thousand of miles to do the same. But I also met a string of spiritual slackers who just talked metaphysics and said: "When the disciple is ready the master appears," the implication being that they need do nothing until a master came along and offered his services to them. But moksha does not come in search of us, we must actively and continually seek moksha on our own initiative.

The Raja of Chandod told me that his family, though of royal lineage, had been living in poverty in Rajasthan. Learning of this, their relative the Maharaja of Baroda wrote and asked them to send him some of their male children of suitable age, one of whom would be chosen to live with him and be educated to become a raja of the principality he intended to form for him out of his own kingdom. Three boys were chosen and sent to him, one of them being the Raja of Chandod's grandfather. The Maharaja had them brought one by one to a room where he was sitting behind a screen. His chief minister, at his instruction, asked each one a single question: "Why did you come here?" The first boy replied: "To get something good to eat." The second said: "Because my mother told me to come." The third, the grandfather of the raja who was telling me the story, told the minister: "To be the Raja." He was chosen by the Maharaja and did become a raja.

It is the same with us. Those who seek God for any other reason than the attainment of moksha do not find God–and so do not attain moksha.

A lot of spiritual layabouts like to tell everyone that only God's grace matters, that nothing we do can liberate us but God's grace. This is a case of Figures Don't Lie, But Liars Figure. Certainly, only the grace of God brings about our liberation, but the ability to engage in spiritual practice and discipline is a manifestation of that grace, proof that God's grace is in our lives. When there is no practice there is no grace, no true life. Saint James wrote: "Show me thy faith without thy works, and I will show thee my faith by my works" (James 2:18). We could paraphrase this: "Show me God's grace in your life without sadhana, and I will show you God's grace in my life by my sadhana."

Everything that exists is the grace of God. We live in and by the grace of God. What the "grace only" people need is to learn from the children's game where there is a division into two parallel lines and one side challenges the other: "Get to work and show us what you can do!" Only those who get to work show that the grace of God is in their life.

What determines the difference in the time moksha is attained? Hunger, the intense desire for liberation, is the determining factor. Ma Anandamayi said: "The desire for God is the way to God." No matter how effective a yoga method may be, if it is not practiced with a heart reaching out with fervor toward God, it will not be maintained and the lukewarm yogi will eventually abandon it and wander on in samsara.

Two friends of mine, Anne and Elwood Decker, had some truly precocious grandchildren, and at the beginning of December one year Anne said to Elwood: "I told them you would write a Christmas play, and we would record it and send it to them." Elwood was amazed and chagrined, but he put his mind to it and wrote a two-character play about the birth of Jesus. Elwood was one of the shepherds the angel told about Jesus' birth, and Anne was an angel who helped him go into Bethlehem and find where the Child was. At the end, the angel tells the shepherd she must return to heaven, and he says: "How I wish I could go to heaven!" She asks: "Do you *really* want to go to heaven?" He says, "Yes," and there comes a great whooshing sound and that is the end of the play. He really wanted it, so he went there. Only intensity of desire had been lacking, and once he had it… whoosh!!!

Madness, Divine and Worldly

The world and its inmates think that the all-consuming intensity needed to find God is insanity. The ideal teacher of this divine madness is Sri Ramakrishna. So here are his words on the subject:

"If you have to turn mad why should you do so for the things of the world? If you are to turn mad be mad for God."

"I said to Narendra [the future Swami Vivekananda], 'Look, God is the ocean of bliss. Don't you feel like plunging into this ocean? Just imagine that there is a cup of syrup and that you are a fly. Where will you sit for drinking the syrup?' Narendra said, 'I will sit on the edge of the cup and sip the syrup stretching my head.' I asked him, 'Why so? Why should you sit on the edge?' He said, 'If I venture to go too far I will drown and lose my life.' Then I said, 'But, my child! There is no such danger in the ocean of existence-consciousness-bliss. It is the ocean of immortality. No one dies plunging into it. A man becomes immortal! A man does not lose his head by becoming mad for God.'"

Vivekananda quoted Sri Ramakrishna, saying: "My Master used to say, 'This world is a huge lunatic asylum where all men are mad, some after money, some after women, some after name or fame, and a few after God. I prefer to be mad after God. God is the philosophers' stone that turns us to gold in an instant; the form remains, but the nature is changed—the human form remains, but no more can we hurt or sin.'"

One of Sri Ramakrishna's spiritual teachers had told him regarding being mad for God: "My son, blessed is the man upon whom such madness comes. The whole of this universe is mad—some for wealth, some for pleasure, some for fame, some for a hundred other things. They are mad for gold, or husbands, or wives, for little trifles, mad to tyrannize over somebody, mad to become rich, mad for every foolish thing except

God. And they can understand only their own madness. When another man is mad after gold, they have fellow-feeling and sympathy for him, and they say he is the right man, as lunatics think that lunatics alone are sane. But if a man is mad after the Beloved, after the Lord, how can they understand? They think he has gone crazy; and they say, 'Have nothing to do with him.' That is why they call you mad; but yours is the right kind of madness. Blessed is the man who is mad after God. Such men are very few."

The last word should come from Sri Ramakrishna himself: "If you see in a man ecstatic feeling and love of God spilling over and see that he is mad for God and is intoxicated with his love, know for certain that God has become incarnated in that man."

Yogananda used to say that everyone in this world is crazy, but people of the same craziness get together and call their craziness normal and say that those who are not like them are the ones that are crazy. Blessed are those who drop earthly craziness to find the only true wisdom in God-realization.

Intelligence is given to us for the pursuit of spiritual liberation (moksha). Certainly we should use it for practical matters in the world. But those who occupy their intellect (buddhi) day and night with things of the external world and never give a thought to the inner world where alone reality is to be found, waste this precious resource and exhaust the positive karma which brought it to them.

The truth is that everything about us—body, mind, intellect and spiritual faculties—is given to us for the primary purpose of attaining spiritual enlightenment. Human birth is intended for the pursuit of evolution of consciousness. To not do so is to be dead while seemingly alive.

Ignoring the life of the spirit is spiritual suicide, though most of the world blithely engages in it. I grew up hearing that being "too religious" could drive you crazy. But the really crazy people I have seen in my life are those without living roots in their own spirit and the Supreme Spirit. Spiritual awakening alone is sanity.

The vision of God is the only real cure for the wrong kind of madness, and that comes only through yoga sadhana which produces the right kind of madness. We continually come across people who insist that since they are the Self they need do nothing but just *be* the Self, that any kind of practice affirms a false identity and is a denial of their real nature, and therefore an obstacle to realization. But how can anything be an obstacle to the Self? Whence comes their fear of delusion if they are nothing but the Self and need do nothing?

We may have two perfectly good eyes, but if our head is wrapped around and around in veils, we will be unable to see. Who but a fool or a lunatic would simply deny not being able to see and say that nothing is needed for them to see? True, they are not blind, but their sight is being blocked by veils which must be removed before they can see. It is certainly true that they can already see, but that which prevents sight must be taken away.

Those in jail would be insane if they went on and on about how by nature they are free and need not be released from the jail. I once watched a parole hearing of Charles Manson. At one point he boasted to the parole board that they had no idea about him, that he was really at that moment driving down a California highway, free and in control of his life. (He also claimed to have a submarine where he produced hit records.)

A lot of craziness goes on under the cloak of "advaita" and "non-dualism." For example, Sri Ramana Maharshi is held up as an example of someone who "did" nothing but entered into enlightenment spontaneously. Not so. Only after he intentionally went through the process of methodically experiencing death did he gain awareness of the Self. So he "did" something just as much as any yogi. Since he was obviously born either enlightened or only a step away from enlightenment, that was all it took. But he did take that step, and so must we whether it be a single step, a mile, or a million miles. And by the way, he did not stay at home and live a "normal" life, but fled to Arunachala. So he did not at all think that for one who knows the Self it makes no difference where the body may be.

When the yogi starts looking at everything, including the world, through the eyes of subtle, spiritual reality, he is considered insane by the truly insane: those who see the appearance and miss the reality completely. The only way to placate these crazies is to revert and become crazy like them. A lot of spiritual aspirants do just that when either threatened or promised benefits. How sad.

Sri Ramakrishna told the following experience: "Once Krishnakishore asked me, 'Why have you cast off the sacred thread?' ...I said to Krishnakishore, 'Ah, you will understand if you ever happen to be as intoxicated with God as I was.' And it actually came to pass. He too passed through a God-intoxicated state, when he would repeat only the word 'Om' and shut himself up alone in his room. His relatives thought he was actually mad, and called in a physician. Ram Kaviraj of Natagore came to see him. Krishnakishore said to the physician, 'Cure me, sir, of my malady, if you please, but not of my Om.'"

The search for mahima—external greatness in the sense of great power, fame, influence, control, and possessions—is one of the worst strains of madness, for not only is it all-consuming it is also virtually impossible to cure. Here, too, those who gain what they want are made utterly miserable and ultimately ruined by it.

"Then said Jesus unto his disciples, Verily I say unto you, That a rich man shall hardly enter into the kingdom of heaven. And again I say unto you, It is easier for a camel to go through the eye of a needle, than for a rich man to enter into the kingdom of God" (Matthew 19:23-24). This applies to any abundance of "the good things" of this world, for they addict human beings mercilessly, and it is a very real addiction. First they compel people to seek so many things, and when they get them, they become compelled to get more and more, and all the time live in fear of losing even the smallest amount of their "treasure." It is a net almost impossible to break free from.

Here is an example from "yoga life." The renowned operatic soprano Amelita Galli-Curci bought a small house in Borrego Springs, a tiny town in the low desert of southern California. After some time Dr. Minot W. Lewis, Yogananda's first American disciple, bought that house and used it as a private meditation retreat. Some time before his mahasamadhi Yogananda told James Lynn (Rajasi Janakananda) about the Borrego area and advised him to make a similar meditation retreat there. After Yogananda's passing he built a small house for himself (where he left the body). But although he was a great yogi and spiritually very advanced, he was still so addicted to making money that even though he was worth millions he just could not stop. So he also bought four hundred acres which he turned into a potato farm and bought up quite a few properties which he rented out. (One of our friends when we lived in Borrego had been his tenant.) After the passing of Doctor Lewis his house became the site of a small chapel and was used as a spiritual retreat, and today is a retreat for the monks of Self-Realization Fellowship. Rajasi's property, on the other hand, was sold off after his passing and his own house was abandoned, becoming a ruin and a haunt of squatters and drug users. Finally a devoted yogi bought it and moved it to his property where he restored it and lived in it himself. There is a lesson here, and not hard to get. This is not a criticism of Rajasi, but an affirmation of what Jesus had to say about "the game" of this world.

I would like to go further in this matter. For many years Rajasi Janakananda was a disciple of Yogananda, who often praised him and lavished great love upon him, and after the Master's passing he became the president of Self-Realization Fellowship. Yet one day after his guru's mahasamadhi a terribly sad fact was revealed. In meditation Rajasi had a vision of Yogananda—the first after his mahasamadhi. He came in great joy to Sister Durga, another advanced disciple of Yogananda, and told her about the vision. In conclusion he confessed to her that all through the years as Yogananda's disciple he kept wondering if Yogananda was so kind and loving to him because he had a lot of money—that it was his money Yogananda was interested in. But after Yogananda came to him in the vision he could at last believe in his guru's love. How tragic! The decades of association with his guru were blighted by doubt, fear, and mistrust—all caused by his money! What a curse his wealth was, for it poisoned that time of his life which should have been the most blessed. He was unable to fully have faith in such a great Master because his money was always looming in the background of his mind, more real to him that his Master's love. As Jesus had warned: "Where your treasure is, there will your heart be also" (Matthew 6:21). Again, this is an indictment of riches, not of Rajasi.

People have all kinds of reasons and justifications for running here and there. How noble so many of them sound! And how wise and even scientific. It is wonderful how "doctors" and "researchers" find that indulging their whims and addictions is actually good for them. For example, a "true Freudian" will tell you Freud claimed that sexual abstinence caused neurasthenia, when in reality he said that sexual *indulgence* produced neurasthenia, and was himself a strict celibate in the latter part of his life, having told his wife that sexual activity was inconsistent with the accomplishment of any great work.

The changeability and consequent instability of the "wanting" mind is a tremendous and a continual torment to the individual and those around him.

The material world and our misperceptions of it not only delude us, but addict us to the delusion. Like any other crazy person we defend our delusions—even hysterically. When many people who think they are religious but are really only deluded encounter the truth, they intuit that its acceptance would wipe out their investment in foolishness and reveal it for what it is. Even worse, they would be obligated to acknowledge the truth and apply it. This would bring down their card house and reveal what they really are—and are not. So they may even become violent in resistance. For many centuries such "religious" people imprisoned, tortured and killed those who challenged their delusions. And a lot of people have a subconscious nostalgia for those days, regretting their passing.

I have met bigots whose major grief was their inability to silence those who spoke contrary to their spiritual hallucinations. So they set about trying to destroy their "enemies" in other ways such as virulent defamation. Bishop Jay Davis Kirby told me that when he moved to Birmingham, Alabama and started a Liberal Catholic church, the Roman Catholic bishop of Birmingham contacted the local FBI and told them Bishop Kirby was a Communist. For as long as he lived in Birmingham his phone was tapped. I could cite many examples, but if you meet it you will know it for yourself.

Manas (Mind) and Buddhi (Intelligence/Intellect)

The mind (manas) and intellect (buddhi) are both two and one. Only the yogi truly understands this. So in this section sometimes "mind" means only the manas, and sometimes it means both the manas and the buddhi together, or the buddhi alone. This is the problem with words. They are only symbols and not the thing at all. But we have to work with what we have.

The illumined-wisdom level of the human being is the refined buddhi or intellect. Its wisdom is intuitive, but it is capable of conveying it in intellectual terms. The energies of which it is composed are so subtle, so rarefied, that they are almost indistinguishable from spirit. For this reason many developing yogis cannot at first discriminate between the buddhi and the Self. But as they continue in their sadhana all becomes clear.

The mind (manas) is higher than the body and the intellect (buddhi) is higher than the mind. The Gita says it simply and completely: "The senses are superior [to the body], the mind is superior to the senses, the intellect (buddhi) is superior to the mind. And much superior to the intellect is the supreme intelligence (param buddhi)" (Bhagavad Gita 3:42-43).

Between the mind (manas) and the Self (Atman) is the buddhi, the intellect. But the buddhi has two aspects or faces, one looking downward and one looking upward. The downward-turned aspect of buddhi is the intelligent, thinking mind. The upward-turned buddhi is literally looking at God, and as I said, it is so subtle that it is virtually indistinguishable from spirit. It is perfectly conscious, but not consciousness itself. It does not think, it perceives and it *knows*.

The manas, usually translated as "mind," is the sensory mind; the faculty that receives the messages of the senses. It has no intelligence, only sense-experience and instinctual, emotional response. Most people live centered in the manas and as a result their lives are disordered, foolish, and pain-filled. They seek all kinds of remedies, none of which solve the problem. In our time psychotropic drugs are a positive curse in many people's lives, for they are the most destructive of false remedies. Religion, too, is a completely pointless resort for those who are manas-driven in their lives.

The buddhi—usually translated "intellect" or "intelligence"—embraces intellect, understanding, and reason. It is the higher, thinking mind which is the seat of wisdom. The manas is completely material in orientation, whereas the buddhi can enter into communication with the Self and be so transmuted by such contact that it virtually becomes spirit. That is why Krishna speaks several times of Buddhi Yoga in the Gita.

If we continually subordinate the manas to the buddhi, ignoring its responses and listening only to our illumined intelligence, we will in time become adept in yoga sadhana, and through that we will fully enter into our Self and attain that mastery we call moksha (liberation), and thus be free forever from the cycle of birth and death.

Right thought is an element of the Eightfold Aryan Path expounded by Buddha. Right thought eventually evolves into right intuition, which is the highest intelligence human beings can achieve, for it leads to liberation.

Chitta is the subtle energy that is the substance of the mind, and yet is consciousness itself. When that is made one with the buddhi, Self-knowledge must result.

I do not think it is a surprise to anyone reading this that the mind is deluded about what is unreal or real, true or false. But in time the mind is transmuted into the buddhi. And that transmutation must be brought about by us through intense yoga sadhana–there is no other way. Until we do so, the mind is completely vulnerable to the three gunas and their operations.

The lower, sensory mind (manas) cannot perceive the Self, but the higher mind, the buddhi, can. This is because the buddhi in its higher reaches merges into the Self at the point where akasha becomes one and indistinguishable from chaitanya, the consciousness that is spirit. This is possible because the entire range of relative existence is really an expansion of Brahman and therefore essentially consciousness/spirit.

The mind must be purified and transformed into a higher mode of function. Basically the lower mind must be transmuted and assumed into the higher mind (buddhi). It is this which is called Buddhi Yoga in the Gita.

Truly the manas, the lower mind, is "like the troubled sea, when it cannot rest, whose waters cast up mire and dirt" (Isaiah 57:20). But the yogi's buddhi can become steady through the Buddhi Yoga outlined by Krishna in the Bhagavad Gita:

"This buddhi yoga taught by Sankhya is now declared to you, so heed. Yoked to this buddhi yoga, you shall avoid the bonds of karma. In this no effort is lost, nor are adverse results produced. Even a little of this dharma protects from great fear. In this matter there is a single, resolute understanding. The thoughts of the irresolute are many-branched, truly endless" (Bhagavad Gita 2:39-41).

"Action is inferior by far to buddhi yoga. Seek refuge in enlightenment; pitiable are those who are motivated by action's fruit. He who abides in the buddhi casts off here in this world both good and evil deeds. Therefore, yoke yourself to yoga. [This is a play on words since "yoke" and "yoga" have the same root: yuj.] Yoga is skill in action. Those who are truly established in the buddhi, the wise ones, having abandoned the fruits of action, freed from the bondage of rebirth, go to the place that is free from pain. When your buddhi crosses beyond the mire of delusion, then you shall be disgusted with the to-be-heard and what has been heard. When your buddhi stands, fixed in deep meditation, unmoving, disregarding the Vedic ritual-centered perspective, then you will attain yoga (union)" (Bhagavad Gita 2:49-53).

"To them, the constantly steadfast, worshipping me with affection, I bestow the buddhi yoga by which they come to me. Out of compassion for them, I, abiding in their own Selves, destroy the darkness born of ignorance by the shining lamp of knowledge" (Bhagavad Gita 10:10-11).

Buddhi Yoga is that which develops the buddhi, the intellect, which in time evolves the faculty of intuition, becoming both intellectual and intuitional. This is the mark of a fully developed human being. Those who do not possess that level of development are only potential humans; they have the human form but not the human mind which is the distinctive trait of a human. Doctor Bronner of Peppermint Soap fame was a friend of our monastery and donated many of his products to us. Once when one of our monks called to place an order, Dr. Bronner spoke with him at length, and more than once in the conversation said emphatically about certain types of undeveloped people: "Not yet human!" He was right.

If our judgment is based on our physical perceptions and experiences it will go astray and prove erroneous. But if it is processed in the intellect, the buddhi, then wisdom and right response (action) will result.

The buddhi must not be merged in the manas, but the manas must be elevated and merged with the buddhi, with the principle of spiritual intelligence within each of us. This is the real "elevation of humanity," an intensely personal endeavor in which each one must engage if humanity is to have any better future. It is not to be found outwardly but inwardly.

The lower mind cannot reach Shiva-loka, the level of consciousness that is divine. Rather, the buddhi must be expanded and refined through effective yoga practice. Then the Self can be known.

The mind must be "polished" continually to keep it bright and unmarred. The foremost way is through meditation, but we must also use our intelligence and continually be expanding our intellectual faculties (buddhi). We must make sure that our minds do not accumulate a layer of dust and dirt that will dull and deaden the mind. It is a constant process to keep our minds in the condition favorable to spiritual growth and ultimate realization.

Intelligence and intuition united is a trait of the successful yogi. Those who establish buddhi, the intellect, as the master of the manas, the sensory mind, are real yogis.

When the buddhi has been purified and refined sufficiently, the eternal verities become perceptible to the yogi. And as he proceeds onward and upward he intuits that in time he will see and unite with the Eternal Itself.

Enlightenment encompasses and transmutes the buddhi, it does not eliminate or transcend it. Therefore intelligence, awareness and intuition can lead us to liberation through (and within) the buddhi.

Intelligence, awareness and intuition are essential ingredients in our attainment of liberation. These three things are faculties of the buddhi and by their nature tend to higher consciousness. Nevertheless we must put forth our will to use them as tools of transformation. But since this is their very purpose, we will not find them hard to use for our benefit.

The buddhi can become one with the Absolute and realize that it is the Absolute, and always has been the Absolute. The external world is not negated, but rather is perceived as not really outside but inside, for it, too, is the Self and the Supreme Self. It does not really *become* the Supreme Being, it is *revealed* as That.

Real viveka, discrimination between the Real and the unreal, between the Self and the non-Self, between the permanent and the impermanent, is produced when the mind merges into the buddhi which is pure intelligence and intuitive insight. Then viveka arises spontaneously.

Pleasure and pain originate in the mind and overwhelm us, but when the yogi by practice learns to center his experience in the buddhi, then they become objective to us, and we will no longer be overcome by them, nor will they agitate us in any way. We can choose to perceive them or not.

The mind, being the root of action, determines the character of our whole life. That is why Solomon said: "Keep thy heart with all diligence; for out of it are the issues of life" (Proverbs 4:23). (The Hebrew word *leb* means mind and intelligence: buddhi.) The mind is the source of life itself–it *is* life. Yet it can be transcended–transmuted.

All good or evil comes to us from ourselves, from our mind. God has nothing to do with it whatsoever. Therefore the Gita says: "Do not say: 'God gave us this delusion.' You dream you are the doer, you dream that action is done, you dream that action bears fruit. It is your ignorance, it is the world's delusion that gives you these dreams. The Lord is everywhere and always perfect: what does He care for man's sin or the righteousness of man? The Atman is the light: the light is covered by darkness: this darkness is delusion: that is why we dream. When the light of the Atman drives out our darkness that light shines forth from us, a sun in splendor, the revealed Brahman. The devoted dwell with Him, they know Him always there in the heart, where action is not. He is all their aim. Made free by His Knowledge from past uncleanness of deed or of thought, they find the place of freedom, the place of no return" (Bhagavad Gita 5:14-17, Prabhavananda translation).

We have to conceive or think good or evil before we can do good or evil. That is why purification and mastery of the mind is the yogi's primary concern all along the pathway. The mind is neutral. It is our will that determines its character. We can turn it to either side. If we let it drift, it will inevitably turn to folly and evil. That is the problematic condition of birth on this planet in a human body. It has a long past, reaching far back into many incarnations. But since it is under the power of the will, we have the ability to turn it around and make it an instrument of good.

It is not the nature of window glass to be black or opaque, but clear, with nothing obstructing the passage of light. So it is with the Self. Yet the mind obstructs the manifestation of the Self as soot inhibits the light from shining through the glass of the lamp chimney. Of course we might wonder whether the mind becomes sooted and needs cleansing, or that the mind itself is soot that needs to be purified and assumed into the clarity that is the Self. Both views will be helpful to us if we pursue them by means of intense sadhana.

The Gita says with great force that the mind must be made an instrument of the Self, otherwise it becomes an opponent of the Self and an obstacle to the Self and its realization.

Karma is also an aspect of the mind, and yoga alone purifies and elevates the mind-substance (chitta) itself. Since karma is conditioning of the mind, yoga is needed to decondition the mind and bring it into alignment with the ever-free Self.

Sri Ramana Maharshi taught that when a person attains Self-realization, his mind which heretofore has been troubling and deluding him will turn into the Self, will be transmuted into atmic consciousness. The mind is the Atman, but it is the Atman that is dominant: the mind belongs to the jiva (individual Self), the jiva does not belong to the mind. In time the mind is assumed into the jiva-Self so that the jiva is no longer being "consumed" by the mind. Now when this happens a greater marvel takes place: the jiva realizes it is Shiva, the Supreme, that it exists in the Paramatman just as the mind existed in it. However, the jiva, being eternally part of Brahman, will not become "lost" in Brahman in the way the mind becomes assimilated into the Atman.

It is the defects of the mind that keep returning us again and again to this world.

Only when we can shed our petty little measure-bound minds can we comprehend the Divine Nature which is our nature.

No matter how real or solid material objects and material existence seem to be, it is really all in our head. It is purely our idea of things. If we think about that, then we can realize what powerful beings we really are. Our minds are reflections of the mind of the Creator of All. Our wills have the power to shape our lives in every birth. We truly are gods.

Attraction is never in the object, only in the mind, and if our mind is free of illusions, nothing in the cosmic dream will be of any special value to us, and nothing can entangle or enslave us. At the moment of death we will fly away into the freedom of the Self, with not a backward glance or thought.

Along with striving for a one-pointed mind, the struggle to control the mind is a source of misery and exhaustion for the unskilled yogi. This is because the gross intellect is completely untamable. The solution is twofold: through inwardness of awareness we should be in touch with the subtle side of the mind that is amenable to the process of meditation and which can be purified accordingly.

But most important is the need to refine the entire mind so it will be completely subtle in nature. When the mental energies of even the external senses have been made pure and refined through diet, moral conduct and (especially) japa and meditation, then troubles with the mind mostly cease. I say mostly, because there is always the chance of the deep inner mind tossing up some samskaras that rock the boat a bit, but not for long if we keep steadily to our practice.

Of course there is no hope of refining the mind if a pure diet is not maintained, since the mental energies are derived from the energies of the food we eat. Moreover, the mind cannot be refined without the steady observance of yama and niyama.

MASTERS, TRUE AND FALSE

There are many ideas about what makes someone a liberated master. Some think a man was a master just because he did not wear clothes, or only a kaupin. All kinds of eccentricities are listed as the traits of avadhutas, but a real avadhuta embodies a single trait: total desirelessness. That is because desire carries a great deal of baggage along with it, not the least being the ego and an entrenched sense of duality. If you have a text of the Bhagavad Gita in your computer, do a search for the words "desire," "desires," and "desireless." You will be amazed at the number of times they occur. Desire and its adjuncts are the major subject of the Gita.

"Knowledge is covered by this, the constant enemy of the wise, having the form of desire which is like insatiable fire. The senses, mind, and intellect are said to be its abode. With these it deludes the embodied one by veiling his innate wisdom. Therefore, controlling the senses at the outset, kill this evil being, which destroys ordinary knowledge and supreme knowledge" (Bhagavad Gita 3:39-41).

That is how to become a master.

Many liberated beings have said that everything was their guru, meaning that they saw the One in all things manifesting as the universe which embodied the wisdom of Spirit. The ability to learn from life itself is necessary as we ascend in levels of consciousness. Further, the Self-realized understand that God is the only guru, teaching us by means of His creation. This is depicted in Swami Sivananda's thrilling poem, *Only God I Saw*:

> When I surveyed from Ananda Kutir, Rishikesh,
> By the side of the Tehri Hills, only God I saw.

In the Ganges and the Kailas peak,
In the famous Chakra Tirtha of Naimisar also, only God I saw.

In the Dedhichi Kand of Misrik,
In the sacred Triveni of Prayag Raj too, only God I saw.
In the maya Kund of Rishikesh and
In the springs of Badri, Yamunotri and Gauri-Kund to boot,
    only God
I saw.

In tribulation and in grief, in joy and in glee,
In sickness and in sorrow, only God I saw.
In birds and dogs, in stones and trees,
In flowers and fruits, in the sun, moon and stars, only God I saw.

In prayer and fasting, in praise and meditation,
In Japa and Asana, in Tratak and concentration, only God I saw.
In Pranayama and Nauli, in Bhasti and Neti,
In Dhouti and Vajroli, in Bhastrika and Kundalini, only God
    I saw.

In Brahmakara Vritti and Vedantic Nididhyasana,
In Atmic Vichara and Atmic Chintana, only God I saw.
In Kirtan and Nama Smaran, in Sravana and Vandana,
In Archana and Padasevana, in Dasya and Atmanivedana, only
    God I
saw.

Like camphor I was melting in His fire of knowledge,
Amidst the flames outflashing, only God I saw.
My Prana entered the Brahmarandhra at the Moordha,
Then I looked with God's eyes, only God I saw.

I passed away into nothingness, I vanished,
And lo, I was the all-living, only God I saw.
I enjoyed the Divine Aisvarya, all God's Vibhutis,
I had Visvaroopa Darshan, the Cosmic Consciousness, only God
    I saw.

Glory, glory unto the Lord, hail! hail! hail! O sweet Ram.
Let me sing once more Thy Name–Ram Ram Ram, Om, Om,
    Om,
only God I saw.

Evil does not exist as an entity but only as a distortion of the good. Just as any object touched by King Midas turned into gold, if an evil person is brought into intimate contact with the good he can change and resume his earlier character as good if he so wills. The beneficial effect of satsang (spiritual association) demonstrates this. This is why throughout history it has been seen that when evil people encounter great holy ones they may became drastically changed and begin living a good, even a holy, life.

In our own time, powerful figures in organized crime in India were transformed by a single meeting with perfected yogis. Oftentimes a single glimpse was sufficient to change them for the rest of their life. This occurred throughout the life of Swami Sivananda and in that of others I met in India.

During my first trip to India I met Girish Chandra Mazumdar, a disciple of Gandhi, who was renowned for curing alcoholism by means of devotional music, especially kirtan, the singing of divine names. Three or four times a day kirtan would be held at his home, and many of those who regularly participated were freed from their addiction. Why? Because they were themselves divine in essence and their degradation was only temporary and superficial.

But what practical value does this have for us? When we meditate we find all kinds of negative and destructive elements and impulses stored in our mind. But if we will introduce into our minds sacred vibrations through meditation and continual japa we will find that these undesirable impulses will become purified and made forces for good in us. This is why we should never try to push away anything that arises in our minds as we meditate. Instead we should scrutinize those things with the "eye" of mantra japa, exposing them to the holy vibrations that will not drive them away or destroy them but transmute them into spiritual benefit. Those who immerse themselves in the sacred power of mantra, especially when joined with the breath, will experience this for themselves.

There is simply no way to overemphasize the truth that without authentic and increasing spiritual experience, the experience of eternal realities, we are speaking into empty air from an empty heart. Only that which is based on personal attainment carries the vibrations of awakening which makes any spiritual teaching of value. False teachers employ all kinds of gimmicks and emotional manipulation to attract and enslave their disciples, but men and women of real spiritual attainment need only the words of teachers which are pervaded by the consciousness produced by their realization.

A friend of mine heard Yogananda speak in the 1920s. He told me: "When Yogananda spoke on the Bhagavad Gita you knew that he understood the Gita as no other person did." Yogananda could do the same with music. My friend said: "When Yogananda played the vina you could feel your own consciousness opening out as though vast cubes of space were opening in your own mind. This was his power."

I would like to tell you a story that bears this out.

One Sunday day morning I was sitting with my friend Jean Page, in the SRF Cafe at the Hollywood center. I did not know it, but it was Jean's birthday. For a few moments she closed her eyes and got very still. As she opened her eyes, the telephone rang in the office of Sister Meera who was in charge of the center and the cafe. Shortly Sister Meera came out of the office and over to our table. "Jean, how would you like a copy of the first edition of *Autobiography of a Yogi*?" she asked. "I would!" exclaimed Jean. "There is a woman on the phone who has one she will sell. Shall I get you her address?" As Sister Meera went back to the telephone, Jean told me: "Just now I closed my eyes and said: 'Master, what are you going to give me for my birthday?' And the phone rang immediately!"

It was not long before we were in Jean's car heading for our goal. When the woman came out with the book, she said: "I would like to tell you about how I got this book. I was raised in the Catholic Church and went faithfully to Mass, but never found any peace of heart. Later I went to various churches and spiritual groups, but still I had no peace. I was always anxious and discontent inside. Then one Sunday my husband and I went to Yogananda's church. When we came in the door, he was playing the organ; and the moment the sound entered my ears it was like my soul gave a great sigh of relief and for the first time in my life I had peace and happiness. Later on I bought this book and have had it all these years. I will never forget Yogananda and how he helped me find peace."

Such was the effect Yogananda had on countless thousands of souls. I met people whose lives he had literally saved, and many whose souls were awakened in his presence. This is the way a liberated master lives in this world. His every word and deed are expressions of his divine consciousness. When we are with such a one we are with God.

Paramhansa Yogananda told his close disciples that God had promised him that anyone who read his autobiography would be given at least one chance to find God in this lifetime. It is amazing the number of people who never finish *Autobiography of a Yogi*. I have had people tell me the most amazing and deluded "reasons" why they stopped reading *Autobiography*. Others have told me that they read the entire book except for the last chapter and "somehow" never finished it, but planned to do so in the future. (Chances are it never happened.) As the Master said: "People are so skillful in their ignorance." And especially in maintaining it!

Yogananda said that wherever a Master goes, his vibrations will remain there forever. The same is true of his words: they will continue vibrating in the subtle levels until the dissolution of the creation cycle. That is why we can tune in with the teachings of all true masters and learn from them directly, as the Venerable Master Chen Kung, founder of the Amida Society, often says. There are no "dead and gone" masters. They are always present, but we must refine our consciousness to perceive them and become their disciples.

Between 1924 and 1935 Yogananda travelled throughout the United States and spoke in nearly all major cities, leaving behind his wisdom vibrating in the ether to be accessed by those yogis that have sufficiently purified and developed their intelligence (buddhi). After his seeming death he was asked by his chief disciple Rajasi Janakananda why he did not come to those who called on him. His reply was that he would no longer come down to this world, that those who wished to meet him must rise up into the Light where he was dwelling. That is true of all masters of all ages. "All that the Father giveth me shall come to me; and him that cometh to me I will in no wise cast out" (John 6:37).

When the finite jiva unites with the infinite Paramatman, the ego dissolves. In the consciousness of the One, selfishness is totally impossible. Once when Yogananda came out into the street from visiting Sri Yukteswar he saw a man looking at his motorcycle. "Do you like it?" asked Yogananda. "Yes!" replied the man. 'Then it is yours," said Yogananda.

The fully liberated are free on all levels, and that includes freedom from the law of death. When they will it to be so, then alone does their body fall away in seeming death. Actually, they walk out of the body as easily as we remove our clothing. For example, Swami Sivananda asked to see an astrological almanac and studied it for a long while. Then he put his finger by a date and commented that no advanced yogi would be able to resist taking advantage of that day. When his close disciples (some of whom I knew) looked at the book after his laying it aside, they saw he was referring to July 14, 1963. On that day he left his body.

Yogananda left his body at will after having warned his disciples for some months. To one disciple he said on the day of his departure: "In a few hours I will be gone." Yogananda wrote about others who left the body at will in his autobiography. Such great ones do not really die, they live forever. Great saviors take up and put down bodies as easily as you and I pick up a book and put it down. They are really never born nor do they die. In one of his recorded talks Yogananda said: "Yogananda was never born, nor will he ever die." Krishna, Buddha, and Jesus are perhaps the most famous examples of those who left the world when they willed.

One thing I have seen in my enounters with saints is their clear-sightedness. The image of the innocent and childlike saint that never sees the negativity in anyone is a wish-fantasy of the corrupt and hypocritical. No one becomes a saint without dealing with his own mind, which includes learning all the tricks of the deluded ego. Having seen it in themselves they can see it in others. Certainly I never met a saint that was cunning, calculating or negatively shrewd, but their eyes were wide open and they saw everything about those who came to them. For example, Paramhansa Nityananda once said: "Worldly people are like someone who defecates in their hand and then holds it out to you and asks: 'What should I do with this?'" This has been my experience for decades. They make the mess and demand that you get them out of it. And they have every intention of making future messes, too.

The word avadhuta means "cast off"—one who has cast off the world utterly. An avadhuta is a supreme ascetic and jnani who has renounced all worldly attachments and connections and lives in a state beyond body consciousness, whose behavior is not bound by ordinary social conventions. Often they wear no clothing. They embody the highest state of asceticism or tapas.

An avadhuta is one who lives both in this world and the higher worlds. This is possible because all worlds are ultimately one, and space is a dream-illusion.

Avadhutas eat, sleep, walk around, and speak to others. How could they do that without some kind of bodily sense and awareness of others? An avadhuta perceives himself, including his body, as pure conscious-ness—as the Self. His body is not a cover of the Self, but a revelation of the Self. He is at all time aware of the Self in all things: "He who is steadfast in yoga (yoga-yukta) at all times sees the Self present in all beings and all beings present in the Self. He who sees me everywhere, and sees all things in me—I am not lost to him, and he is not lost to me. He, established in unity, worships me dwelling in all things. Whatever be his mode of life, that yogi ever abides in me" (Bhagavad Gita 6:29-31).

Sattwa, rajas, and tamas do not exist for the avadhuta, because they are simply three modes of energy behavior in Prakriti. But for the avad-huta there is only Purusha, which transcends Prakriti.

Sunlight is the same whether it shines on sea water or fresh water, whether it is at sea level or on top of a hill. If, however, our attention is on the water or the location, we will miss this fact. Light is light, wherever it is; and light is everywhere.

If light is what we are after, then no matter what the environment or the source, it will all be the same to us. But this will only be the sit-uation if we have truly experienced light and come to know its nature and purpose. Just to see something with the eye is not enough. Consider how many people have seen great saints and masters, yet have not known what they were seeing–not at all. The capacity people have for seeing but not seeing is remarkable, especially in the spiritual realms. Few indeed have the eyes to really see. "But blessed are your eyes, for they see: and your ears, for they hear" (Matthew 13:16).

We should be intent on what a thing actually is, not how it is packaged or presented. We must not be influenced by the snobbery of "civilization," but perceive with the eye of intuition what is the value and true nature of a thing or person. I have seen glitter gurus in India who had a great following because they "looked like a sage" and had lots of rich and powerful disciples.

On the other hand, one of the most remarkable yogis I knew was a small, unassuming and rather comic-looking man who walked unsteadily because he was born with deformed feet and had deformed hands, as well. As a consequence he had less than a dozen disciples, in contrast to the hundreds and thousands that flocked to the popular teachers. Yet my dear friend possessed all the yoga powers (which he rarely used), daily entered into profound samadhi, and was very beloved to some of India's greatest (and genuine) saints. He lived in a tiny room, had two changes of clothes, meditated all night rather than slept, and tirelessly worked for the free education of the poor villagers of India. Yet who wanted to hear what he had to say? If he could have increased his height, corrected his hands and feet, grown luxuriant hair on his head and face and developed shiny, glowing eyes, "walked like an elephant" and gave polished but empty talks, he would have had a large following. (In India the people know more about spirituality than those in the West, but they do not have much more sense).

As long as he was robust in health, had a resonant voice, and gave lectures, my beloved Swami Sivananda drew big crowds to his ashram. But when I knew him he was failing in health and gave no talks at all, but in the satsangs asked riddles, told jokes, and in general had great fun. How we loved it—and him! He was giving away divine awakening with both hands as a god walking among us. But most people said he had gone senile, and in all that huge ashram we only had about twenty people at the morning satsang and forty in the evening satsang. How blessed we were. Those times with him are the most precious of my life. Yes, we laughed and enjoyed ourselves, but in each satsang there were moments of profound spiritual awareness. It often seemed to me that we could not be on earth. Other times I felt that time had reversed and we were sitting with one of the primal sages of India, whose very sight purified the heart. And yet the sophisticated and "wise" stayed away. They had no time to waste with such undignified and superficial goings-on. What they missed! But we did not, for which I will be forever grateful.

One of the greatest yogis I met was a woman wandering around rural Bengal pretending to be insane. Everyone was laughing at her, but she let me know her real character and blessed me greatly.

A friend of mine, part of the UN Mission to India, once asked a knowledgeable Indian man who was the greatest saint in Benares. He smiled and said: "The greatest saint in Benares is a dirty 'beggar' that sits all day opposite the main post office and seems to be crazy. But if you go there, don't go near him with the intention of speaking to him or getting his blessing. For if you do, he will shout at you and run away!"

The essential fact is this: we should decide what we are after and care nothing about externals, and especially care nothing about what "the public" values. Our sole question as sadhakas should be: "Does this take me to God?" and that should be the sole test.

Non-yogis are always trying to figure out or imagine the state of consciousness of a liberated person—something that is as absurd as a child attempting to understand the full mind of an adult. These people often write books on the great masters and thereby give a completely mistaken and even distorted impression of them. Their sincerity of intention matters not a whit.

Those of us who admire and love Paramhansa Yogananda like to read books about him, especially the memories of his close disciples. But those accounts give us an insight into how really close–spiritually speaking–to the Master the authors really were. Some accounts leave us inspired, feeling that we have somehow momentarily been with the Master. Others, though, feel like an encylopaedia article, not really living or even personal. Once I read a long account of a disciple's memories of Yogananda and literally felt like I was reading fiction. It was not that I thought the author was lying, but that somehow there was no reality, no life, behind the words. This saddened but did not puzzle me, because nineteen years of frequent contact with Anandamayi Ma had shown me that there were people who traveled with her constantly that were never affected by her company in any way. One devotee who had known Ma from the first time she came to Benares told me: "I assumed that everyone around Ma had to be a great soul, especially those that lived and traveled with her. But one day I told this to Ma, and she pointed to her hand and said: 'Baba, even flies sit on this body.' Then I understood." And so did I. Once a devotee relayed to me something about someone who had stayed around Ma's body for decades. All I could say was: "It's a pity he never met Ma."

This all relates to the attempt to intellectually comprehend a liberated master. Some have come up with the absurd proposition that absolute masters are not even aware of anything, that it is only their bodies that move about and even speak to others (supposedly because to them "there is no 'other'"). This is what comes of trying to get the intellect to comprehend those that are beyond the intellect.

Being enamored of the body and its possibilities for enjoyment, even those who claim to be interested in spiritual life always want a yogi to be diseaseless and ageless.

How well do I remember meeting a famous yogi at an airport when he landed in America for his second visit. A large number of admirers were there, and as we were all walking along after him I heard a flurry of chagrined whispers about how the last time his hair had been totally black, but now he had so much gray in his beard. Not a few were quite disturbed by this, and I heard about it later on, too.

One time when Swami Vivekananda visited London he found that his most fervent and devoted "disciples" had actually fled the city so as be sure they would not meet him. The reason? They had learned that he had been seriously ill some months before. Declaring that a master could never become sick, that sickness was sign of a mental flaw, they renounced and denounced him bitterly.

His teacher, Sri Ramakrishna, had been very popular and respected in Calcutta, but when he got throat cancer the "devoted" disappeared–some because they believed a master could not get such a disease, and others because they were afraid they might be asked to help with his medical expenses! He himself said that the purpose of the disease was to separate the wheat from the chaff–and there was a lot of chaff.

Many disdained Paramhansa Yogananda because of his illness and handicap in walking at the end of his life. (On occasion he swept the illness away and did what he needed to do and then brought it back. That is real mastery.) One of his disciples told me: "There were people who said that Master could not be a master because he was too fat. Others said he could not be a master because he sweat too much." Those people really had earthbound consciousness!

People I knew said that Swami Sivananda could not be a master since he "died" of diabetes, even though it is known that he chose the day and hour of his departure from the body.

Regarding a liberated person and suffering, the Bhagavad Gita says: "Having attained this [enlightenment], he regards no other gain better than that, and established therein he is not moved by heaviest sorrow" (6:22). No suffering can overshadow or cloud the yogi's inner vision, no matter how terrible or prolonged it may be. Two events come to mind that illustrate this.

Sri Ramakrishna was in the final stages of throat cancer. Its ravages were terrible. One day he began pathetically describing the horrible pain to a disciple. After listening a while, the disciple interrupted him, vehemently saying: "No matter what you say, I see you as an ocean of bliss!" Sri Ramakrishna smiled, turned to a disciple standing nearby, and said: "This rascal has found me out!" And that was the end of the subject.

Toward the end of his earthly life, Paramhansa Yogananda had severe trouble with his legs, at times being unable to walk. Sometimes when the pains were so bad that he could not sleep, close disciples would sit with him in his bedroom. Often he asked them to play recordings of Indian devotional music to take his mind to higher levels. Once, though, he fell asleep as his first American disciple, Dr. M. W. Lewis, and his wife kept sad vigil in his room. After some time, Yogananda began to softly moan, and then his groans became increasingly louder and more expressive of the awful pain. Both devoted disciples began to weep in sympathy for his sufferings. Instantly Yogananda stopped groaning and began laughing. Then they understood: the great Master was always immersed in divine bliss, however much the body might suffer.

The wise aspirant never listens to the glorification and praise (and promotion) of a supposed guru, but looks very carefully at his disciples. There the whole story is told.

Conditioning of the mind comes from the company we keep or the environment in which we live. Just as the two situations—being in intense light or intense dark—cause the person to be unseeing when they go into the opposite situation, in the same way people's habitual mode of life can blind them to the truth of things, either about themselves or others. And this is especially true when people encounter saints. Since their daily life is totally opposite to the atmosphere or aura of a saint, when they meet them they either consider them nothing or they dislike them, not realizing that the defect or lack is in themselves.

It is wisdom for us to remain intent on our own mind and its development and leave others to do the same, or not, whichever pleases them. The Gita's descriptions of the enlightened consciousness underlines this. Only the individual knows whether or not he is in that state described by the Gita. Sri Ramakrishna often jokingly commented that a man of realization does not grow two horns by which we may recognize his realization. Someone once asked Sri Ma Sarada Devi: "Mother, does the vision of God mean the attainment of knowledge and spiritual consciousness? Or does it signify something else?" To which she replied: "What else can it mean except the attainment of these? Does anybody mean to say that a man of realization grows two horns?" Consequently we should not be interested in whether someone is wise or ignorant. The only relevant question is: What am I? And that should be the focus of our endeavors.

Various things that appear essential to the person without higher experience (and therefore without higher consciousness) become worthless and even a hindrance when higher experience and consciousness are attained. Before such attainment it would be foolish to discard them, and after attainment it would be foolish to retain them. Unfortunately ego gets in the way and makes many people act in the way they think the enlightened should act. So they toss aside what they still need and adopt ways which are beyond them, even resorting to fakery when they cannot really do what the master yogis do easily.

I have seen people in both East and West faking samadhi—and very badly, too. Of course I had the advantage of having seen the real thing. At one time I was living in a simple Indian ashram literally in the middle of nowhere. Every day I saw a yogi in samadhi and got to know both its appearance and feel. The supreme experience was seeing the great master Swami Sivananda in samadhi. It was a transcendent experience that I cannot put into words, but I knew I was seeing divinity. I also saw Anandamayi Ma a few times in samadhi, and it was indescribable. No one can begin to imitate the real thing, for it also conveys to the observer a definite spiritual experience.

One of the most perilous decisions a person can make is to decide to learn and practice meditation. Not only does only one in thousands seek God (Bhagavad Gita 7:3), only one guru or teacher in thousands really knows how to find God, but nearly all lead their disciples in the byways of delusion and futility, the same byways they themselves are (often sincerely) hopelessly lost in.

For some reason in the West talk passes itself off as reality, especially in religion and even more so in yoga. But we need solid experience, not the flimsy and foolish nonsense that many people claim for their "enlightenment experience." I have heard astonishingly obvious falsehoods passed off by supposedly enlightened people. Some of them were tricksters and confidence men, others were dupes of phony gurus, and some were genuinely mentally ill. I have witnessed the entire range of deception over the decades. Their antics in attempting to appear enlightened and in sahaja samadhi are often very funny as well as tragic.

One of the biggies of India once came to a conference (Samyam Sapta) sponsored by the Anandamayi Sangha. Of course he did not come for the whole thing, he just whizzed in and whizzed out with a large amount of devotees in attendance. He gave a talk that was thoroughly hilarious because it was so silly and exaggerated. I was delighted at every moment and wished I could laugh outright. After his talk he remained about an hour as one of the genuine mahatmas gave a talk. I was watching him throughout with great interest, especially his big gold cufflinks that were attached to his kurta (shirt) that had no cuffs, just holes for the cufflinks to be put in. But the most telling thing was his blasé expression as he looked up and around, and the way he had taken off his sunglasses and was idly swinging them back and forth like a worldly sophisticate indeed.

As I watched the sunglasses rotate I thought: "That gesture tells the whole story. What a fake!" And then I thought: "What am I doing? I could be looking at Ma [Anandamayi] who is just a few feet from him!" So I looked over at Ma... and saw her leaning forward and intently watching his sunglasses display with a speculative expression on her face that indicated she, too, considered that it told the whole story. Jai Ma! (You might be interested to know that this man's carryings-on and posturings failed utterly in America. So there is some hope for us.)

Often in India those who live in an utterly psychotic and chaotic manner are thought to be great yogis and siddhas. Furthermore, the reasons given for considering them holy are philosophically obscure and often simply foolish. I would like to give you an example. Someone once wrote about a local mahatma in India: "A confluence of feelings in his eternal heart is the mark of the ever free consciousness of the mahatma, wherever may be his place and time in this phenomenal world. The life of S. M. depicts the very essence of vairagya—complete resignation and detachment. He rests in a natural spiritual state of Turiya. That is the superconscious soul-perception in which all identification with one's physical and mental person is lost." That sounds grand, does it not? A tremendous amount of similar blather follows. Then we get a description of the mahatma. Consider this:

S. M. lived on a veranda surrounded by burlap curtains. He gave darshan sitting on a bed-sized billiard table. Its legs had been cut off to convert it into a swing that was suspended from the ceiling by iron chains. It moved at a slight push.

S. M. was wearing about twelve shirts, one on top of the other, and nothing else. As he sat there he ate nearly all the offerings people brought. Rather than let them have any as prasad (the usual custom) he only let two sadhus that lived with him and cows and dogs eat the rest.

S. M. had been giving darshan on that billiard-swing for twelve years. He had never moved away from there even for toilet or bath. The stools he passed right there used to be dry and without any smell. They were hard and if broken looked like ash. The explanation given (who would want any?) was that his internal yogic fire must have burned up all impurities that normally come to the physical body. That condition of his defecation was the sole proof given of his having extraordinary yoga powers. When he wished to communicate with others he spoke loudly in garbled Hindi that every one could hear but not understand. The words had no meaning; made no sense.

On occasion he unexpectedly slapped, struck and kicked people who approached him with devotion. The right response was for them to massage his hand or foot lest *they* had hurt him by being so hard to strike. After all, a blow from a saint is considered a very special blessing. Everyone was in awe of him and considered him to be one of the rarest among human beings. (I am not being sarcastic.) Some devotees tried to clean him up by giving him a bath, but immediately after his bath, S. M. would rub mud and sand on his body.

If this is not psychosis, nothing is.

If we read the Gita each day and carefully consider the descriptions given there of those who have attained true realization, we will not go wrong in our evaluation of supposed yogis, nor we will ourselves wander off into some exotic byway that in the final analysis is mental illness.

A friend of mine was once asked to help a phony American "Mataji" to her car. She was weaving all over the place, supposedly in exalted consciousness and mostly unaware of this material world as he tried to guide her toward the street. At one point she announced in a very sharp manner: "Watch the curb, boy!" My friend stepped back and said: "I think you can manage on your own now." And you know what? She did!

One famous "shaktipat" guru in America kept saying to me: "I have no idea where this shakti is coming from," and asking my opinion about its origin. Since my opinion was just that he was deluded and in danger by following a deluded guru, I avoided giving an answer. When the public crash came a few years later it was colossal and permanent.

MAYA

Maya is delusion about what is real. Many people think that the world outside is maya, but maya is the mistaken way we see, experience and look at the world. Maya is totally interior, in the mind alone, just as is karma. It begins and ends in us. Maya disappears in us through the practice of meditation.

Maya means "The Measurer," a reference to the two delusive "measures" Time and Space. Maya is the dream from which we all must awake. However, just as we have a lower and higher Self, and conquer the lower self through the higher Self, in the same way maya is dual, consisting of maya and Mahamaya. Mahamaya is the "Great illusion," also known as Mahashakti, the Great Power, the divine creative energy. Maya is the power of illusion, and Mahamaya is the power of awakening from illusion. Yoga invokes the Supreme Power, Mahashakti, which delivers us from the binding power of maya/materiality. It is the Absolute which frees us from the relative. Only the yogis really understand this. (See *Philosophy of Gorakhnath* by Akshaya Kumar Banerjea.)

Nothing is ever destroyed in essence, only the temporary forms. Maya is the net in which we are caught, the prison which confines us. We do not need to tear it apart or destroy it, we need only let it melt away at the advent of our Self-realization.

Krishna spoke truly in the Gita when he told Arjuna: "All this world is deluded by the three states produced by the gunas. It does not perceive me, who am higher than these and eternal. Truly this maya of mine made of the gunas is difficult to go beyond. Verily only those who attain me shall pass beyond this maya" (Bhagavad Gita 7:13-14).

It is interesting that Saint Anthony the Great, the first "official" monastic in Christianity, said: "I have seen the snares of the Wicked One spread out upon the face of the earth." This he said in reference to the catching of birds in nets spread on the ground. Getting their feet tangled in the net they cannot escape. So it is with human beings, as well.

All sentient beings are caught in the net of rebirth. To escape that net is both difficult and rare. "Helpless, the same host of beings being born again and again merge at the approach of the Night [the dissolution of a creation cycle] and emerge at the dawn of Day [the beginning of a creation cycle] (Bhagavad Gita 8:19). "Whatever be the forms produced within all wombs, the great Brahma is their womb, and I the seed-casting Father" (Bhagavad Gita 14:4).

Just as salt is extracted from water by dehydration and can be melted back again by mixing it with more sea water, so the dream we call maya emerges from Brahman and returns to Brahman, Brahman alone having really existed at any time.

Before samsara begins at birth, and when it stops at death, the real nature of the person is glimpsed, but not to much use, since samsara in another world begins to take over. Therefore from birth to death it is all maya and must be understood to be so in order not to get hypnotized or drawn into its illusions.

This is extremely important: the universe is not just Shiva at its roots in the most subtle chidakasha, but on the very visible, material level as well. The universe is not a disguise of Satchidananda Shiva, but is a revelation of the Infinite Spirit. When we see the world we are seeing God. The problem is that our mind (manas) and intellect (buddhi) are distorted and even corrupted, so we mistake the Spirit we are seeing for matter. Our mind itself is maya.

Impermanence is the nature of this visible world. Things in the subtler astral and causal worlds last much longer, many times more than on earth, yet they too break up and dissolve. So although the invisible lasts longer, the wise seek to transcend the visible and invisible and enter into the Imperishable Reality.

In India it means something to be a beggar, truly destitute and with no prospects of a better life. Calling someone a beggar in a spiritual sense, then, carries real weight. Three kinds of people are spiritual beggars: 1) those that have not realized God, 2) those that have not dispelled delusion from their minds and hearts, and 3) those that remain on the downward path of the world.

Human beings are running frantically after what is basically nothing: mere shadows. This world and all within it is really insubstantial, a mirage. Yet from life to life people struggle for things of the world and suffer when they cannot get what they want, and suffer even more when they do. What a horrible paradox!

When I was small, I had the most peculiar delusion. I believed absolutely that if I could hold on tightly enough to something in a dream, I would be able to bring it over into the waking world. Sometimes I just came upon the thing in a dream, and sometimes I found myself in a store like Woolworth's, which was a paradise for a child. Being alone in the store, I would run around in a frenzy of greed, grabbing as much as I could hold of what attracted me. Then I would sit down and hold on as tightly as I could. The strain of that would of course wake me. I would look down at my arms: empty. After a while I gave up. But humans take dozens if not hundreds of lives to get the idea.

People think it is clever to say: "I only believe in what I can see," so in their ignorance they do not seek the invisible spirit, though it is the only Reality, the only thing they can really make their own. Their suffering is colossal, stretching through life after life, until they get the right idea and seek God.

The adharmic center themselves in the world. Their thoughts, words, and deeds are hollow echoes of the world and its ways. They are absorbed in the world. The dharmic are just as centered and absorbed, but in the spirit-Self. They are poles apart, which is why they really cannot communicate with one another.

When you get into a train you just sit and it takes you to its destination. If you do not want to go there, that is unfortunate, because you are definitely going to end up there. Once we enter into prakriti, into relative existence, we are completely under its influence and like a swift river we have fallen into, it sweeps us along. All the talk of free will matters little, since hardly anyone really controls their life to any meaningful degree.

Sri Ramakrishna said that human beings are like animals tied to something. They can move around all they like within the length of the rope that binds them, but that is all. And most people are on very short tethers.

It is literally true that most people cannot help what they think or do; they are carried along by the current of material existence. Rebelling against this situation does very little but make us miserable. The only way to not be in the jail is to get out of the jail. Otherwise "around and around it goes and where it stops nobody knows." People would like for things to be different, but they do not want to let go of the wheel. Some aspiring (and failing) poet once wrote: "I just love the world so much,/Seems I can't hold it close enough."

Not to worry—the world had that "poet" held tightly in its grasp (a stranglehold, actually). There is no complete or lasting freedom for any but the yogi who extricates himself from prakriti, not just in this world but in all the worlds. Only in the boundlessness of Spirit is there any freedom.

Samsara usually binds us, but we can make it a springboard to a leap into the Infinite. Only when we undergo suffering do we seek the cessation of suffering. Only when we feel the pangs of separation from God are we impelled to seek union with God. So we need to clearly see "what" we are right now and begin to work toward being "that" which transcends all samsaric existence.

First we experience the frustration of bondage and then we take up the path to liberation. After understanding the nature of relative existence as a dream, only then can we intelligently seek awakening. Samsara is not real, but it leads us to the Real. It veils the Face of God, but its very presence tells us there is a Face behind it that we may seek and see.

We cannot really transform the world, only our idea about the world.

Edgar Allan Poe wrote in a poem: "All that we see or seem is but a dream within a dream." And that happens to be true to some degree: all our experience of the outer world is through the senses which only relay electrical impulses to the brain which translates those impulses into sensory impressions. (I am oversimplifying.) So what we know of the world is completely in our head, as insubstantial as a dream. On the other hand, though we do not perceive the actual world directly, it is real because is is a manifestation of divine intelligence and power. But for a the yogi it is good to keep in mind that what we perceive of creation is in our mind. Therefore we should deal with the world as an interior as well as an exterior entity. And cultivation of the interior life through yoga is the best preparation for dealing with the world meaningfully or successfully.

We must realize that maya/samsara is a dream, a dream of God in which we are dreaming our own part of the cosmic drama. Awakening is the only antidote to the dream. And then we will discover that the dream was nothing at all. This is very important. Awakening alone should be our interest. And yoga is the process of awakening. This is why in his incarnation as David, Jesus sang: "I shall be satisfied, when I awake, with thy likeness" (Psalms 17:15). And: "When I awake, I am still with thee" (Psalms 139:18). Wherefore we must say with his son, Solomon: "When shall I awake? I will seek it yet again" (Proverbs 23:35).

Maya does not seize us, we seize maya. But in time our involvement with maya seems the other way around. This is what we call delusion. We must recognize the truth of the situation and shake off the paralysis it has induced in our will.

Involvement with maya is really a form of addiction. The first few times a person willfully takes an addictive substance, but eventually the substance "takes" the person who becomes a slave, sometimes even dying if the substance becomes unavailable.

It is an interesting fact that we can become addicted only to what is bad for us, not what is good. People who avidly eat certain foods are often found to be allergic to them or harmed by them in some way. So our problem is not maya: it is us. And we can solve the problem only if we hold that perspective and work from there.

Even as a child I was astounded at the ability of people to completely fool themselves about every aspect of life, and especially about their own thoughts and feelings as well as their ideas and attitudes toward others. Human beings truly are "dwellers in the mirage." Everyone has their personal maya-illusion within the greater cosmic illusion. First we must break out of our personal maya into realization of the truth about the cosmic illusion and then out of that.

Poe was absolutely right in his poem, "A Dream Within a Dream."

Take this kiss upon the brow!
And, in parting from you now,
Thus much let me avow–
You are not wrong, who deem
That my days have been a dream;
Yet if hope has flown away
In a night, or in a day,
In a vision, or in none,
Is it therefore the less gone?
All that we see or seem
Is but a dream within a dream.

I stand amid the roar
Of a surf-tormented shore,
And I hold within my hand
Grains of the golden sand–
How few! yet how they creep
Through my fingers to the deep,
While I weep–while I weep!
O God! Can I not grasp
Them with a tighter clasp?
O God! can I not save
One from the pitiless wave?
Is all that we see or seem
But a dream within a dream?

His problem was that he saw only half of the truth, the illusion, but not that divine state into which we will all eventually awaken.

Perspective on anything can either reveal or conceal its true nature. For example, there is a story of a king who called in an astrologer to tell him his future. After drawing up the king's horoscope, the astrologer told him: "I am sorry to tell you, your majesty, but all those close to you are going to eventually die and you will be left all alone." This so infuriated the king that he had the astrologer executed, then called for another astrologer, who had heard about the fate of the first one. So he drew up the horoscope and then said: "Oh! your majesty, your health and vigor are going to last your entire life, so much so that you are going to outlive every one of your family and friends." The king was greatly pleased and gave the astrologer much wealth and honor.

We must realize that although we are presently immersed in the dream, we are destined to awaken into Infinity. Even though our mind and personality are really constantly shifting mirages, we need to see what is (at least presently) true about them. Therefore a yogi comes to know his own defects and merits and faces and deals with them in wisdom. Equally, the yogi comes to perceive all the desires in his mind and resolves them through purification of the mind. Then he will be able to differentiate between the impermanent and the eternal, between the unreal and the real. He will no longer be deceived by mere appearances, but will know the truth of things.

MEDITATION

The basis of the search for God is daily meditation and constant japa. Those who purify and elevate their minds in this way will rise above the detrimental influences of the world, including worry. "Thou wilt keep him in perfect peace, whose mind is stayed on thee" (Isaiah 26:3).

Meditation is the sure way to Live in the Light, for it lights up our inner and outer being. That is why Krishna said: "Even a little of this dharma protects you from great fear" (Bhagavad Gita 2:40). But to be without meditation is to live in uncertainty and fear. As Krishna also said: "For him who does not meditate there is no peace or happiness" (Bhagavad Gita 2:66).

All the good and evil in the world comes from the human mind exclusively. That which appears to come from outside the mind comes only because of the karmic forces set in motion by the mind itself. The entire world is a mirror, a sounding-board, for humanity. Therefore the solution for all evil and suffering lies right inside each human being. It is not the world that needs changing, but each one of us.

Since the mind is the power of the Self it can accomplish all that is necessary. But knowledge of the way to use that power is needed, and that way is Yoga.

"For the undisciplined there is no wisdom, no meditation. For him who does not meditate there is no peace or happiness" (Bhagavad Gita 2:66).

"The yoga-yoked sage quickly attains Brahman" (Bhagavad Gita 5:6).

"With mind made steadfast by yoga, which turns not to anything else, to the Divine Supreme Spirit he goes, meditating on him" (Bhagavad Gita 8:8).

The mind which is such a botheration to us, which seems the embodiment of all that binds us to the wheel of birth and death, can through the cultivation of awareness through japa and meditation eventually unite with the Infinite Consciousness that is Brahman.

The secret of detachment from worldly objects is to be totally attached to God. Then lesser attachments will vanish. Continual practice of japa and meditation is the way to accomplish this.

Since the Self is within, we can maintain awareness of it whatever the external sensory experiences might be. If the inner awareness is fixed on japa, even when acting the yogi is meditating. Meditation alone develops the mind, intellect and consciousness. To find out for yourself how this is done and what is it like, see *Soham Yoga, the Yoga of the Self.*

"Verily; that Self is (abides) in the heart. This one is in the heart, thereof it is the heart. He who knows this goes day by day into the heavenly world" (Chandogya Upanishad 8:3:3). To be immortal, the yogi must lead his awareness into the cave of the heart, the core of his consciousness. Meditation is the way.

The Canadian humorist, Stephen Leacock, wrote a wonderful satire called *Sorrows of a Super Soul,* in which a complete fool tries to commit suicide by keeping poison and bullets by her bed. Every morning she is astounded to find herself still alive. Silly as that is, this foolishness is a commonplace in human life, especially in the field of religion. Even though true religion is the science of the spirit, people confine it to externals, the result being that people remain in ignorance, and often hypocrisy, all their lives. For religion must be thoroughly internalized to be of any real value and effect. Sadhana alone is the process to accomplish the necessary internalization.

However holy an external object or person may be, our approach to it must be internal. Consider Krishna, the archetypal divine yogi. There were those who did not benefit a bit from being around him. Some hated him and a few tried to kill him. But Arjuna was transformed by being with him. Arjuna, you see, was a yogi, and that made all the difference. He internalized and assimilated the wisdom of Krishna, making it his own.

It is in the stillness of meditation that we find the path to liberation (moksha). It can be found nowhere else.

It is not enough to intuit the existence of God, to "somehow" know God exists. We must know where God is in a twofold manner. First we need to know that God is everywhere–not like some invisible, pervading gas, but rather as everything that exists–that God is not just inside all things, God *is* all things. Second, and most immediate, is the knowledge that God is within us as the core, the essence, of our being. God is the Soul of our soul, the Spirit of our spirit. Therefore to find God we must not just look within occasionally, we must become always aware within and look outward with the inner eye of unity, not just with the physical eyes of duality. Japa and meditation is the way to ensure this.

As long as we perceive the many we have not entered the True and the Real. Our meditation must reflect this principle by being focused on the One Transcendent.

In the Bhagavad Gita we find this very significant verse: "Like the ocean, which becomes filled yet remains unmoved and stands still as the waters enter it, he whom all desires enter and who remains unmoved attains peace" (Bhagavad Gita 2:70). This indicates that forces of negativity, ignorance and evil can be encountered and even "touched" by the minds of those living in the human body. Good and evil are "offerings" to the human being who either responds or does not react to them. When Patanjali speaks of the yogi's mind having no waves (vrittis), he means that the adept yogi's mind is insensitive to outward stimuli unless he wills it otherwise. He has the power to respond or not respond and remains always in command of his entire being.

Since duality is the foundation of relative existence, positive and negative, light and dark, good and evil constantly flow toward each sentient being. To attempt to simply cut this off is ultimately ineffectual. Japa and meditation make us untouched by negative bombardment, just as being inside a house makes us untouched by wind, rain, hail or snow.

Many people who enter conscious spiritual life, especially meditation practice, expect their practice to be perfect and to become enlightened right away, or at least in a few weeks. But time is needed for the unripe to become ripe, for the sour to become sweet.

I met a swami on my first trip to India who was a genius but eccentric to the point of craziness. He was quite advanced in age, and had been just as odd throughout decades of sadhu life. Whenever I would go to the ashram where he lived I would be sure to meet him so I could enjoy his weirdness and have some funny stories to relay back home. Actually, I greatly respected him, as did the members of the ashram, though they had plenty of hilarious stories to tell about him. He was very kind to me, but that did not decrease my amazement at his strange behavior and words. The last time I met him I took one of our ashram members, promising him a good show. But we got something better. When I found him sitting outside, he was very quiet, and emanated a divine radiance. He was so still, so still, and so filled with bliss. We sat with him for some time, savoring the holy moments. That was our last meeting. It had taken time—over fifty years I would estimate—but the fruit had become ripe and sweet.

There were others I met who at our first meeting were not at all admirable, even a bit objectionable, but years later when I met them they had become utterly transformed, awesome even. It had just taken time. The one thing they all had in common was perseverance. As Yogananda used to say: "A saint is a sinner who never gave up." Certainly I have seen proof that steadfastness in yoga works transformation undreamed of. We just have to wait and work. Yogiraj Shyama Charan Lahiri was fond of saying: *Banat, banat, ban ji!* Working, working, done! (Or: Making, making, made!). Certainly, time is necessary, but we should be assured that the result we desire will come in the form of spiritual growth.

Do you know yogis that somehow cannot pull their minds together and focus? Their minds shift in and out of focus seemingly of themselves, whimsically, the yogis being unable to direct them. It is their meditation method that is at fault. They think they are being "spiritual" and beyond materiality, but they are in grave danger of keeping on until they are nothing but a mass of silly putty. I knew a man that lost the ability to focus his eyes through prolonged practice of a wrong meditation technique.

When I began meditating I was really annoyed with people who did not meditate telling me that meditation was dangerous. But after years of experience and observation I realized that *wrong* meditation can be very dangerous, indeed. I saw many people seriously harmed through false systems of meditation, all of which were marketed as the highest and the best. Some became mentally ill, and others became physically and mentally impaired to varying degrees. Many just became pious sillies and liked it that way.

We must realize that meditation should help us to gather in our mental energies, then still and focus them. When the mind matures in yoga, expansion will as naturally follow as does the growth of a child into adulthood, but until then it needs confinement within so it can eventually expand within.

Although it happens imperceptibly, everything about a yogi is made different by his sadhana.

A fundamental effect of meditation is calm and clear mental states which actually enable the yogi to go beyond the mind and see the deeper reality of his entire makeup. This is the touchstone of right yoga and right practice of right yoga. All kinds of amazing and cataclysmic experiences have nothing to do with authentic yoga, most especially not "kundalini experiences."

A yogi must be after consciousness itself, not all kinds of modifications of the mind and psychic energies. Teachers who go on and on about energy and vibration are harmful in the long run, though they appeal to people who have a background in hallucinogenic drugs. A true spiritual teacher and yogi will speak of consciousness and point the student to higher levels of consciousness, instructing him in the way to move into those levels and be established in them.

Prana

All sentient beings share a common makeup. All have the same number of bodies and the evolutionary process is the same for all. The prana in all beings is the power of Divine Consciousness and must be understood and directed to its ultimate purpose.

In the human body the prana is divided into five forms: 1) Prana, the prana that moves upward; 2) Apana: The prana that moves downward, producing the excretory functions in general. 3) Vyana: The prana that holds prana and apana together and produces circulation in the body. 4) Samana: The prana the carries the grosser material of food to the apana and brings the subtler material to each limb; the general force of digestion. 5) Udana: The prana which brings up or carries down what has been drunk or eaten; the general force of assimilation.

These five pranas are the "clockwork" of any living organism, yet are really the single, first-listed Prana operating in five different ways. That is, the upward-moving prana is the "original" prana that in the body also functions in four other modes, in much the same way that Prakriti is the basic substance and the three gunas are its modifications or variations.

"Prana" can also be translated "life" as well as "breath." That being so, life is exclusively internal, that all external phenomena are "living" but not Life itself. This is an important point because, as in most things, the West sees things opposite to the view of the East. For example, the West thinks that matter is the source of consciousness, that consciousness (and therefore intelligence) evolves from matter, whereas the East considers that matter proceeds from consciousness, that matter is really the vibrating effect of consciousness and of buddhi (intelligence). This is a great difference in viewpoint and colors just about all the thought and behavior of both East and West. In the same way, the West confuses the "signs of life" with life itself, rather like confusing art with the artist and concluding that the painting has produced the artist. Yes, it is just that dramatically absurd, a kind of intellectual psychosis.

The conclusion we need to draw is that if we really want to live in the fullest sense we will become internally oriented and internally conscious: this in contrast to the West which thinks that the more frantically and variedly active we are the more we are "living," when really all we are doing is hallucinating. Psychosis, again.

There are five modes of subtle life force in the body we call prana, but the supreme Prana of the yogis is the Living Self or Pranatma. It is Brahman, the One.

The pranic force that manifests in the form of breath is the very power of life itself. It causes us to live and gives us the possibility of evolving. Therefore, the breath-prana is the fundamental power within the yogi. Through it he can become free. Then the Self is revealed as the sole controller, the sole potentate on the throne of liberated consciousness.

Prana goes upward and downward and causes our consciousness to go upward and downward with it. Therefore the yogi must ensure that the upward flowing prana is usually dominant within him. This is done by constant japa and meditation.

Although prana is a kind of all-purpose word for breath and the life-force moving within the body, it is also a technical term meaning the upward-flowing life force in the body. In correct meditation, this becomes dominant and the prana begins to flow up into the Sahasrara through the subtle passages or nadis in the various bodies of the yogi, not just in the sushumna nadi. As a result the centers of higher perception in the Sahasrara are stimulated and activated and the inner, spiritual senses awaken. The full opening of the Sahasrara is the means to enlightenment and liberation, therefore the prana accomplishes the goal of human life. The Gayatri–both the Vedic mantra and the ajapa gayatri, Soham–are intended to polarize the prana to flow upward into the Sahasrara, as well. (Again, see *Soham Yoga: The Yoga of the Self*.) Joy or bliss experienced in meditation is an indication that the prana is flowing upward into the Sahasrara, therefore it is called yogananda: yogic bliss.

The sages of India realized that augmentation and direction of the prana was necessary for fulfilling the purpose of life: evolution. The upward flow of prana must be constant, though it may vary in intensity. The yogi must control the quality of his prana, mostly through diet, since prana is derived from food. Then he maintains the upward flow of prana through the perpetual practice of japa and meditation. When this is done strictly according to the principles of yoga, the yogi's unfoldment takes place without hindrance or delay.

It is necessary to polarize the prana so it flows continually upward into the thousand-petalled lotus (sahasrara), the astral/causal equivalent of the physical brain. The sahasrara contains many subtle centers of awareness that must be awakened and developed. This is accomplished by the simple expedient of immersing them in a high concentration of prana, much like getting seeds to sprout by continually immersing them in water.

The sahasrara is the "paradise" from which all human beings have fallen, and we must return there if we are to be liberated. Unfortunately, the subtle prana has become negatively polarized so it continually flows downward, making us body-conscious and almost completely under the control of material forces. This condition is spiritual death, spiritual enslavement. Unless the pranas are repolarized to flow upward perpetually, there is just no hope, no matter how religious or fervent we may be. Only an eventual falling back into the darkness can be our fate. That is why it is so necessary to become a yogi.

The prana was originally concentrated in our head, and it must be returned there to regain our original state of spirit-awareness. Those who accomplish this return are truly human; the rest are mere soulless bodies, as the first great Christian theologian, Origen, was wont to say.

Mere "good" behavior is not virtue. Only those who have re-entered the awakened sahasrara and come to dwell there, continuing in the process of yoga, possess true, divine virtue.

When we become aware of the internal movements of prana, the inner world is seen. I am not speaking of wandering through all kinds of astral/psychic experiences and gaining "powers" of various kinds, but attaining the perception of Infinity. As the boundless sky can be reflected in an earthen pot of water, in the same way through our inner vision we can come to see and merge into the Chidakasha, the Sky of Consciousness which is Brahman Itself and ourselves as well. All boundaries are dissolved and Pure Being becomes our Abode, becomes Ourself.

When we keep our awareness centered within, not letting our attention or the subtle life force (prana) "leak" out, then all the power we possess will be internalized and used to develop our entire being. Unfortunately, most people "bleed" out their vitality in a myriad of ways and consequently amount to nothing from life to life. I think one of the most striking things I observe in many people is how lifeless they are, devoid of vitality (shakti) and personal presence. Dreariness is the key trait of many people and their lives.

Those who attempt drawing up the pranas into the brain with various forms of breathing exercises will harm themselves. Unless the prana moves in the subtle nerve channels (nadis) exactly where it should, and to the level it should, we do not really live at all. When that does not happen, then nothing worthwhile happens to us, we are only walking corpses. Without the working of the inner fire, our life is nothing but death. By means of yoga we kindle and direct that fire and truly live.

There is a great yogic secret here. When the inner breath comes to function on the conscious level, that is when the kundalini rises. Unless the yoga practice is directly intended to produce this, we are wasting our time.

Raja Yoga

Raja Yoga is the science of Prana, the breath being the main yogic instrument for its accomplishment. It is much more than controlling or refining the breath (for real pranayama is refinement, not control), it is the Way of Unity. Raja Yoga both leads to and is the experience of unity with the Self and Brahman. Total unity is its only goal. This is important to recognize, because Raja Yoga involves mastery of our inner and outer life, which inevitably involves the emergence of inner powers which can easily be wasted or misapplied.

It is pointless to tell a yogi to "shun the yoga powers" any more than it would be to tell a child to avoid adulthood. Certainly, an adult is subject to many more delusions and addictions than a child, and certainly has the ability to work much more harm to himself and others. Nevertheless, adulthood is inevitable. And so it is with the yogi: these powers will manifest in him. If he keeps his eye upon the goal of liberation in Brahman, those powers will ripen into something more, into spiritual realizations, much the same way that sexual energies conserved are transmuted into far higher and greater forces within the consciousness of the yogi. Both sexual energy (and all the body-energies) and the yogic powers are the ore that can be refined into the gold of Self-realization. Those who misdirect and waste them become lost in the maze of illusion, including illusions of enlightenment. But a worthy Raja Yogi stays intent on Unity and lives in that context alone.

There is externalized practice that is really just Hatha Yoga with a veneer of Raja Yoga. This is most important to understand, because in our time Raja Yoga means just about everything it is not. A great deal of physical involvement and cultivation of bodily control is believed to be Raja Yoga. Body identification is at the core of such activities that are not only not sadhana, but the destroyers of authentic sadhana.

Nearly everything called Raja Yoga in India is this fraud. Because of this, and lest I fall into a yoga pit, one day in Varanasi Mother Anandamayi spoke to me very plainly about Raja Yoga. "Raja Yoga deceives its practitioners," she said, "by giving them just a touch of what they should attain. Then after years of practice it evaporates and leaves them totally empty." This I have observed myself through the years. The number of burnt-out Raja Yogis I have seen shuffling around with dead eyes and blank faces and speaking in weak, hoarse voices, having ruined their throats and vocal cords with their thoroughly material and abnormal practice, I cannot calculate. And then there are those with the neurological problems brought on by it, and those who have become alcoholic through it. Truly pathetic are those with dementia. I have known them all. And it was a result of their false yoga. Sincerity did not save them.

Of course, Ma was not speaking of the real Raja Yoga, but of the delusive imitations. As the ads used to say in my childhood: Accept No Substitutes.

Only those yogic processes which take place in the Sahasrara are the true Raja Yoga. The process of liberation begins at the Ajna, but eventually pervades the entire Sahasrara.

The real purpose of Hatha Yoga was the maintenance of the health of hermit-yogis whose way of life precluded normal physical exercise. The main object was the ability to sit for many hours (even days and weeks) in meditation without it being detrimental to the yogis' bodies. Spiritual life not health was their sole interest.

There are masters who insist that there is a bold line between Hatha Yoga and Raja Yoga. Not that they disdain Hatha Yoga, but they object to its being over-valued and believed to be equal to or the same as Raja Yoga.

Raja Yoga is the seat of non-dual consciousness, of liberation. In its highest level Raja Yoga is spiritual consciousness. Raja Yogis are following the path of Spirit, of moksha. Nevertheless, there are those that consider themselves Raja Yogis who engage in pranayama so overtly (and often strenuously) physical and so dependent on the body and its condition that they are really Hatha Yogis in Raja Yogi clothing. Oftentimes they are very good and sincere people who have simply been sold a sham practice and told it is the highest.

Those who engage in Hatha Yoga with the understanding that it is a system of physical culture are perfectly right in doing so. But those that think it is a system of spiritual culture are gravely mistaken.

The distinction between the two systems may seem obvious and even unnecessary to us here in the West, but I have encountered "yogis" in India who knew nothing of even the simplest spiritual principles, but who because of their expert knowledge of Hatha Yoga passed themselves off as great Himalayan yogis.

At the Kumbha Mela these types gain a great deal of notoriety and money. One yogi boasted to me of making nearly one hundred and fifty thousand rupees at one Mela, and that was in the days when the rupee was worth over five times more than it is now. This is because they can impress people by their physical demonstrations. The yogi I just mentioned could float, sitting on water and playing the harmonium!

But what "show" will an enlightened Master give? He can only sit there and be what he is. And how many people can perceive his inward state? The blowhards have lots of loudspeakers and give hours of discourses interspersed with scriptural recitations and singing by their groupies. Some of them bring acting and dancing troupes along to literally give a show. The man of wisdom just cannot compete, and does not want to.

This is why the intelligent pilgrims at the Kumbh completely bypass the big tents and sideshows of the mela and wander through the areas of the unmoneyed (and therefore "unimportant") who have no assigned "camps" but are on the outer areas of the mela grounds. There they may find real treasures sitting at peace. One of my friends only goes to the other side of the Ganges in Prayag during the Purna Kumbh, where he has met many great souls over the years.

Brahmanirvana, the state of liberation (nirvana) that results from total union with Brahman, is itself Raja Yoga—not a practice but an attainment. It is transcendental and therefore beyond all qualities and forms. It cannot be expressed or explained, but it can be experienced and made one's own natural state.

All things are formed of the Vaishwanara, the Cosmic Fire Element. It is only symbolically called Fire, for it is very subtle. Yet it is the power which enables the universe to take on limitless and numberless forms, and is the power of spiritual transformation, as well.

In the human being it is the gastric, digestive fire (energy). The so-called "Cosmic Om" or "Cosmic Motor" sound heard by some yogis who plug their ears and listen for it is only the astral sound of the fire element in their bodies. A person who hears that sound is hearing the astral vibration of the process of his digestion and metabolism—nothing more. That this is so is shown by the following upanishadic statement: "This *fire* which is within a man and digests food that is eaten is Vaisvanara. *Its sound is that which one hears by stopping the ears*" (Brihadaranyaka Upanishad 5.9.1). It is psychic, not spiritual. Buddha described how during his intense practice of various yogas he became adept at hearing this astral sound, assuming that it was a spiritual experience, until after examining its effects he realized it was just a psychic distraction that led nowhere, and abandoned it.

Reincarnation

We do not incarnate aimlessly or randomly, even though nearly all people (including the believers in reincarnation) have no idea why they are here. We incarnate for a very real purpose that leads to our eventual liberation. The idea that our life is something for us to fiddle around with and use for whatever small-term goals our deluded minds and egos can come up with is a terrible mistake, and results in wasting lifetimes. It is an invitation to more and more suffering and frustration. Finding out our purpose is not really difficult. The Bhagavad Gita presents the full picture.

Human birth is not easy to attain because we cannot be conceived and born if both parents are not compatible with our karma and a match for our entire psychic background. This is not common, so a person can wait decades or even centuries to find parents who can produce the body needed to manifest his karma. Therefore it is a great shame that when we do get human birth we waste it in pursuing little ego-goals, leaving aside the Great Goal.

Those who have recall of their pasts lives, including the experience of birth and death in those lives, say that it is easier to die than any other phase of life. Death itself is not pain, but release from pain, for entry into the astral world is less confining than earthly birth. To die is to be delivered, at least for a while.

Human beings often behave like animals rather than humans, reverting to the ways they followed in their lives before reaching the human level. Being in a human body is no guarantee of true humanity.

The only way to conquer birth and death is to transcend them by full entry into the consciousness of the Self and rising above them. Death and all that leads to it must be removed from our consciousness and therefore removed from our karma. Otherwise there is an inevitable slipping back into the realm of birth and death.

RELIGION

Religions have different names and concepts of God about which they argue, but if they came to know God then all argument would cease. Yogananda said: "If we could put the founders of the world religions into one room we would have paradise, but if we put their 'followers' together we have a war!" It is the difference between knowing God and only believing in God. Yogananda also wrote in a chant to God: "Thou art the sweetness which I do seek." God is the sweetness that enters our heart and unites us to himself. Then all difference disappears because our silly little egos vanish in the Divine Light.

In the beginning, good deeds, good ideas, and religiosity are lights in our darkness. But they can only illuminate a bit of our spiritual environment. This may not be understood by us at first, but when the sun of spiritual experience arises in us, and the Self begins to shine and give light to our whole personal world, we will understand. Not that we will despise and consider our former lights as valueless, but we will have a right perspective on the matter and realize that if the sun had not risen we would still be fundamentally in the dark, or at least in the dim. The Gita tells us: "When the whole country is flooded, the reservoir becomes superfluous. So, to the illumined seer, the Vedas are all superfluous" (Bhagavad Gita 2:46). And the same is true of all external good words, deeds, and thoughts when the Self becomes active in our consciousness.

A great deal of religion just keeps us going round and round on the wheel of samsara. What we need is the spiritual outlook and practice that gets us out of maya and into the Absolute. A lot of people's religion consists of holy toys that amuse and distract them but in no way free them from delusion and bondage, because they are themselves delusion and bondage. And that includes any philosophy that is just talk and no practical application.

Maya is delusion, whether gross or subtle, and we should have nothing to do with it or we will suffocate in its numberless manifestations, which can include religion. We should carefully study our religion and see what it is really doing to us, and get rid of it if it is not taking us to moksha. True religion is the path to liberation, whatever form it might take.

Unless their conscience is blunted by ignorance and frustration, the truly sincere followers of external, exoteric religion are inwardly tormented by the fact that their beliefs and their religious observances cannot purify or correct their minds and hearts. "What lack I yet?" (Matthew 19:20) is their cry, even if only secretly in their heart. Their religion will never give the needed answer. But they will find it in the vision of the Indian sages. Only by the light of the Self, only by entering into and experiencing the Self, will their impurities and the impulse to negativity be destroyed. For Krishna is speaking as the Self in each one of us when he says: "Free from greed, fear and anger, absorbed in me, holding fast to me, purified by knowledge-based tapasya, many have attained my state of being" (Bhagavad Gita 4:10). There is no other answer but experience of the Self.

If our goal is realization, then that which does not lead to realization is worthless, actually detrimental. All kinds of devotional and religious actions can be a tremendous block to genuine spiritual life. The only good action is that which reveals the Self to us.

A religion which does not teach the fundamental truths of karma, rebirth, and evolution of consciousness which results in the revelation of innate divinity and liberation is a soul-killing delusion, an enemy of God and man. To say that all religions teach the truth and lead to the same goal is irresponsible. Only those with the characteristics I have listed are teaching the truth and leading to the one Goal. They alone are dharma, the others are adharma.

In religion we have people that bully or cajole others into doing what they want them to do. They often do it to bolster their religion and keep people moving through the religious assembly line, and often they really are concerned about the person and truly are doing it "for their own good." But it never works, and often creates hypocrisy and misery.

Regarding this, Sri Ramakrishna said: "You must remember that nothing can be achieved except in its proper time. Some persons must pass through many experiences and perform many worldly duties before they can turn their attention to God; so they have to wait a long time. If an abscess is lanced before it is soft, the result is not good; the surgeon makes the opening when it is soft and has come to a head. Once a child said to its mother: 'Mother, I am going to sleep now. Please wake me up when I feel the call of nature.' 'My child,' said the mother, 'when it is time for that, you will wake up yourself. I shan't have to wake you.'" And on another occasion: "I want you to remember this. You may impart thousands of instructions to people, but they will not bear fruit except in proper time."

Dedication to God and the pursuit of higher consciousness can only occur when a person has an intense desire to end the mirage of this earthly life and ascend into the divine life.

This is the only true religion there is: the path of return to God. Everything else is a myth. It does not matter what formal religion a person professes, if he is not a yogi then he has no religion at all.

When Saint Paul was speaking to the philosophers on Mars Hill in Athens, he declared what God had ordained regarding all human beings: "That they should seek the Lord, if haply they might feel after him, and find him, *though he be not far from every one of us*: for in him we live, and move, and have our being; as certain also of your own poets have said, For we are also his offspring" (Acts 17:27-28). That is why Saint John the Apostle wrote: "*Now* are we the sons of God" (I John 3:2). It is our eternal being. Jesus spoke for all of us when he said: "*I and my Father are one*" (John 10:30).

So we should pay no attention to those religionists who would presume to say who is near or far in relation to God. Certainly the consciousness of some is near to God and the consciousness of some is far from God. But the essential being of both is the same, and it is the destiny of every one of us to take the journey to God, a journey that takes place in our consciousness. A person who today is a sinner may quickly become a saint when he turns around. And someone considered a saint may fall into delusion before the day is over.

The Gita says this: "They who worship me with devotion are in me, and I am also in them. If even an evildoer worships me single-heartedly, he should be considered righteous, for truly he has rightly resolved. Quickly he becomes a virtuous soul and goes to everlasting peace. Understand: no devotee of me is ever lost. Truly, those who take refuge in me even though they be from wicked origins, they also attain the Supreme Goal. Having come to this impermanent and unhappy world, devote yourself to me. With mind fixed on me, devoted, worshipping, bow down to me. Thus steadfast, with me as your supreme aim, you shall come to me" (9:29-34).

A friend once said to me: "The problem with nearly all religions is that they try to tell God what he can and cannot do." And regarding the "only true" religions "outside which there is no salvation," he commented:

"They are terrified at every moment of making of a mistake since they are 'infallible'!"

Some things have life inherent in them, and others do not. If we sow a seed in the earth it will grow and produce fruit containing other seeds, ensuring that life will continue in a perpetual cycle. But stones will not. The sadhaka must be careful to only sow life-bearing things in the field of his sadhana. The externals of religion may be impressive and even inspiring, but they cannot produce any growth in the individual—no evolution of consciousness. Only the internals of religion give us life and increase that which we already have.

Shraddha, faith, is an intuitive knowing, not just an intellectual conviction. It arises from spiritual experience which is possible when the necessary degree of evolution is attained. Because of this, Max Heindel insists in *The Rosicrucian Cosmo-Conception* that the most negative state possible for the human being is unbelief, lack of faith.

There is no "getting beyond" God, although those of atheistic bent like to pretend that we can transcend "the need for God" and therefore God himself. We cannot transcend either faith or God. Since faith is the highest thing in this world, we should cultivate it assiduously.

The opposite of faith is not unbelief, but ignorant gullibility. Those who think they are sophisticated and beyond faith and religion are not hard-headed rationalists as they like to consider themselves. Rather, they are ignorant and spiritually unintelligent, having no basis or stable point of intellect by means of which to measure truth or untruth, and consequently are taken in continually by the craft of evil people: people who like them are usually without personal faith.

We love to think of and experience that in which we have firm faith. This being so, a truly religious person loves involvement in religion and looks upon everything in the context of his religion. Those who can only endure an occasional religious activity have no faith and therefore no real religion.

Those who have faith in God continually think of God and make him the center of their life. The highest manifestation of faith is dedication to yoga sadhana. It is the yogi who has the highest and truest faith.

SAMADHI

Samadhi is not just going into some unusual state such as cessation of breath and heartbeat (though this can occur), but it is an attainment of consciousness, of being established in the awareness of Divine Unity embracing all things. It is seeing God.

We are used to the mistaken idea that it is the norm for holy people to flip in and out of samadhi, or an altered state mistaken for samadhi. Whatever the religion, there is a great deal of talk about those who get "overcome" or enter into exalted states against their will. This is nonsense. A master is someone who has mastered something. A master yogi is in perfect control of his body-vehicles. Everything is under his direction. He is in total command. Otherwise he is not a master but a servant of "divine moods" and other such nonsense.

Our intention as sadhakas is to return to the Infinite, but we can make a mistake understandable in people brought up in the West. Just as we think "eternity" is time without end, when in reality it transcends time and is beyond it, in the same way we think of Infinity as being infinitely big and without boundaries because it is too large to be encompassed, when actually it is beyond large or small. Even though it encompasses everything, it does not do so in a spatial sense, but in *consciousness*. Many yogis worry about their progress in meditation because they do not swell out like a cosmic balloon, but instead become more and more intent inwardly, deepening their awareness. They will themselves often quote: "The kingdom of heaven is within you" (Luke 17:21), but then forget that when they sit to meditate.

In an article entitled "Different States of Samadhi" (*East-West*, April, 1933), Yogananda says: "In the most advanced, or Nirvikalpa Samadhi state, the soul does not expand itself into the big Spirit, but realizes itself and Spirit as existing together." Although it is usual for a yogi to have some experience of savikalpa samadhi, it is possible to almost right away pass to the nirvikalpa state in meditation and work within it for realization. Yogananda said that his greatest disciple, Sister Gyanamata, had gone far beyond the savikalpa samadhi state without ever experiencing it.

It takes a while for the subtle yogic forces to manifest themselves and for the yogi to be in complete charge of them. When proficiency in directing the prana upward is managed, then it is as though the whole world is at the yogi's fingertips.

Many things are claimed to be the way to liberation, and they usually are external acts or attitudes. But since the very cause of bondage is the condition of our gross and subtle bodies, our spirit-Self being ever perfect and unchangeable, only yoga provides the means to liberation. We must all become urdhvareta yogis in whose subtle energy system the pranas, the life energies, are predominately flowing upwards into the Sahasrara, the thousand petalled lotus of which the brain is the physical counterpart. Our immortal, eternal spirit abides in the Sahasrara united with God the Absolute Spirit, the finite with the Infinite. Therefore the permanent urdhvareta state leads to liberation.

Right now the consciousness of the jiva is spread throughout the various bodies, although it is always centered or rooted in the Sahasrara. But it gathers itself up, so to speak, and becomes fully present in the Sahasrara through the process of yoga within the buddhi, the extension of the Chidakasha at the heart of the Sahasrara. This process is accomplished by japa and meditation. Nothing else accomplishes this, though many things can and must support it.

Samadhi occurs when the prana flows upward into the Sahasrara. It is simple. The upward prana is itself called the Taraka Brahman, the Delivering Brahman. We must remember that the consciousness/ energy duality we think of so readily is really not true. All is Brahman. Therefore it is God Consciousness that arises in the subtle nadis and pervades the Sahasrara.

Sahaja samadhi is the established state of the advanced yogi. All yogic phenomena are normal for such a yogi and he is at home in all conditions. Everything is natural for him and causes him no doubt or confusion. Swami Sivananda was the most natural person I have seen, and some of his advanced disciples were very like him in being perfectly normal. After all, what is more normal than God Consciousness? Another living embodiment of this supernatural normality was Sri Swami Muktananda Giri, the mother of Anandamayi Ma.

A great deal of busywork in the form of techniques are dear to the hearts of those caught in the compulsion to act. But true spiritual life is an awakening. Even more to the point, it is an establishing of the consciousness in its true home.

SADHANA

Since the Self is always right at hand, the path to Self-realization is always right at hand. This is a very important point. If our sadhana does not begin with experience of the Self, even if only to the slightest degree, then it will not lead to the Self. Only that sadhana which is itself the revelation of the Self, even though it may take time for the fullness of that revelation to occur, is true sadhana. This is why nearly all "yoga" is ultimately useless, though it may be entertaining and produce the fireworks of many phenomena. The only question to ask is: Do I know the Self any more than I did at the beginning? Otherwise years are wasted in practice that leads nowhere but back to samsara. This is tragic but true.

The spiritually mature truly grasp that God is their origin, indeed that God is all. As the Gita says: "At the end of many births the wise man takes refuge in me. He knows: All is Vasudeva [He Who Dwells in All Things]. How very rare is that great soul" (Bhagavad Gita 7:19). For once it is understood that they come from Brahman, then the desire to return to Brahman arises and they begin the return through yoga sadhana.

We must experience the Self by means of Atma Yoga—by sadhana. We "began" in the Self and shall "end" in the Self. If we did not begin in the Self we could never end there. Originally we were just the Self, but we "borrowed" the various bodies, entered into relative existence, and began to evolve within it. But we must grow beyond the need for all those "things" and surrender them back to the cosmos and rise into absolute Freedom. If we have broken or damaged anything it must first be repaired and corrected by us.

Each one of us is a world, a cosmos to itself. And that is what Jesus had in mind when he said: "This gospel of the kingdom shall be preached in all the world for a witness unto all nations; and then shall the end come" (Matthew 24:14).

The Bhagavad Gita tells us more than once that our divine Self and God, the Self of our Self, lives forever in our hearts (10:20; 13:17; 15:15; 18:61). Yet if we do not possess direct experience of our Self and God, simply believing that does us no good at all. We all, and always, have the Divine within us, but we must experience that for it to mean anything. Yoga is the key to that blessed experience.

If something does not fulfill the purpose of its existence, then it is, practically speaking, nothing at all. For example, if there is no oil inside a lamp, it cannot be kindled to give light. In the same way, "empty" people devoid of Self-awareness are not really people, but just shells. We must be "full" of consciousness within; then we will be conscious without, as well. This is the gist of Jesus' parable (Matthew 25:1-12) about the wise and foolish virgins waiting for the bridegroom. Only those that had oil were able to light their lamps and meet the bridegroom. The others missed the groom and were not admitted to the wedding. The groom, of course, is the Self, and the wedding is the realization of the Self. Only those with "oil" in their "lamp" are worthy spiritual aspirants. How do we get the oil? Through intense sadhana.

The invisible is both the subtle levels of our existence and the supremely subtle levels of the universe, which is both spirit and Spirit, both our individual existence and the Cosmic Existence. Many times in my life I have remembered what the resurrected Lahiri Mahasaya said to his grieving disciple, Panchanon Bhattacharya: "You do not live just in this world. You live with me." It is a wonderful thing to be aware that even now eternity is our present home if we will keep ourselves attuned to that reality by constant sadhana and aspiration for ultimate liberation.

A teacher of wisdom, of sadhana, shows the way to liberation and encourages and blesses those who follow the way. The value of contact with such a person is beyond all calculation, yet the seeker, who should certainly be grateful to all of his teachers, must realize that it is his own effort, his own will, that will achieve his liberation. A teacher may give him the map to freedom and advise him about the journey, but he must traverse the route himself by his own inner power, which is divine power: atmic power. Ultimately, God alone is the Guru, of Whom we are an eternal and inseparable part. This Sadguru works from within and without us to bring about our liberation, but all along the way it is our assent and our effort that is needed.

It may be hard to believe, but in India it has been very common for centuries that many people receive initiation from a guru with no intention to do sadhana even once. Their idea is that the guru will have to guarantee their salvation, that nothing more is needed, because at the moment of the death the guru will liberate them. This happened over and over with Sri Ma Sarada Devi, much to her chagrin. Some people receive initiation from several gurus, hoping that the best one will deliver them from rebirth at the time of death. The great fallacy is the ignorance of the fact that nothing whatsoever can affect us that is not interiorized. All the poisons and bullets in the world cannot harm us if they do not get inside us. Sadhana is the way in which the divine life begins flowing within us and moving us along to the goal, for sadhana is a totally interior process. That is why it works. Nothing else does.

Practice, practice and more practice is needed to gain the knowledge of God. For as both Vyasa and Shankara explain, yoga itself becomes the teacher, revealing subtle facts that cannot be conveyed through speech, only intuition. This is one of the reasons why total dependence on any teacher or verbal teaching prevents perfection in sadhana.

At some point the sadhana itself must become the yogi's teacher and authority. This happened in the life of Swami Ramananda of Almora. His experience did not agree with his guru's teaching, and he said so. The guru insisted that his statements on interior life and practice alone were true. So Swami Ramananda severed his connection with the guru and struck out on his own, becoming one of the most brilliant and powerful yogis of twentieth century India.

A Zen master taught for many years: The Buddha is the Mind. One day he called in a disciple and told him: "I have realized that all these years I was wrong in teaching The Buddha Is The Mind. The truth is: No Buddha, No Mind." He then told the disciple to seek out one of his earlier disciples who lived far away in a mountain range doing meditation and tell him of the change in the Master's teaching. The disciple managed to find the hermit and told him that the Master now taught No Buddha, No Mind, so he should change his belief. "Well, I still say The Buddha is the Mind," responded the hermit. Fueled by indignation the disciple went running back to the Master and told him: "When I found him, I told him he should believe No Buddha, No Mind, as you now teach. And he had the temerity to say that he still believed The Buddha Is The Mind!" The Master smiled and said: "I see he has attained maturity."

Our inner, spiritual potential is like the inner potential of seeds. If we just hold on to our potential but do nothing to evoke it, then we shall not have a fruitful life. But if we provide the right environment, as we do with seeds, our potential will manifest. As yogis, then, we must engage in regular and diligent sadhana and gain the experience of our true nature. The thirteenth chapter of the Bhagavad Gita is entitled: "The Field and Its Knower." Our body is the field and we are the knower of the field. The most meaningful experience of divinity we will ever have in this world is that of our own divinity which is made manifest through the divine seed of yoga. This is the purpose of life itself, and if we do not apply ourselves we live in vain.

In the beginning of sadhana we assiduously turn from the world, reminding ourselves that it is unreal. But once we experience the Light of Spirit we will see that the entire universe of made of that Light. That is why the opening verse of the Isha Upanishad says: "All this should be covered by the Lord, whatsoever moves on the earth." In other words, we should not see God inside material objects, but rather see them within God. There is a profound difference. The first view comes to the progressing yogi, but the second one comes to the perfected yogi.

When we get inside the passions–come to understand their nature and are withdrawn from the outer phenomena that incite them–we are no longer coerced by them. Part of being "inside" them is understanding what produces the things that provoke them: our own karma. We understand that all which we respond to negatively is really our own doing, that we ourselves are the source of all aggravation. When we see this through our buddhi clarified by sadhana, we understand the meaning, the lesson, that is to be learned. Then we are free. This is perfection.

If a seed is fried or boiled, the heat destroys its geminating properties so it cannot sprout. In the same way, karmic "seeds" can be rendered sterile by spiritual practice, by tapasya, which literally means to generate heat. In the upanishads we find the simile of two sticks (aranis) being rubbed together to make heat that will produce fire. Such is the process of sadhana–japa and meditation.

Knowing about karma intellectually is a great help to understanding life, but it is of no use whatsoever in freeing ourselves from karma and its power to force us into rebirth over and over. There are those who are utterly addicted to "knowledge." So they become those whom Saint Paul describes as "ever learning, and never able to come to the knowledge of the truth" (II Timothy 3:7). Sadhana alone cuts through the bonds of karma.

It is not only our ideas which must be changed, for that is just a renovation and rearrangement of mental furniture. What is necessary is a change of consciousness. And this is accomplished only through yoga sadhana, without which there is no prospect for the human being other than rebirth.

Faith implies awareness of both the value and the purpose of something. So everything in our sadhana should be done with understanding and intellectual assent. Nothing is more destructive than rote religion which is followed just because we are afraid to do otherwise, or have been bullied into it or sold on the idea. Everything we do must reflect our insight and reason. True, sometimes we must do something to experience its value for ourselves. But doing something over and over without perceiving any value or purpose in it is willful stupidity. And that gets us nowhere.

To become established in non-dual consciousness we must develop subtle discrimination (sukshma viveka). The only way to do that is to refine the mind, the buddhi, through yoga sadhana to such an extent that it becomes extremely subtle itself. When that is done, it will function as a reflection of the Self. It will not be a matter of affirming or keeping an idea of unity in mind. It will *see* unity at all times. It is not a way of thinking but a way of perception.

It is essential that we remain centered in the buddhi, in our intelligent mind, at all times without break. Human beings are either rational or instinctual, and most are instinctual and therefore sense-oriented. We

must be fully rational. It is interesting that in Eastern Christian writings
the disciples of Christ are called "rational sheep." Only through continual practice of yoga can we become and remain rational beings. Here is
what the Gita says about the matter:

"He who is without desire in all situations, encountering this or that,
pleasant or unpleasant, not rejoicing or disliking–his understanding
(wisdom) stands firm. And when he withdraws completely the senses
from the objects of the senses, as the tortoise draws in its limbs, his
wisdom is established firmly. Sense-objects turn away from the abstinent,
yet the taste for them remains. But the taste also turns away from him
who has seen the Supreme. The troubling senses forcibly carry away
the mind of even the striving man of wisdom. Restraining all these
[senses], he should sit in yoga (yoked), intent on me. Surely, he whose
senses are controlled–his consciousness stands steadfast and firm. For a
man dwelling on the objects of the senses, attachment to them is born.
From attachment desire is born. And from [thwarted] desire anger is
born. From anger arises delusion; from delusion, loss of memory; from
loss of memory, destruction of intelligence (buddhi). From destruction
of intelligence one is lost. However, with attraction and aversion eliminated, even though moving amongst objects of sense, by self-restraint
the self-controlled attains tranquility" (2:57-64)"

I expect most of us have had friends who, when a beloved animal
friend died, said vehemently that they would never have another and
repeat the grief. But they did. In the same way people are buffeted by
life and for short periods of time feel disillusioned and detached. But
it is all ego-based and therefore evaporates. Only the detachment that
is based on perception of our spirit-nature can really last, and there is
no way to be firm in spiritual consciousness other than continual and
regular sadhana.

Viveka is discrimination between the Real and the unreal, between the Self and the non-Self, between the permanent and the impermanent. It is not intellectual, but intuitive discrimination. Only through diligent yoga practice is it developed and maintained.

Enlightenment does not strike like lightning, and especially does not occur without a cause, and producing the cause depends on us. Spiritual development comes about through our own effort. Although we can certainly be encouraged and inspired and instructed along the way, it still is our effort alone that produces the spiritual result.

Only those totally committed to realization will attain it. Every sadhaka must be like Buddha, who took the vow that even if his flesh and bones melted away, he would not abandon his practice until he attained nirvana.

Day and night the process of sadhana in the form of japa and meditation must go on. Naturally this cannot be done right away, but those who really try will find themselves eventually able to do so.

If sadhana is practiced ceaselessly, unbrokenly, the yogi will attain success (siddhi–perfection) in his practice, just as a tender plant can break up stone and drops of soft water can wear down stone. Persistence is the key.

Yoga sadhana is a continuous process that must pervade our life. Whatever our external condition may be, no matter who we are with, inwardly we must be in the limitless sky of consciousness (chidakasha) through constant japa. Then we will live and move in moksha.

The six enemies (shadripu) to realization of the Self are: desire (kama), anger (krodha), greed (lobha), arrogance (mada), delusive attachment (moha) and jealousy (matsarya). They are overcome only by yoga abhyasa, the practice of yoga. All the philosophizing in the world and resolving to "be good" in the future accomplish absolutely nothing in relation to these six, for they are delusions of the mind, not weaknesses and failings as Western religions suppose. Therefore only a change in consciousness will overcome them and render them ineffectual.

In a moment the benefits of sadhana can be wiped out without a trace remaining. There is a tradition that da Vinci took many years to complete the Last Supper because of the time taken by his search for the ideal models. Early on he had found a young man whose face and manner were the embodiment of grace and goodness, so he painted him as Jesus. Finally after years the single remaining face he needed was that of Judas. Wandering around in the worst part of town, da Vinci saw a man whose face was the expression of depravity and cruelty. Assuming that the man was a professional murderer, he hesitated to approach him, but then he realized that he might never see him again, so he spoke to him. To his amazement, the man smiled and called him by name. When da Vinci asked how he knew him, the man was surprised. "But don't you recognize me?" he asked. "You painted me some years ago as Jesus in the fresco of the Last Supper." Just a few years had destroyed all the purity and goodness.

I have known some yogis who were radiant with innocence and devotion. Seeing them a few years later I literally did not know who they were. Physically they were completely altered, coarsened and without conscience, spiritually devastated. One young man lived in our monastery for some time. He told me he wanted to travel to India, and I encouraged him to do so. When I saw him there a few months later I found that he was making all kind of excuses to leave India, even though Sri Anandamayi Ma had told him he could live in the Almora Anandamayi Ashram. I urged him to follow Ma's advice, and promised him that we would regularly send him money so he would lack for nothing. Over the years quite a few Western men had asked Ma if they could live in one of her ashrams and she had always refused. Now this rare blessing was offered to him freely. But all he would do was dream up problems that might arise and keep insisting that he was "not ready" to live in India, even insisting that Ma had told him to live in India so he would discover that it was not really what he wanted to do! The next time I saw him (in America) I did not know who he was. Everything about him was altered. Even his voice was different. And he looked nothing like he had previously. His life was dissolute and dedicated to self-destruction. Eventually he died horribly of AIDS, stubborn and conscienceless unto the last breath. Even after death he continued to harm himself by the negative and foolish terms of his (legal) will.

One of the saddest possible experiences is meeting with strayed and fallen yogis, monks and nuns.

Mastery is a positive necessity for those who would truly live, evolve and attain the destiny of all sentient beings. For a while (sometimes a very long while) we just coast or mosey along, developing in a kind of hit-or-miss manner, letting lifetimes slip out of our grasp through not just centuries or millennia, but even for creation cycles. Finally we must take ourselves in hand literally and stop all delays, impelling ourselves forward and upward through intense yoga sadhana. Spiritual adulthood must be assumed and maintained. Few things are more deadly to the individual than the attitude of having all the time in the world with no need to stop wasting life after life. In this way we silence the inner voice that urges us onward and upward, and become no more than driftwood on the sea of life. This is one of the most dangerous states we can lapse into, sleeping the deadly sleep of heedlessness and indifference.

The way to divine union is that union itself. This sounds like word juggling and mystification, but it is not. In the very highest levels of spiritual consciousness the dual light becomes one and therefore the cause becomes the effect, or rather returns to being the effect, having previously become the cause into order to initiate the jiva's entry into relative existence. Enlightenment itself has manifested as sadhana, and the sadhana resumes its original status as enlightenment. There is no duality at all, and there never has been.

When philosophical concepts are dispelled by actual atmajnana then we see That which is real and true. There is a knowing that leads us onward to unknowing that is the real Knowing. This, too, is achieved only through sadhana. Careful and frequent study of the Gita makes the way to attain this clear.

Genuine (not synthetic) camphor burns up totally, leaving no ash or soot. When it is gone, it is gone; no trace remains. In the same way the lower, sensory mind ruled by ego and material consciousness must be "evaporated" by the heat of spiritual attainment, by the fire of yoga practice. There is nothing that the Spirit cannot transmute into Consciousness, back into Itself. So that materiality which is worshipped by bound souls must be dissolved for them to be free. And that dissolution must be done consciously and intentionally. Otherwise nothing will happen. We are wise if we keep this fact in mind.

DEDICATION TO SPIRITUAL LIFE

A great number of people ascribe to spiritual philosophy, but few follow the practical means to realization and prize them more highly than anything else on earth. Every day people are forsaking spiritual life for that which they desire more, or to avoid that which they fear or dislike. In all viable spiritual traditions those who seek higher life are sometimes likened to dedicated soldiers: ready to give up all, even their life, in the struggle for enlightenment. As was said about the Westward Expansion in America: "The cowards never started and the weak died along the way."

As Saint Teresa of Avila said, worldly people want to go to God the way a chicken walks. In case you have not seen a chicken walk, I will describe it to you. They meander around, never in a straight line, scratching and pecking at the dirt, often lifting one foot and then standing still as if they are in a coma. They literally veer to the side frequently and often walk backwards a bit. If they run, it is only for a few feet and then they stop and wonder what they are doing. Everything they do is "in a bit," in little spurts and stops. As I said, they meander, they do not really walk. It is purely a matter of lack of intelligence, and therefore lack of good sense. Further, as they walk they often croon to themselves in an aimless and patternless manner, as if trying to figure out if they are even alive, much less where they are–and why. Yet people prefer to live in just such a way, and are proud of it. As Yogananda said: "People are so skillful in their ignorance."

We are so used to hearing "sadhu" applied only to monastics, that we forget (or never knew) it is an adjective with a great deal of positive qualities. *A Brief Sanskrit Glossary* says it means: straight; right; leading straight to a goal; hitting the mark; unerring; straightened; not entangled; well-disposed; kind; willing; obedient; successful; effective; ready; prepared; peaceful; powerful; fit; proper; right; good; virtuous; honorable; righteous; well-born; noble; correct; pure; excellent; and perfect. "Sadhuguna" is a Sanskrit word not used very often. It includes all these traits, all of which come from non-attachment: vairagya. And vairagya is non-attachment; detachment; dispassion; absence of desire; disinterest; or indifference, especially towards all worldly things and enjoyments. This is simple to say, but very hard to do, and impossible for those who are not yogis, for yogis certainly are sadhus whatever their external situation.

Vairagya is detachment, absence of desire and disinterest in all worldly things and enjoyments. A lot of people are disillusioned and disgusted with certain things in the world, but their basis is ego and not awareness of the emptiness of the world and its ways. Further, true vairagya is an active force like burning fire. Real vairagya burns up illusions and attachment, which are the fabric of the world and relative existence. The world becomes a bridge which the sadhaka burns behind him after having safely crossed over it. If we do not see this process in the mind and life of an aspirant we can know that his aspiration is a mirage.

Having incinerated ignorance, attachment, desire and egotism, the glory of the Self begins to be revealed in the very appearance of the yogi as well as his daily life. Swami Sivananda of Rishikesh was an embodiment of the atmic glory in all aspects of his life. Never was it veiled. At all times the splendor was there for those who had eyes to see.

In truth, for us there never is any time but "now." The past and future are both unreachable for us. There are people who obsess on past spiritual experience as though that is sufficient, and there are those who make big plans about how dedicated to spiritual life they are going to be in the future when things are "right." I have seen my good friends that were yogis letting spiritual opportunity slip away from them because of this kind of delusion. How many spiritual layabouts have told me that they were "not yet ready" for dedicated spiritual life! (Usually "I am not ready," means "I don't want to.") Some of them said so decades ago and today are still not ready: bound in material life, spiritually stagnant and spiritually dead. Their life was over the day they decided to fool themselves into delay. "Just a day or so more," they tell themselves, until death ends the whole pretence. As Jesus said, grieving for such people, not condemning them: "If thou hadst known, even thou, at least in this thy day, the things which belong unto thy peace! but now they are hid from thine eyes" (Luke 19:42).

"Behold, now is the accepted time; behold, now is the day of salvation" (II Corinthians 6:2). The wise know this to be true and act on it. Swami Sivananda wrote a song in English simply called "D.I.N.," in which he sang the refrain: "D.I.N., D.I.N., D.I.N.: Do It Now, Do It Now, Do It Now." Now is all we have or ever will have.

If you are breathing and conscious: Today is your day.

I told someone who kept going on "retreats" that had no real lasting benefit: "You mistakenly think that you can sit out in the world and roast in the fires until it becomes unbearable, and then 'go on retreat' for a week or two and cool off, only to go right back out and roast some more. It won't get you anywhere. Get out of the fire!"

Someone once asked Yogananda if he believed in hell. The Master smiled and asked: "Where do you think you are?" We can live in the fire and not be burned if we know how. The yogis who study the Bhagavad Gita and conform their lives entirely to its teachings will become fireproof and live at peace, untouched by the flames. And then after death go on to higher worlds where there are no flames.

The purpose of a fruit tree is to bear fruit. If it does not, it is worthless and usually cut down. The purpose of human life is to realize God. Therefore a life not dedicated to that purpose is a waste and the person is a fruitless tree. In the sight of the wise such a person is meaningless. Those who do not realize God or advance toward the realization of God are failures in life.

Unfortunately few have this perspective. Even the yogis are willing to just mosey through life in a pious manner, which is why so many emphasize devotion instead of knowledge, when it is progress in yoga sadhana that is the only worthy endeavor and emphasis. And even though they defensively talk about how there is no need to be a monastic to realize God, they excuse their minimal discipline and progress by saying: "We are householders with responsibilities, not sannyasis." But every single one of us has the responsibility to seek God first. Those who are continually complaining that householders are considered second class aspirants are perfectly willing to *be* second class, and proud of it.

Please remember this: What we do not sow we cannot reap.

It is generally supposed in both East and West that the grihastha, not being a sadhu, can live his life as he pleases, completely according to his wish and will except for a few token religious/spiritual observances and practices. But that is not so. The family is the basis of society. If that basis is not dharmic, then the society is not dharmic, either.

I have lived in ideal dharmic households in India. As my sannyasa guru, Swami Vidyananda Giri, said to me after I had described my stay in the home of a disciple of Swami Keshabananda, who is written about in *Autobiography of a Yogi*: "There are many households that are spiritually superior to many ashrams." When the members are dedicated yogis, this is definitely so. Daily worship, meditation and observance of yama and niyama transform the members of the family, including the children.

I have had some American yogi friends who sincerely wanted to have completely dharmic homes but did not know how to go about it since they were completely unaware of the traditional ways of an Indian household. Meditation is not enough for anyone to succeed in spiritual life. There is an entire world to be entered and perpetuated wherever the yogi may be.

Renunciation and vairagya are as necessary for grihastas as they are for sannyasis. I know many Indian grihastas who far outdistance the institutional monastics I have seen in India. Yoganandaji often told people: "Make your heart a hermitage," and that hermitage must be in conformity with the thousands of years' discipline and wisdom embodied in dharmic Indian households even today. Ishwarapranidhana is the fundamental character of the life of anyone, whatever their ashrama: brahmachari, grihasta, vanaprastha or sannyasi. We must all live our lives as an offering to God.

Here is what Saint Paul said about it: "I beseech you therefore, brethren, by the mercies of God, that ye present your bodies a living sacrifice, holy, acceptable unto God, which is your reasonable service. And be not conformed to this world: but be ye transformed by the renewing of your mind, that ye may prove what is that good, and acceptable, and perfect, will of God" (12:1-2). "Know ye not that your body is the temple of the Holy Ghost which is in you, which ye have of God, and ye are not your own? …therefore glorify God in your body, and in your spirit, which are God's" (I Corinthians 6:19-20). Everyone, whatever their state of life, needs to follow this counsel.

Some years ago I stayed at a Trappist convent and spoke to the nuns in the evenings. The subject arose of how a person could know whether they should take up the monastic life. I pointed out the irony of the attitude that a man or woman should do all kinds of praying and agonizing over whether or not to be a monastic, even consulting spiritual advisors on the matter. But no one was supposed to take such care about entering the householder life. Just pick out someone to marry and do so and it would be God's will. What hypocrisy! And what a slighting of non-monastics. Isn't their life as important as a monastic's? Does it not matter if their lives are lived carelessly and according to egoic will rather than according to divine wisdom?

The householder life is not something to be lived merely because a person wishes to. It is an ashrama, a stage of life that obligates those in it to as seriously regulate their lives and follow the principles of dharma as does any sannyasi. It is not my place to instruct married people how to live, so I will not expand on this subject. But I urge serious married yogis to search out Yogananda's teachings on this subject. Also valuable are the words of Sri Ramakrishna to be found in *The Gospel of Sri Ramakrishna*. Just look up the world "householders" in the index.

The inner and outer life of the grihastha must be as pure, and therefore as disciplined, as that of a sannyasi. Many householders try to excuse slackness in their life by protesting that they are not sannyasis, but grihasthas. A grihastha is as much a Sanatana Dharmi as a brachmachari, vanaprasthi or sannyasi. And purity and discipline are demanded of all.

Every day should be one of conscious renunciation for us. One evening in Aswan, Egypt, I was sitting outside with Bishop Hedra, the Coptic bishop of Aswan, and a group of laymen. He told the people to ask me questions, which they did. One lady told me that the fundamentalist Protestant missionaries were just then making a big fuss about when the end of the world would occur, and asked my opinion. I told her: "A true Christian 'ends the world' every day." All agreed.

This principle that every day should be a day of renunciation is very important, for so many begin as fervent renouncers and then not only fall back into their old ways, but start accumulating more and more attachments, until they are more materialistic than ordinary people.

It is also important that renunciation be extended into every aspect of our life, otherwise all kinds of things slip through and render us hypocrites. For example, one time in Kanpur a famous swami was giving a series of talks on the Srimad Bhagavatam. In one talk he made the silly remark that if we have a kaupin (a strip of cloth traditionally used as underwear) it should be very narrow—and he showed with his fingers how narrow it should be. This was supposed to be an ideal of simplicity and renunciation. Yet I had noticed that every day he had worn a different expensive sweater, and I knew that he had hundreds of thousands of rupees in the bank.

In keeping with this guru's hypocrisy was a young "sadhu" disciple of his that was living in a thatch hut in Brindaban. He was always well trimmed and well-oiled as he daily displayed himself, walking along the road barefoot with a tiny cloth around his waist and a picturesque (equally well-oiled) kamandalu in one hand. The purpose was obvious: he would live like this for a few years so it would look good on his "resume" when he finally emerged to head a big ashram, all togged up and riding around in his auto with a driver to appointments with his accountants. (Of course, he already had his M.A. degree).

So renunciation is a continual practice.

Although certain external factors (or their absence) can be conducive to spiritual life, it is a grave error to think that of themselves external conditions are going to enable us to live a spiritual life. And it is positively deadly to delay spiritual effort, telling ourselves that when the fortuitous externals have been gained, then we will really get busy and dig in and have a strong spiritual life. Two of my friends frittered away their lives in this way. They always had big plans, often involving moving to another place and getting another job, that were going to enable them to dedicate themselves seriously to spiritual endeavor. But in the present they were neglecting spiritual life, supposedly because of factors that would removed in the future. Foolishly they thought they could slack off by daydreaming of a brighter tomorrow in which their progress would be effortless. That tomorrow never came, and in time they abandoned spiritual life and lived in embittered and self-justifying delusion, desolate and dreary.

A lot of people claim to burn their bridges behind them, but in the future it develops that they just camouflaged them and kept them ready to retreat over. Sri Ramakrishna often said that when people go into the Ganges their sins jump off and perch in the nearby trees. Then when they come out of the water they jump back on them. Unless something is truly destroyed and cannot ever be revived, we must not think we are rid of it. That is why the scriptures speak so often of roasting karmic seeds or burning negativity to ashes. We must be sure that we really are free of something before we decide we are, and then in the future find it was only hidden. One of the reasons Shaivites smear themselves with ashes is to remind themselves of this truth.

We often become temporarily desireless or develop an aversion to something when it causes us pain or we see its repulsive aspect. Certainly at such times a slight vairagya arises, but almost always only to subside sometime later. That is the deadly secret of the body: any detachment or disgust is sure to eventually subside and the old addiction that was established in numberless previous lives will reassert itself.

Therefore we must never trust a seeming indifference to either our own or others' bodies. The conditioning from past lives is utterly subliminal and instinctual, and all mental and philosophical analysis intended to block that conditioning is useless—worse than useless because it is deceptive. The body is a danger at all times until we are enlightened, and people who think they are enlightened almost never are. So keep the red lights on in the mind and avoid the danger.

SELF-REALIZATION

The cave of the heart is the dwelling place of both the individual spirit (jivatman) and the Supreme Spirit (Paramatman): "There are two selves that drink the fruit of Karma in the world of good deeds. Both are lodged in the secret place (of the heart), the chief seat of the Supreme" (Katha Upanishad 1:3:1). The Advaya Tarakopanishad in verse eight says: "One tries to find the turiya state hidden in the cave of the heart," turiya, pure consciousness, being the essential nature of the Spirit-Self.

To "dwell in the cave of the heart" is to have our consciousness established fully and permanently in the Self. That, and that alone, is the goal of our life. This is not something that takes place after death, but an experience that can be lived right now in the material body, for matter is simply frozen spirit and not inconsistent with spiritual realization. It is our delusions which make the separation and blind us to the ever-present reality of Spirit.

All sentient beings are headed toward divinity, not just sainthood. We must aim for the top because that is our inherent destiny, and in the process we may help others along the same path.

Not even material embodiment can diminish the power and glory of the Self (Atman). Therefore when we correctly enter into the experience and consciousness of the Self we shall be in touch with that power and attain perfect (and permanent) realization when we are established in it.

It is commonly thought that the way to be free from desire is to fulfill all desires. But that just keeps us in the cycle of ever-rising desires. Trying to stop them by fulfilling them is like pouring gasoline on a fire. It will only get worse. The only way is for us to find and possess that which renders all other things pointless, revealing them as nothing. The sages of India have told us this one thing is the Self which is to be united with the Supreme Self–the jivatman with the Paramatman. Therefore the only path to moksha is the yoga which leads us to that Supreme Attainment, the Paramartha. And only the persevering yogi will succeed in that path. The Bhagavad Gita tell us:

"He whose happiness is within, whose delight is within, whose illumination is within: that yogi, identical in being with Brahman, attains Brahmanirvana" (5:24).

"The yogi whose mind is truly tranquil, with emotions calmed, free of evil, having become one with Brahman, attains the supreme happiness.

"Thus constantly engaging himself in the practice of yoga, that yogi, freed from evil, easily touching Brahman, attains boundless happiness.

"He who is steadfast in yoga (yoga-yukta) at all times sees the Self present in all beings and all beings present in the Self.

"He who sees me everywhere, and sees all things in me–I am not lost to him, and he is not lost to me.

"He, established in unity, worships me dwelling in all things. Whatever be his mode of life, that yogi ever abides in me.

"He who judges pleasure or pain by the same standard every-where that he applies unto himself, that yogi is deemed the highest" (6:27-32).

The faith we need is faith in the truth of the Eternal Self and the possibility of regaining full awareness of the Self: Self-realization. With-out this, desirelessness is impossible, for what else is there but material existence if the realm of spirit is unknown to us? Of course we will run after all the mirages within the big mirage of maya, for they alone will be real to us. Consequently only bondage is possible for us, and liberation will be unthought-of and therefore unattainable.

To be an authentic Sanatana Dharmi is a lifework requiring continual study and application of what is learned. As Vivekananda said in *Jnana Yoga*: "Say to your own minds, 'I am He, I am He.' Let it ring day and night in your minds like a song, and at the point of death declare 'I am He.' That is the Truth; the infinite strength of the world is yours. Drive out the superstition that has covered your minds. Let us be brave. Know the Truth and practice the Truth. The goal may be distant, but awake, arise, and stop not till the goal is reached."

To not seek Self-realization as our prime objective in life is to waste incarnation after incarnation, compounding our ignorance and rendering that realization more and more difficult to attain when we do develop the intelligence to turn back from the unreal and seek the Real.

Satchidananda is in us as our essential being just as we are in Satchidananda as Its essential being. Though two, we are one. This cannot be perfectly comprehended by the human intellect, but as Yogananda said, it can be known by the yogi in direct realization. This is what yoga is all about. This unity must be recovered, although it has not really been lost to us—it has been forgotten. Self-realization is a remembering of our Self and of Brahman, the Self of our Self.

Although we experience the world as a prison, the bondage is not only in our mind, it *is* our mind in its present state. There is only one solution: the attainment of liberation in which only freedom is perceived.

Self-realization is the only purpose of life itself. To not pursue that realization is to be totally without purpose and therefore to live in confusion and frustration birth after birth. Those who think that the pursuit of liberation is a kind of secondary purpose to life and that it can be relegated to second place are profoundly deluded. Those who offer God second place offer him no place. No matter how many karmic strands we may have to manage in our life, still our realization must be first in priority at all times.

"Night and day, night and day, I look for Thee night and day. Door of my heart open wide I keep for Thee." During part of my university years I used to sing this chant of Yogananda's in desperation as I walked across the UCLA campus where everything was being sought except God. "Will my days fly away without seeing Thee, my Lord?" I sang, having seen the truth of Lahiri Mahasaya's words: "If you don't invite God to be your summer Guest, He will not come in the winter of your life."

I had read more than once the words of Yoganandaji in the twenty-fourth chapter of his autobiography: "To allot God a secondary place in life was, to me, inconceivable. Though He is the sole Owner of the cosmos, silently showering us with gifts from life to life, one thing yet remains which He does not own, and which each human heart is empowered to withhold or bestow–man's love. The Creator, in taking infinite pains to shroud with mystery His presence in every atom of creation, could have had but one motive–a sensitive desire that men seek Him only through free will. With what velvet glove of every humility has He not covered the iron hand of omnipotence!"

As Yogananda's greatest disciple, Sister Gyanamata, often said: God First. God Alone.

When liberation is only a theory to us, and we have not really grasped the implications of the nature of our own divine Self, we think that moksha is not just in the future, but "way over there" in a vague pseudo-metaphysical way. Mostly this is because the erroneous concepts of the Western religion we grew up in or were surrounded by are ingrained in us to some degree. But when we shake them off and take the Upanishads and Gita at their word and understand what they say about the Self, then we know that we *are* the Self right now and only have to experience that. And since the Self is within us, there is nowhere to go or any external acts for us to do. We need only learn the way to turn within and enter fully into Self-experience, and it is done—not as quickly as it takes to say that, but still not countless lifetimes away as most people (even in India) think. Our search must be intelligent through our mind becoming completely directed and illumined by the buddhi. Intelligence and discrimination are absolutely necessary lest we mistake some stage along the way for the Goal. (This is a common error.)

Self-realization is the eternal state of the Self. That alone is liberation. Yogis wander through lifetimes because they do not one-pointedly seek the Self. Readers of *Autobiography of a Yogi* will remember the accounts of Swami Keshabananda there. I knew some disciples of Keshabananda, and they told me amazing stories of his yogic powers. Keshabananda even materialized after his death when he so willed. Yet Master Yogananda said that he did not attain liberation in that life because of his attachment to miracles.

To become totally liberated is a matter so great and high that it is beyond our conception. Because we do not realize its nature we can mistake a point on the way for the end. Those who are being taught by Sri Yukteswar in Hiranyaloka would seem God to us if they incarnated now, but they still need to keep moving onward through yoga even there at the heights of the astral world. And when they graduate from there they will have the even vaster reaches of the causal world to traverse! Those who do so and return to this world are avataras.

Yogananda described the experience of God as "ever new joy," implying that enlightenment is not a static condition, but is ever new. The Self possesses a perennial newness; it is always sunrise, always looking forward to new heights and new depths. Just how this is, or how it can be, is for us to find out by experiencing It ourselves.

Every moment of our lives we are being tested—not to reveal to God our worth, but to reveal to us our true worth or lack thereof. *Satyam eva jayate*. The truth alone will prevail.

To know the Self and God the Self of the Self is the eager yearning of each one of us. But lifetimes of karmic debris (samskaras and vasanas) have either buried or so distorted it that practically speaking we have lost it. Therefore we have no lasting happiness or peace because we continually violate our nature at every moment of our ego-directed and materialistic life. Only the yogi has the possibility of everlasting peace and joy in the Self.

SHIVA-SHAKTI

Shiva is consciousness and Shakti is the creative power directed by consciousness. Shivashakti is the sadhana shakti that is the perfect union of Shiva and Shakti which carries forward the spiritual development of the yogi. Therefore it is the process of salvation, of liberation, for it is the power of the One Indivisible God. Shivashakti manifests as the subtle power in our various bodies that moves upward and establishes itself in the Sahasrara chakra, the physical, astral and causal brain. This force is both breath and prana polarized to the highest centers of awareness in the brain. It is the ascent of consciousness in the yogi.

Usually in contemporary writings "Shivashakti" means both the consciousness and energy of Shiva the Infinite. Shivashakti is the totality of life and life forms. There is nothing outside its domain, and when yogis use the term they mean the spiritual power whose interior action accomplishes the perfection of the yogi, changing him into a siddha. Without the action of Shivashakti in our life there can be no evolution, no liberation. Even the idea of liberation cannot arise in the mind except through Shivashakti. Authentic spiritual consciousness and practice are manifestations of Shivashakti which has become awakened in the yogi. Shivashakti is the beginning, middle and end of the yogic process.

In the West masculine is considered active and feminine passive, no doubt because the West bases its ideas on external, material experience and social customs (especially before the twentieth century), whereas the East bases its ideas on interior, subtle and spiritual experience. So in the East it is just the opposite: the purusha is the non-acting, passive witness of the activity of prakriti. The eternal male observes the cyclic dance of creation performed by the eternal female. The concept of Shiva and Shakti is not just an idea, but a practical awareness of the nature of the evolutionary process of the universe.

The yogi is aware that as a human being he is both Shiva and Shakti, and orders his life, especially his sadhana, accordingly.

Shiva and Shakti are the same thing, like the two sides of a coin. But in relativity they appear to be not only two but separated and needing unification. In the dream of life this illusion pervades, but we can also dream a process of unity, and that is yoga sadhana. The union of Shiva and Shakti is in the core of the Sahasrara, the chidakasha. There is located the power of the supreme jnana.

Shivashakti effects the union of the individual with the Absolute. When Shivashakti is steadily increased, the person begins entering into levels of evolution beyond humanity and ultimately becomes one with Brahman.

Shakti is usually equated with maya, but in the Nath Yogi tradition expounded by the Master Yogi Gorakhnath (see *Philosophy of Gorakhnath* by Akshay Kumar Banerjea) Shakti is really Shiva in his dynamic aspect. They are not two, but one, and Shakti reveals the Self and liberates the individual spirit or jiva. Maya, on the other hand, blinds and binds everyone under her power. Those of spiritual consciousness do not fear Shakti, but take refuge in her, while those of material consciousness are addicted slaves of maya.

When the yogi awakens the divine power that pervades his bodies, unifies and directs it upward into the Sahasrara, in time the core of the Sahasrara will be awakened and the subtle power will be drawn into it, completing its existence. Symbolically this is called the union of Shiva and Shakti. Shakti merges into Shiva and becomes Shiva. Duality ceases to exist and the consciousness of the One Only Without a Second (Ekam-evam-advitiyam) remains. This is liberation—moksha.

For a genuine Shaivite, Shiva is the infinite, non-dual Reality, not a mythological figure. Such a Shaivite fixes his awareness on that Reality, knowing that It alone existed in the beginning, even now alone exists, and in the future will be revealed to the yogi along with his life-force, his prana or shakti, as his own Self. Even before the beginning there existed the One that was Two: Shiva/Shakti. And in the end That alone will exist. So now That must fill the yogi's mind.

Is there such a thing as matter? Is there such a thing as energy/shakti? Yes and no. There is the idea and the experience of energy, yet ultimately there is only consciousness. Therefore the mind as an idea/concept is a "fragment" of the Self. In actuality we do not "drop" anything, but rather through sadhana we transmute it until it is revealed in its true nature as spirit/consciousness. Just as we do not really die, but rise to higher life, in the same way the gross and subtle bodies are assimilated into the Self from which they originated, in which they evolved and into which they return. In the great mystery drama of the lives of Jesus and Mary, the Resurrection-Ascension and the Assumption represent this return. This is liberation.

SPIRITUAL EXPERIENCE

Countless sadhakas have mistaken their perceptions for genuine realization. If the perception can be described and conveyed to another, it is not perception of the Self. Perception of the Self is beyond words. Just remember this: no one can describe the taste of salt except to say that it is salty, and that conveys nothing. So if a material element such as salt cannot be described, what possibility is there for anyone to describe the transcendental Self? None.

Master Yogananda emphasized that the light seen in profound meditation is God, and that Light is the highest form of God, as he describes in the first chapter of *Autobiography of a Yogi*. The adept yogis of India insist that formless Light is the highest form of God, and that visions of various forms, however beautiful or fascinating, are greatly inferior. In Christianity for over a thousand years the only spiritual experience considered valid was the vision of infinite Light, and awareness that the mystic was one with that Light. This changed toward the end of the Middle Ages to the permanent and present detriment of the Western Church. However, this remained stable and traditional in the Christian East. Here is how Saint Ambrose of Optina, a nineteenth century Russian Orthodox saint, describes one of his visions.

"Suddenly I was in another world, quite unknown to me, never seen by me, never imagined by me. Around me there is bright, white light! Its transcendence is so pure and enticing that I am submerged, along with my perception, into limitless depths and cannot satisfy myself with my admiration for this realm, cannot completely fill myself with its lofty spirituality. Everything is so full of beauty all around. So endearing this life–so endless the way. I am being swept across this limitless, clear space.

My sight is directed upwards, does not descend anymore, does not see anything earthly. The whole of the heavenly firmament has transformed itself before me into one general bright light, pleasing to the sight.

"But I do not see the sun. I can see only its endless shining and bright light. The whole space in which I glide without hindrance, without end, without fatigue, is filled with white light....

"...Not a single thought of mine is any longer enticed by anything earthly, not a single beat of my heart is any longer moving with human cares or earthly passion. I am all peace and rapture. But I am still moving in this infinite light, which surrounds me without change. There is nothing else in the world except for the white, bright light...

"My rapture at all this superseded everything. I sank into this eternal rest. No longer was my spirit disturbed by anything. And I knew nothing else earthly. None of the tribulations of my heart came to mind, even for a minute. It seemed that everything that I had experienced before on earth never existed. Such was my feeling in this new radiant world of mine. And I was at peace and joyful and desired nothing better for myself. All my earthly thoughts concerning fleeting happiness in the world died in this beautiful life, new to me, and did not come back to life again. So it seemed to me at least, there, in that better world.

"...This did not seem at all to be a dream. Actually, about earthly things I no longer had the least notion. I only felt that the present life is mine, and that I was not a stranger in it. In this state of spirit I forgot myself and immersed myself in this light-bearing eternity. And this timelessness lasted without end, without measure, without expectation, without sleep, in this eternal rest."

Although in meditation we may see only darkness, light is at the heart, the core, of that darkness, and in time it will reveal itself. On the other hand, at the heart of material, earthly experience there is darkness, because it is an illusion, not reality. We can say it this way: There is light in inner darkness and darkness in outer light. We must learn which to trust.

Relative existence is actually darkness, but if we penetrate that darkness we will find light is its essence.

What is written in books is not worthy to be compared with personal experience, because such experience proceeds from our Self and we have no idea of the source of what is found in books, whatever claims might be made. Therefore we must seek to know for ourselves the way to higher consciousness. As Paramhansa Nityananda often pointed out, we were born with a brain but not a book.

To seek liberation in a book rather than in the Self is a vain endeavor. We must be much more intent on the illumination of our intelligence (buddhi) than on someone else's words. Those who speak from books and not from brains are worthless indeed. In both East and West professional religionists speak as though they had a library of audiobooks in their head rather than a brain. I do not think there is anything more inane and tiresome than present-day Indian pundits and gurus that are what Yogananda called "spiritual phonographs" with never a glimmer of a functioning brain.

We can read all the spiritual books we like and read the descriptions of others' spiritual experiences, but it will add nothing to our development. We must have divine experience for ourselves. Then we will be living books of spiritual wisdom. All true scriptures are written from the basis of the authors' personal illumination. Nothing is true just because it is in a book, but a book can be a presentation of truth when it comes from an enlightened consciousness.

In his autobiography Yogananda tells of once visiting the great yogi, Nagendranath Bhaduri. "The saint and I entered the meditative state. After an hour, his gentle voice roused me. 'You go often into the silence, but have you developed anubhava?' He was reminding me to love God more than meditation. 'Do not mistake the technique for the Goal.'"

Anubhava is direct, personal experience, especially of the yogi's identity with Brahman.

Nevertheless, I would like to recommend the *Gospel of Sri Ramakrishna* to you. It is a unique spiritual record of Sri Ramakrishna's teachings and interchanges with various levels of aspirants. A friend of mine was wandering through the library of his college one day and came upon the *Gospel*, which is a very large book. He was so intrigued by it, that he checked it out. In the school parking lot a friend asked him: "Are you going to read all that book, Charlie?" Charlie laughed and said: "If I can get through this book I will never be the same!" He got through it, and never was the same.

THE SPIRITUAL TEACHER

A guru or teacher is something or someone which gives us a push in the direction of higher consciousness, who teaches us to see farther and deeper than we have before. Sometimes a book does this, and sometimes a single word spoken by someone who had no idea it would have that effect on another person. And for those of great good karma it is possible to meet a great soul who can lift them to a higher level of awareness by various means, including their mere presence. But some impetus to awakening is necessary for all of us. Of course, that awakening ultimately comes from within, but since we are so outward-turned it almost always requires an external stimulus of some sort.

As the yogi goes through life in the maze of this world he picks up a great deal of practical understanding on his own. This is why the company of a seasoned yogi is so valuable. For he knows volumes of wisdom gleaned not from books but from observation and experience, things that could not be guessed at by beginners.

All do not attain enlightenment at the same time, nor do all follow the exact same path. All cannot be teachers all the time; they must also be students. Moving between the two, in time they transcend both and simply ARE.

A worthy teacher can help anyone who wishes to change, for the divine Self is within all, and the moment anyone desires higher life he is ready and able for it. In the lives of great yogis we find examples of every kind of degradation being dispelled by their merciful teaching. What value would they be if this was not the case? The principle is that those who have dug themselves into a hole can climb out if they have a competent teacher. This is true for all. The sole factor is their intention and will.

The teacher may show the water in the well, but the student is the one who brings out the water from the well, for it is his own Self that is the well! Certainly a teacher can instruct in the way to access the water, but the student does the rest.

A true and worthy guru or teacher (acharya) will freely teach anyone who is sincere and willing to follow instruction. He will care nothing about their background or their past. A mentally disturbed man tried to kill Swami Sivananda, who forgave him and asked him to live in the ashram and do sadhana. A man was hired by jealous Brahmin pandits to poison Sri Brahma Chaitanya of Gondawali because of his open attitudes and ways. Knowing that if he refused the offered poison the man's intention to kill him would be revealed and he would be punished, Sri Brahma Chaitanya took the poison and swallowed it. Seeing this, the man fled in terror. By his yoga powers the saint did not die, but he developed chronic asthma. Such was his love and mercy.

There was a great spiritual guide (elder) on the island of Aegina in Greece named Ieronim. Once a monk I knew came to visit him. As he prepared to leave, the monk asked the elder to pray for him. "No, I won't," replied Fr. Ieronim, much to the monk's surprise. "I can't eat or sleep for you and I certainly can't do what you should being doing for yourself. You pray for yourself and I will pray for myself. Then we will both benefit." This is true: no one can live our spiritual life but we ourselves. Spiritual growth is a purely personal matter. Others can inspire or encourage us, but spiritual practice is ours exclusively.

People ignorantly think that a teacher's body is the guru. This is really only to be expected, because however philosophical we may think we are, we are very body-identified. It is a matter of conditioning from nearly all our previous lives. So of course we will identify a guru or teacher with his body and become dependent and even obsess on it. This is not just a serious obstacle to spiritual life, many "disciples" make it a substitute for spiritual life. What we should be intent on is the wisdom teaching of the guru. We need to listen, learn, and apply. And that is all.

If the guru's body is far away or no longer alive, we will be in no way hindered in our progress. That of course is easy to say, but human beings are addicted to attachments of all sorts, including spiritual attachments. I will admit to you that I wish with all my heart that I could have even just a few minutes again in the presence of the great souls I have known in the past. There is no substitute for the company of the holy, for it can change us in subtle ways we often are not aware of until that company is lost. But since Brahman Itself is "mighty world-destroying Time" and "all-devouring death" according to the Gita (11:32; 10:34), we shall certainly lose the company of the holy, and it is wise to be ready for that. We must strive to embody the wisdom they teach us so in us that wisdom shall live on in us, and after our death we can ascend to those worlds where such great ones abide.

A true guru is a living example of what he teaches, and he continues to observe himself all that he teaches to others. You know you are within the gates of a guru-cult when your hear: "Maharaj no longer needs to…." Buddha meditated until the day of his passing from this world, and he followed all the disciplines that even the youngest of the monks observed. He went on the alms-round just like everyone else: no special cook and kitchen for him. Nor did he make his advanced age an excuse for slacking off. The same was true of Swami Sivananda. What he told others to do, he himself did until the last breath.

A true spiritual teacher does not have the idea, "I am a guru." He sees divinity within all, equally, and never see them as disciples. Once a vain young Brahmin man went to Rishikesh to see Swami Sivananda. He was one of these "I bow to no one" simplistic non-dualists. He was wondering how he would get out of bowing to Sivanandaji, since others would be doing so. In his egoic dilemma he went into a small alleyway to ponder what to do. In a matter of moments Swami Sivananda entered the alley, came up to the young man and bowed down and touched his feet! He got the message.

There are a lot of "jewel in the lotus" gurus in India, but there are real gurus that treat everyone like their own family, often to the shock of those that have only been around the "jewel" type. That is why, although he was inexpressibly great, when I speak of Swami Sivananda I can so readily call him "my friend." One morning in satsang I sat there looking at him and knowing: "If there is anyone in this world who loves me, it is this man." And I did not mean love in the egoic sense of normal human emotion. He loved the true Me: my Self, not my masks and labels.

Truly: Sivananda was God and God was Sivananda.

Only those who are consciously one with Satchidananda Itself should be sought out by us. If we know no embodied ones that are in that state, then we should read the lives and teachings of those that lived in that state in the past. They are eternal, and our attunement with them can bring their blessings to us. For example, Sri Brahma Chaitanya of Gondawali in Maharashtra left his body in 1913, yet on occasion he has emerged from his samadhi shrine and spoken with sincere seekers. Time and space do not exist for such embodiments of the Eternal Joy. I can assure you that Swami Sivananda is present in his samadhi shrine at Sivanandashram in Rishikesh.

The Supreme Self (Paramatman) and individual Self (jivatman) alone are the "world-teacher," for the impulse to seek enlightenment comes only from deep within each of us. And it is our will alone that maintains our sadhana.

When you enter the presence of one who has attained the highest you can feel the sacred vibrations all around him. Further, he radiates light and peace and you will find yourself uplifted by merely sitting in his aura. If he speaks, listen with your heart as well as your ears.

We must be the same in relation to both living and departed teachers whose wisdom we have studied, and in relation to our own soul-intuition, for the ultimate guru is our Self.

Our mind must not waver like agitated water, but must be steady and calm. Only then can we truly hear and apply the teachings of the wise, and thereby ourselves become wise. "Therefore be a yogi" (Bhagavad Gita 6:46).

No one is to perpetually grovel at the feet of a supposed guru—something a true guru would never allow. But if we find a real master teacher we should happily sit at his feet and actually learn—not adore vacuously.

Here is an example from the life of Jesus that applies exactly to the situation: "Now it came to pass, as they went, that he entered into a certain village: and a certain woman named Martha received him into her house. And she had a sister called Mary, which also sat at Jesus' feet, and heard his word. But Martha was cumbered about much serving, and came to him, and said, Lord, dost thou not care that my sister hath left me to serve alone? bid her therefore that she help me. And Jesus answered and said unto her, Martha, Martha, thou art careful and troubled about many things: but one thing is needful: and Mary hath chosen that good part, which shall not be taken away from her" (Luke 10:38-42).

Think of all the busybodying "disciples" you know, who are running here and there "serving the guru," or at least the guru's organization—which in time will be identified with the guru so that whoever questions or leaves it will be declared guilty of doubting or rejecting the guru. They are selling books and magazines they have never "had time" to read, arranging seminars and world tours, setting up interviews with the rich, the powerful, and the media, immersed in busywork (oops! karma yoga) to avoid facing this utter emptiness—and often with the intention to become a big cog in the guru's machine and maybe in time be the guru's successor. Whether the guru is a fake or not is irrelevant. They are so frantically cramming activity into their lives they could not benefit from the greatest of teachers.

On the other hand there are those that sit their bodies and minds down and listen and learn and apply. Wherever their body may be, by always following what they have learned, they never leave the feet of the guru.

The proof of a true guru is his imparting freely to those around him both awakening of consciousness and instruction in the yoga that bestows liberation. Swami Sivananda Saraswati was such a one. Many of his disciples became great enlightened beings. I met several myself.

In the nineteenth century the proof of the enlightened status of Yogiraj Shyama Charan Lahiri Mahasaya was the number of disciples who became siddhas themselves. Just as a candle can light other candles, so a true guru does the same spiritually.

One time Dr. Lewis, the first American disciple of Paramhansa Yogananda, went to visit his guru in California. He arrived in the evening at the hermitage in Encinitas and Yogananda cooked dinner for him. He ate the food and talked with the master, then went to his room. But his mind was flying so high in the sky of consciousness that he could not sleep, and meditated throughout the whole night. When he told

Yoganandaji about it the next day, Yogananda nodded and said that when he had cooked the food he had been very absorbed in God. A true guru can impart consciousness even in such an unexpected way.

One time Sri Ramakrishna said to his disciple, Prasanna, the future Swami Vijnananda, "Let's have a wrestling match." Prasanna was very athletic and liked sports, including wrestling, so he agreed. Sri Ramakrishna stood against the wall of his room and Prasanna took hold of his wrists. Suddenly a tremendous wave of bliss came from Ramakrishna and overwhelmed him so much that he dropped Ramakrishna's hands. Sri Ramakrishna smiled and said: "You win!"

I urge you to obtain and carefully read *Sivananda Yoga* by Swami Venkateshananda, one of Sivananda's most advanced disciples, whom I was privileged to meet. In his book he presents what a true guru is and does. The most important is the guru's ability to communicate his consciousness to another. Sivananda imparted awareness of the Self to those around him. In his light he revealed their light.

One of Sivananda's unique characteristics compared to even the great yogis I met was the fact that when I entered his presence I became deeply Self-aware, my mind illuminated with Self-perception. Although Sivananda was glorious and for me God in flesh, yet I tell you that I never for a moment lost my Self-awareness or became absorbed in awareness of him. Rather, by means of my deepened perceptions I could comprehend that his greatness was beyond my comprehension!

Bullying is a common tool in religion and also in yoga, especially bullying of innocent, trusting people who have wandered into the clutches of a fake yoga cult or fake guru cult. This takes the form of badgering the disciple with dire warnings of the terrible fate awaiting those who "lose attunement with" the guru or "abandon" the guru–and the cult. Fear is a powerful tool of moral and emotional enslavement.

Vivekananda once asked a very devoted disciple: "If you find a guru who can show you the way to God better than I, will you leave me and follow him?" Without hesitation the disciple said: "Yes." Vivekananda embraced him and said: "Now I *know* you are my disciple!"

The amazing yogi, Sri Yogeshwar Brahmachari, told me that he had been initiated by twenty-two gurus, and had spent a great deal of time with others, including Sri Yukteswar Giri, about whom he told me: "I was simply mad for him!" As a result, instead of spending time with his guru (Tincouri Lahiri, the son of Lahiri Mahasaya), he would go early in the morning across the alley and be there with Sri Yukteswar until late at night. Having all those gurus and association with saints had certainly worked for him.

The truth that we can reach a level in which external teachers and teaching are no longer needed is unacceptable to nearly everyone who ascribes to the belief in the eternal relationship between guru and disciple. But many true gurus have said otherwise. Many times the great Swami Sivananda would tell a person who had lived two or three months with him: "You now know all I have to teach you. Go and attain everything yourself." No true teacher cultivates dependence, but rather gives independence. For the only eternal relationship we have is with God, and a true guru shows us the way to recognize and live that relationship, ourselves becoming eternal in that recognition.

When that has come about the guru remains the closest and dearest to the disciple, but the guru is never confused with or mistakenly identified with God. Certainly in relativity there is no one more important to the liberated yogi than the guru. But still he knows the difference between God and guru.

Emotional exaggeration of the guru's relation to the disciple is not devotion but ignorance and addiction. Yoga cults use it all the time to enslave their dupes. It is one of the most poisonous tools of evil teachers and their henchmen. As Sivananda said: "Emotion is not devotion," and: "I abhor gurudom."

It is not the guru that matters ultimately: it is the realization made possible by the guru's teaching. So a disciple is one who applies the teaching and attains. As Buddha said, a teacher is a finger pointing at the moon. Once the moon is seen, who looks at the finger? Obsession with personality is just another way of perpetuating the ego.

I have lived with or spent time in close association with great yogi-teachers, and my memories of them are the dearest treasures of my heart. I am endlessly grateful for their teaching, without which I might not have persevered in spiritual life. *But realization is my own to gain*, something to which I must ever look forward, and not waste my time looking backward and idolizing those names and forms.

Onward, Ever Onward, must be the motto of the serious sadhaka. The guru is meaningless if the student does not apply his teachings and progress.

In India the guru is rated above God, for throughout the subcontinent people are assured that if God is angry and the guru is pleased, then the disciple is safe; but if the guru is displeased or angry then even God cannot save you. Of course the same people will just as easily assure you that God cares nothing for the sin or virtue of human beings and that gurus are established in a consciousness of Unity and Bliss that renders them incapable of being upset at any unpleasantness. So how could they ever be displeased? Often the publicity for these gurus speak of "unconditional love" and "love beyond description."

What has gone wrong? All institutions hate independent and creative thinking. Most hate any kind of thinking at all. Do not be mistaken: the East is just as lockstep ignorant as anywhere else, it is just that the principles recited robotically are wiser than the stupid stuff that flows out of the mouths of Western religionists.

A glorious exception was Paramhansa Nityananda, who was no standard item, and did not fear or hesitate to speak out the truth as he saw it. For example, someone once told him: "In the Gita *Krishna* says…," and he interrupted, saying: "No. In the Gita *Vyasa* says Krishna said." Not the expected response.

A true guru does not just impress: he transforms. Then the aspirant is empowered to follow the path of Self-realization and the guru shows the way and the disciple attains everything, becoming himself what the guru was before him. And let me assure you that a true guru never promotes himself or allows his followers do so, either.

A lot of fakery goes on with supposed yogis pretending to be in all kinds of states. I have seen a lot of play-acting going on in the yoga world, from the "enlightened" gurus at the top down to the foot-soldier disciples at the bottom.

I wish I had videos of the aftermath of special, long meditations I attended where the participants were drifting around in "angelic" states and coming up to one another and saluting or holding hands in divine silence. Ultimately it all came to nothing, and in some cases resulted in a very bad end. God is truth and you cannot draw near to him through pretentious actions and words, what the Greeks call *Agia Fania*: Holy Show.

It is a favorite ploy in India to claim that you spent decades doing intense tapasya in the Himalayas. I personally know one Big Baba of Bengal who claims he spent over twenty years in the Himalayas, when investigation easily shows that he was a building contractor in Calcutta all the time!

Swami Sivananda humorously wrote some instruction for these people. First, he said, rent a little house (kutir) in Rishikesh or Hardwar for six months. Arrange to have your food brought to you, and never be seen by anybody. Sit around inside and do what you like, including a lot of sleep. During that time write two or three trash leaflets (his expression) and a couple of bad devotional songs (bhajans). Then at the end of the six months go down to the plains and put it out that you have been living in silence (mauna) for many years way up in the Himalayas, even beyond Uttara Kashi. Arrange for yourself a few meetings where you will talk aimlessly, sing your bad songs, and give out your worthless leaflets. In no time at all you will be a sought-after guru, and maybe even an avatar.

This is no idle allegation. Once in Rishikesh I was stopped and grilled by a fairly well-educated sadhu who begged me to tell him how to get to America and make a splash. On another occasion in holy Naimisharanya a monk told me that if I would spend a few hours with him each day for a week, "I will show you how to get the people of America in the palm of your hand." That is how these people think.

Excusing a guru's materialism on the ground that "for him these are just toys" or "he is showing us an example in how to deal with them/it" is nonsense. Get straight and get honest. If it walks like a duck, quacks like a duck, and swims like a duck, it is a duck—not a guru or an avatar whose advent has ushered in the Satya Yuga.

It is not unknown for those that set themselves up as spiritual teachers to teach what they think will sell, and keep the worthwhile knowledge to themselves. This is often the case with meditation teachers. One world-renowned meditation teacher claimed the practice he peddled was the highest and best, having been given to him by his guru, a truly great master. But to me he admitted that he had invented the method and the way he initiated people into it. I know of at least two other teachers with followings around the world who just looked through some books and then made up what they hawked as ancient tradition. The practices of all three of these charlatans actually harmed many, but it was the money that counted. They led others into the jungle of harm, themselves being the beasts of prey that lived off of them.

No one can build an empire on real yoga, for that is against its nature. But they certainly can build one on false yoga. And it does not matter if the yoga "does things." It is possible to wander for lifetimes in the psychic regions opened by false (or misapplied) yoga. One of the reasons for this is the sad fact that Jesus revealed when he said: "Men loved darkness rather than light" (John 3:19). False seekers desire false teachers. I have seen people going from one fake to another while refusing to even listen to or read the teachings of a true teacher.

In India there is a great deal of fussing about the yoga powers (siddhis) and how they must be avoided and how wrong it is to use them. But nearly all the biographies of those the authors consider master yogis or siddhas are little more than a string of accounts of their miraculous powers.

There is a very important principle. A true siddha does not just act in an inexplicable or apparently supernatural way to arouse the wonder of those around him. Rather he teaches and makes clear the path to perfect realization, because his interest is in enabling his hearers to attain exactly what he has attained.

If we visit ashrams in India what we usually find is one person who is the jewel in the lotus, a giant being served and adulated by adoring pygmies who themselves never become anything. Miraculous things are related to prove the jewel's worth, but none of the followers ever get anywhere.

There are many very pure and highly evolved people who in their sincere compassion for others are willing to take up the role of guru, but it does not work. On both sides, guru and disciple, sincerity may be undoubted, but the person thought to be guru cannot do what a true guru does easily: transference of consciousness and opening of atmic awareness. It is beyond high and low, inside and out, because the Self is beyond all these things.

This is why I warn people away from becoming a disciple of someone that is not really a sadguru, however holy and highly evolved they may be. Until you are there, you are not there. And to attempt to do for others what only a siddha can do is to harm both oneself and the erstwhile disciple.

An aspiring individual can have many teachers to his benefit, but he cheats himself if he connects with a guru that may work miracles and seem omniscient, but is not perfectly God-realized. In India you can find many good souls that, not having had a true guru themselves, do not realize that they cannot be a guru.

When my friend, Dr. Mukherji, met his guru, Swami Purnananda, a disciple of Mahavatar Babaji, he asked to become his disciple. "No," said Purnananda, "you do not know me. First you must get to know me thoroughly." For three years Dr. Mukherhji spent as much time as possible at Purnanandaji's ashram. Then he became his disciple—a true disciple of a true guru. I wish you could have met Dr. Mukherji. He lived in the highest consciousness, yet was so loving and approachable. His personal knowledge of yoga practice and experience was vast. The hours I spent together with him generously sharing his bounty were among the most blessed and happy of my life. Yet he would never have presumed to be a guru.

A worthy teacher first of all knows the royal road himself and never holds any knowledge from his students. Those who do less must be prepared for the karmic consequences.

Then there are those teachers that dribble out their teaching, especially those that have a series of "initiations" to impart an ascending series of techniques. Since nothing they teach really works, they keep their students in anticipation of the next "higher" technique that surely will begin doing what they promised at the beginning. This is sheer trickery, but what else can they do, since they really know nothing?

But those who do know something worthwhile share it freely, openly, and completely right now, for the future certainly is unsure, but karma is not.

There are two levels of guru: primary and secondary. The primary guru is God himself, human gurus being only secondary and temporary. (They are called "upagurus" in yogic tradition.) A human guru shows us the way to know God and then his work is done. But the Guru God abides with us forever. Paramhansa Nityananda said that a third class aspirant thinks he needs initiation to begin spiritual life, a second class aspirant gets himself a human guru, but a first class aspirant turns to God and becomes His disciple, for as the Yoga Sutras (1:26) say about Ishwara: "Being unconditioned by time he is guru even of the ancients."

Commenting on the Yoga Sutras, Vyasa says: "It is yoga that is the teacher. How so? It has been said: 'Yoga is to be known by yoga. Yoga goes forward from yoga alone. He who is not careless [neglectful] in his yoga for a long time, rejoices in the yoga.'"

Yoga truly becomes our teacher, revealing to us that which is far beyond the wisdom of books and verbal instructions. Moreover, it is practice of yoga that enables us to understand the basis and rationale of its methods and their application. The why and wherefore of yoga become known to us by direct insight. In his commentary on Yoga

Sutra 2:28 Vyasa says: "From practicing yoga, illusion [ignorance] is destroyed and perishes. When it is destroyed, there is manifestation of right vision. In proportion to the practice done, illusion is dispelled. In proportion to its destruction, the light of [spiritual] knowledge increases correspondingly. This increase is an experience of increasing refinement up to the realization of the true nature of the purusha [spirit]."

The Yoga Vashishtha says it clearly and truly: "God Consciousness is not achieved by means of the scriptures, nor is it achieved by the grace of your Master. God Consciousness is only achieved by your own subtle awareness." When Gorakhnath asked: "Who is the Guru that leads to the Goal?" Matsyendranath told him: "Nirvana itself is the Guru that leads to the Goal." That is, the liberated condition of the Self, though presently buried beneath the debris of lifetimes of ignorance, is itself the inspirer and guide to the revelation of our eternal liberation.

SUBTLE ANATOMY

It is good for the aspiring yogi to have some theoretical knowledge of his subtle anatomy, for that is the inner mechanism which comes more and more into function on the conscious level as he progresses further and further toward enlightenment. The three major channels within our subtle bodies, Ida, Pingala and Sushumna, carry not only the movements of the highest, rarefied spiritual energies which evolve us, but through them consciousness itself moves and manifests.

The supreme center of conscious in the individual is the Sahasrara, the thousand-petalled lotus located in the head, corresponding to the brain, for it is the astral and causal brain. It is the place where Self-realization takes place, and where we should keep our awareness centered. For in the head we find the Brahmanadi, the channel in which the consciousness rises upward from the body into the head, through which it moves as liberation is attained, and through which we ascend beyond the bodies into Spirit Itself at the time of death.

It is crucial for the yogi to realize that the chakras and major nadis found in the body are only subordinate reflections of the chakras and nadis in the head, where true sadhana takes place and true enlightenment occurs.

In meditation yogis experience the reality of these things which at first encounter in yogic texts may seem baseless mythologies. But this is the glory of yoga: we can experience those realities for ourselves. Many yogis have doubted various statements or descriptions in the ancient texts, but as they progressed in their practice they experienced the truth of those statements for themselves, much to their surprise.

Leave the downward path and come to the central path. The central path of the sushumna leads directly upward into the Sahasrara, the place of liberation.

The beginningless and endless Infinite is embodied in the Sahasrara-chidakasha. "If a thousand suns should rise together in the sky, such splendor would be like the brilliance of that Great Being" (Bhagavad Gita 11:12). And that Great Being is revealed in the Sahasrara-chidakasha when the attention of the yogi is always oriented toward that both in and outside of meditation.

Human beings are literally miniature universes. I remember vividly the first time I experienced this while meditating. I wrote about it in this way: "While meditating one day all ordinary physical sensation vanished. Spatial relation ceased to exist and I found myself keenly aware of being beyond dimension, neither large nor small, but infinite (for infinity is beyond size). Although the terminology is inappropriate to such a state, to make it somewhat understandable I have to say that I perceived an infinity of worlds 'within' me. Suns—some solo and others surrounded by planets—glimmered inside my spaceless space. Not that I saw the light, but I felt or intuited it. Actually, I did not 'see' anything—and yet I did. It is not expressible in terms of ordinary sense experience, yet I must use those terms. I experienced myself as everything that existed within the relative material universe. Or so it seemed, for here, also, there are two interpretations, one dramatic and self-glorifying, and one the simple truth. The first opinion can be that I had come to experience myself as the totality of universal being, that I had realized that I myself was the Absolute Being, that God and I were the same entity, that I was God and God was All. And then the truth: The human body is a miniature universe, a microcosmic model of the macrocosm. The physical human body is a reflection of the universal womb that conceived it. I had experienced the subtle level of the physical body that is its ideational (i.e., causal) blueprint. On that level it can be experienced as a map of the material creation. Having experienced that for myself I now knew it to be true...." It is this mirroring of the universe that makes humans the highest organisms on the earth.

We are not just miniatures of the physical universe. Since we possess many subtle bodies we are also miniatures of the astral and causal worlds to which they correspond. Actually we are living in/on all worlds simultaneously. Since we are self-conscious entities, humans are embodiments of the entire creation on all its levels. As God pervades all worlds on the macrocosmic levels, we pervade them all as microcosms. Birth and death in any of the worlds is a simply matter of tuning in and tuning out.

Kundalini is essentially not energy (shakti), but the bliss consciousness of Shiva (Brahman). I learned this from Swami Rama of Hardwar many years ago when I was visiting his ashram at Ram Kunj. It is Brahmic Consciousness that must arise in our consciousness and unite us with Itself.

That which gives us light is within. Divine Light lies within the inner world, in our inner mechanism or antahkarana. If we eliminate all that veils it, true jnana will illumine us.

Kundalini is the Brahma Jyoti which is the essence of the light of the sun. For the sun is formed of spiritual energies which gives life to all sentient beings on the earth and awakens and develops their consciousness. That is why at dawn and sunset the Gayatri Mantra, a prayer for enlightenment, is recited facing the sun. The Ajapa Gayatri, the Soham mantra, is the essential mantra for invoking the solar energies at all times, intoning *So* mentally during natural inhalation and intoning *Ham* (pronounced: "Hum") mentally during natural exhalation. For more about this, see both *Soham Yoga: The Yoga of the Self,* and *Light of Soham.*

An urdhvareta yogi is one in whose subtle energy system the pranas, the life energies, are predominately flowing upwards into the Sahasrara/ chidakasha in which our immortal, eternal Self abides, united with the Paramatma, the Supreme Self–the finite with the Infinite.

When the urdhvareta state is established in the yogi, there is a separation of the energies so the subtler can become dominant and bring about the transmutation of the grosser into the subtler, and from there into consciousness.

The third eye, the ajna chakra, is in the brain, not between the eyebrows where it is reflected, but halfway between the point between the eyebrows and the medulla. In the physical body this manifests as the pineal gland, from which physiologists say our two physical eyes have emerged. This gland is affected by light, just as are the two eyes. This is the "single eye" spoken of by Jesus (Matthew 6:22). This is the point of pure consciousness in the body. There awareness rests in the Self.

That inner power which becomes wasted by flowing down and out must be conserved and directed upward into the head, into the sahasrara. Then nothing worthwhile remains unattainable to the yogi. When this is done, the subtle magnetism of the brain begins to draw the straying energies back inward and upward, literally making the yogi "whole."

Sahasrara awareness is an important help in daily sadhana, especially outside meditation when it is so easy to become distracted and lose the thread of spiritual awareness.

Brahmarandhra means "the gate of Brahman" and is the chakra located at the very top (crown) of the head. The liberated yogi departs from the body through this "door" into infinite consciousness.

The chakras correspond to the various levels of consciousness. In the *Gospel of Sri Ramakrishna*, Sri Ramakrishna said: "The Bauls will ask you, 'In which station are you dwelling?' According to them there are six 'stations,' corresponding to the six psychic centers of Yoga. If they say that a man dwells in the 'fifth station', it means that his mind has climbed to the fifth centre, known as the Vishuddha chakra. At that time he sees the Formless."

After saying this, he sang:

Within the petals of this flower there lies concealed a subtle space,
Transcending which, one sees at length the universe in Space dissolve.

In the same conversation, Sri Ramakrishna said: "The Bauls will ask you, 'Do you know about the wind?' The 'wind' means the great currrent that one feels in the subtle nerves, Ida, Pingala, and Sushumna, when the Kundalini is awakened."

Within the Sahasrara there is what yogis call "the Agni Mandala," the sphere of internal fire. In the Fire of the Spirit all that is not either the Self or a purified and necessary vehicle of the Self will be consumed.

As Yogananda said, the book of Revelation in the Bible is not prophecy but a yoga treatise utilizing symbols to convey its message. (He wrote a commentary on the entire book, but it has not yet been published.) There the Agni Mandala is spoken of as a lake of fire: "And the devil that deceived them was cast into the lake of fire and brimstone, where the beast and the false prophet are, and shall be tormented day and night for ever and ever.... And I saw a great white throne, and him that sat on it, from whose face the earth and the heaven fled away; and there was found no place for them. And I saw the dead, small and great, stand before God; and the books were opened: and another book was opened, which is the book of life: and the dead were judged out of those things which were written in the books, according to their works. And the sea gave up the dead which were in it; and death and hell delivered up the dead which were in them: and they were judged every man according to their works. And death and hell were cast into the lake of fire. This is the second death. And whosoever was not found written in the book of life was cast into the lake of fire" (20:10-15).

These verses are symbolic representations (too complex to comment on here) of the final transmutation of the yogi's entire being into divinity. The process is awesome and tremendous. Just after his resurrection the bodies of Jesus were undergoing this process. If anyone had touched him they might have been harmed by that divine energy-power, the way light can pain those with eye defects. That is why Jesus said to Saint Mary Magdalene: "Touch me not; for I am not yet ascended to my Father" (John 20:17). When the transmutation was complete, then he could be touched. When he appeared to the disciples he said: "Behold my hands and my feet, that it is I myself: handle me, and see; for a spirit hath not flesh and bones, as ye see me have" (Luke 24:39). And to Saint Thomas, who had not been there at his first appearance, he said: "Reach hither thy finger, and behold my hands; and reach hither thy hand, and thrust it into my side" (John 20:27).

THE WORLD

The dwandwas, the pairs of opposites inherent in nature (prakriti), such as pleasure and pain, hot and cold, light and darkness, gain and loss, victory and defeat, love and hatred are always present in this world. The pleasant ones attract us and the unpleasant ones repel us. In this way we are impelled back and forth continually, hardly ever coming to a state of real rest and calm. This is the basic condition of samsara.

Before we came into relative existence, the creation (samsara) was eternally present to those within it, and after we have transcended creation and left it behind, it will still be going on, a dream bubble that encompassed us for a while, yet from which we will have been freed. But the ever-changing drama of creation will go on forever to those within it.

It difficult to get into the stream of effective spiritual life. Seeing how difficult it is, many decide that it is beyond their strength, not realizing that once one is fully in the stream most of the difficulties are over. The "luggage" of the world and our accumulated ignorance not only does not bother us, it fades from our mind. The "stuff" of this world no longer matters, for our attention is focused on the practical aspects of living the yoga life that leads to liberation, to perfect freedom.

Entering the spiritual stream is a result of discrimination between the real and the unreal, between the perishable and the immortal. When discrimination (viveka) is ripened in us, then the silly toys that occupied us from life to life are of no interest any longer.

Truth is stable and lasting, and so is the spiritual illumination of those who seek and unite themselves with the highest truth: God. But the thought and words of those immersed in the world and its ways are like letters written in chalk: they quickly fade, become meaningless and eventually non-existent.

The so-called worldly wise are really only worldly fools. All the good will in the world felt toward them cannot reach them. Through the ages holy people and masters have loved such people and did all they could to help them, but it has never worked. For they are just insubstantial chalk until they themselves evolve and change. And that change comes only from within.

Once a friend of mine was with Ma Anandamayi in Delhi when a large group of Europeans came to the ashram. My friend was asked to translate for them. Throughout their time with Ma she said many funny things and even told some jokes. As they were laughing heartily after one joke, Ma said to my friend: "Well, at least I can make them laugh." On another occasion Ma pointed to some Westerners who considered themselves her devotees and said in Bengali to the Indians standing there: "Do you see these people? I can't do anything with them."

WORSHIP

One of the requisites for liberation is understanding Krishna's words in the Bhagavad Gita: "Others, sacrificing by the sacrifice of knowledge, worship me as One and Manifold, variously manifested, omniscient" (9:15). All the many gods worshipped in India are symbols of the many aspects of the One Infinite God. There is nothing wrong with these symbols or their depiction in pictures or images. In fact we can approach God through reverence for them and can worship God through them, even with offerings. It is a matter of right understanding. And since God is everything there is nothing wrong in looking upon an image as God as long as the worshipper does not think that is all there to God, that God is confined to that image and is not all-pervading Spirit. Regarding astrology, Swami Sri Yukteswar said: "Charlatans have brought the stellar science to its present state of disrepute. Astrology is too vast, both mathematically and philosophically, to be rightly grasped except by men of profound understanding. If ignoramuses misread the heavens, and see there a scrawl instead of a script, that is to be expected in this imperfect world. One should not dismiss the wisdom with the 'wise.'" It is the same with the use of holy images. "Idolatry" is a matter of the individual's mind and belief. Here, too, discrimination is a requisite for liberation.

I think because "idolatry" is such a bugaboo to western religion, those Westerners that become involved with Indian dharma and yoga shy away from or ignore it or convince themselves that people such as they have gone beyond the need for "such things."

Once a Trappist monk who had observed a special worship (puja) in our ashram said to me: "But you only worship what the image represents—not the image itself—right?" "No," I said, "we worship the image because everything is divine. Of course it is our intention to worship the Absolute, but as I say, That is all-embracing."

Seeing images is not seeing God if we see only with the two material eyes, even if we worship them. But if we look at them with the one eye of spirit, we will see the One in them. And validly worship them.

Sri Ramakrishna said that water is everywhere, but we must go where it is to be found in its complete, liquid form. One place is in a temple. Shankara established many temples, and he was the supreme non-dualist.

A pitcher is not water, but water can be in the pitcher. It is the same with holy imagery.

True worship is internal, and that should fulfill the words of David: "Bless the Lord, O my soul: and all that is within me, bless his holy name" (Psalms 103:1).

Yoga, the Body and the World

No one calls their house "me," but we constantly call our body "me." That is how deluded we have become through countless lifetimes. The purpose of the body is to get out of it, like the nest of a bird. No bird can fly and carry the nest along with it, and we cannot fly in the Sky of Consciousness if we are tied down to body awareness and body identity.

We must cultivate the discrimination (viveka) that enables us to distinguish between our two dwellings: the mortal body and the immortal Brahman. Body consciousness is really a sort of death, but Brahma-vidya, the realization of Brahman, is true life. We have always existed in Brahman, and our incarnation in a body is but an illusory dream. The subtle discrimination we need is in no way an intellectual process, but the direct realization which meditation alone can give.

As long as we know only the body we are beggars and miserable, but our real nature is Brahmic bliss that is beyond description. How wonderful is Sanatana Dharma! It alone of the world's philosophies tells us the full truth of our immortal, divine Self and calls us to its realization. Most other (not all) religion is obsessed with sin and punishment and "the good life" here on earth and in a pointless heaven. True Dharma also tells us that we need not go groveling after God, for we are eternally a part of Divine Being. We need only awaken into Brahman, and Sanatana Dharma tells us how through Yoga.

Sanatana Dharma is the understanding that our eternal Self is the only truth of our being and that we can realize and demonstrate that truth.

Sattwic people identify with spirit; rajasic people identify with the mind—manas and buddhi; and tamasic people identify with the body. Consequently, tamasic people become obsessed with hatha yoga and diet, especially fasting. No matter how defiled their minds and personal lives are, they obsess on "purification" which they think is achieved by colonics, stringent diets, and prolonged fasts. I have nothing to say to them, as they are unreachable. But I mention it here so sincere seekers will not think they should take up the same obsession or blame themselves for not being interested in such pointless exercises in self-loathing.

Tamasic people love sleep, and we must not become tamasic in that regard. However, in modern life, especially in America, most people do not get enough sleep, and even those who get eight or more hours of sleep may not be truly rested from the sleep. Such people should consult a physician and have a sleep study done. Also, excessive sleep can be a sign of a physical problem, so a physician should be consulted. I knew a yogi who craved sleep and seemed unable to get enough. It turned out that he was pre-diabetic and his body was signaling him in this way. So do not condemn or force yourself in the matter of sleep. Get qualified health advice.

Since the body is meant to be the instrument of enlightenment, we should care about maintaining our bodily as well as our mental and spiritual health. What is inappropriate is obsessing on the body and all things related to it. Oliver Black, one of Paramhansa Yogananda's most advanced disciples, once said to a group of people (including myself): "You can tell by a person's conversation where their consciousness is centered. A lot of people who think they are yogis and spiritual spend most of their time talking about both ends of their digestive tract. They are either going on and on about their diet or about their bowel movements and colonics. They haven't any idea about how much their consciousness is really tied down to the body." It is this mistake we must avoid.

Yogananda insisted that yogis must care for the body, especially its diet, but only in a sensible, practical way.

There is a great deal of exposition in both East and West of how awful certain things are, how ugly, loathsome and disgusting they are. But people are still not only attracted to them, they are positively addicted to them. In India there is a great deal about the human body and how it is filled with disgusting elements and is the source of misery. One of my favorite Hare Krishna stories is about a true incident. One time in San Francisco two male devotees were walking along a street and one began to stare at a girl who was coming from the opposite direction. "You shouldn't be looking at her," admonished his companion. "After all, that body is nothing but blood, pus, feces, urine, bile and other repulsive things." "Yeah," replied the man, continuing to stare, "but in all the right places!" Certainly the admonishing man was speaking the truth, but age-long attachment and infatuation won the day. Attachment for various things can be suppressed and seemingly eliminated, but they always return if they are not dissolved in the awakening of enlightened consciousness through meditation.

"Truly this maya of mine made of the gunas is difficult to go beyond. Verily only those who attain me shall pass beyond this maya" (Bhagavad Gita 7:14). Only yoga can free us from addictions we formed long before we even reached the human form. Yoga is the sole means to take refuge in God and become one with him. Freedom from earthly and egoic desires is not just difficult, it it impossible to anyone but the adept yogi.

We should respect and care for our physical vehicle, for it is the instrument of yoga and enlightenment: of evolution. But a delusive attachment (moha) for it and a kind of body-worship is folly of the worst sort. That is because such attitudes arise from identification with the body, which is as silly as identifying our body with a mirror in which it is reflected. The body, too, is a mirror, a fleeting image in the greater mirror of the cosmos. It is never "us" at any time. We should not have the slightest selfish, egoic attachment to it, or to anything else, for that matter. But such a high ideal can only be attained by one who transfers his identity to the Self through the practice of yoga. And he who knows the Self comes to know the Supreme Being in everything and everywhere.

The body is solely a means to an end: union with Brahman. Therefore we are misusing the body and wasting this inestimable treasure, the means to divinization, if we do not make the realization of God our primary interest and endeavor in life.

The body, being part of the lowest level of samsara, is in constant flux and usually in some form that will cause pain or confusion. Like the description the prophet Isaiah gave of the troubled sea, the body perpetually "cast[s] up mire and dirt" (Isaiah 57:20). Just think, we put on clean clothes and in a short time we need to change them even if we have done nothing that would make them dirty. Rather, the body itself by constantly exuding various things, makes the clothes dirty. If there is anything in the world that is unclean, it is the human body which is a conglomeration of impurity and corruption. Why? Because the body follows the mind, which is itself a collection of imperfections and impurities. But the bodies of those who have purified themselves completely do not produce any uncleanness of any kind and often after death do not decay.

Those who identify with the body, mind and the world around them cannot help but be deluded, for the things they identify with are delusive. Those whose minds are linked to the Self are not fooled by the appearances of samsara. It is very much like the audience in a motion picture theater. Some react to the movie as though it were real, and others do not.

If we dip water from the sea in a bucket we will only get the amount that fits in it. If our bucket is small, we will get little; if it is large, we will get much. The mind of a human being is like a bucket. Small minds get little from life and large minds get much.

The universe is a field, an ocean, of consciousness and we will draw from it according to the scope of our consciousness. Yogananda often spoke of the need to expand our consciousness by diligent yoga practice. Life itself is consciousness. The more conscious we are, the more alive we are. Yoga, then, is the key to ever-increasing life.

DHARMA AND ADHARMA

Adharma: Unrighteousness; demerit; failure to perform one's proper duty; unrighteous action; lawlessness; absence of virtue; all that is contrary to righteousness (dharma). *(A Brief Sanskrit Glossary)*

Dharma: The righteous way of living, as enjoined by the sacred scriptures and the spiritually illumined; law; lawfulness; virtue; righteousness; norm. *(A Brief Sanskrit Glossary)*

To be truly human is to be awakened enough to knew what is dharma and what is adharma and to hold to dharma and eschew adharma. That is why in the Yoga Sutras yama and niyama, the principles of right thought and deed, are the first step of yoga. And those who do not take the first step cannot really take any others, though a lot of people are fooling themselves about that fact.

Without a clear awareness of dharma and adharma, and a life perfectly conformed to dharma, we are not truly human. But those who know the distinction and live according to dharma are truly human beings.

The state of liberation is the sole virtue. All other lesser virtues lead to that. All the powers of the individual must become united through yoga and manifest that unity.

YOGA: THE SUPREME DHARMA

Wheat a few thousand years old was found in an Egyptian tomb. Some of it was planted and it grew. If our divine potential is closed away inside us, unknown or forgotten, nothing will come of it. But if it is put in the right environment, it will grow and bring about undreamed-of results in the form of evolution of consciousness. One seed of wisdom can produce thousands of others. One virtue can multiply into many. All that is needed is the right surroundings. If yoga is not supported by an environment that is totally conducive and consistent, it will either not grow or be stunted and weak and eventually die. I have been watching that happen for over fifty years.

A great deal of religion is cosmetic, just a cover-up or a repression rather than a real purification. All kinds of ineffectual things are considered to cleanse the individual but they really do not. The only thing that purifies is the evocation of higher consciousness, the consciousness that is the our true Self (Atman). And yoga is the process of purification, the first step of which is yama-niyama. Those who have an aversion to those purifying principles will not be cleansed or purified.

Just as drinking alcohol can wipe out memory, in the same way things that are contrary to yama and niyama will wipe out the effects of yoga practice. But the yoga will have worked, even though the person then destroys its effects through negative and self-destructive actions.

If someone challenges me: "What good has yoga done for India?" I can point to thousands of years of great souls (mahatmas) and unparalleled teachers who adorn India's history like blazing jewels, including today. But after over a century, what good has yoga done in America? The truthful answer is: very little good and a great deal of harm. Why? Because it has not been rooted in yama and niyama. Yama and niyama are the seeds of yogic attainment, which is why Patanjali lists the results of perfection (siddhi) in those "ten commandments of yoga." (See *The Foundations of Yoga*.) A yogi is not above or beyond yama and niyama, he is the living embodiment of those principles.

"When I was a child, I spake as a child, I understood as a child, I thought as a child: but when I became a man, I put away childish things" said Saint Paul (I Corinthians 13:11). This is a matter of evolution. When a person truly evolves he understands the ins and outs of all things, including external conduct. Such a person will not act contrary to dharma, for dharmic behavior will have become natural to him. Like God, "he cannot deny himself" (II Timothy 2:13). Evil becomes as impossible for the perfected yogi as it is for God.

Many methods passed off as yoga are not yoga at all. Well-meaning men and women spend years practicing them and getting nowhere. Once a man wrote to me who had been practicing a worthless yoga technique for over thirty years without making any progress. Although he lamented his lack of progress, he was so brainwashed by the yoga cult that he asked me what was wrong with *him*. The truth was that nothing was wrong with him. The method was worthless and the cult repressive and destructive. But I knew that he would go to pieces if I told him that, so I urged him to pray and look within for the answer. There was nothing else I could say. People who are entrenched in personal delusions are unreachable. I have never come across an exception.

If you have a translation of the Gita on your computer, you will find it very instructive to do a search for the word "senses." It is surprising how much of the Gita deals with the subject of the senses. Here are the most relevant passages:

"The intelligent, buddhic awareness of him whose senses are withdrawn from the objects of the senses on all sides will be found firmly established" (Bhagavad Gita 2:68).

"He who by the mind controls the senses, and yet is unattached while engaging action's organs in action, is superior" (Bhagavad Gita 3:7).

"He who possesses faith attains knowledge. Devoted to that pursuit, restraining the senses, having attained knowledge he quickly attains supreme peace" (Bhagavad Gita 4:39).

"That firmness of intellect or purpose by which through yoga the functions of the mind, the vital force (prana) and the senses are restrained, is sattwic" (Bhagavad Gita 18:33).

Total mastery of the senses reveals the Self. And yoga produces that mastery.

"One acts according to one's own prakriti–even the wise man does so. Beings follow their own prakriti." (Bhagavad Gita 3:33). There is no means for finding or developing qualities which one's prakriti does not possess. What you have, you have; and what you do not have, you do not have. If this little bit of reality cannot be seen or admitted, then no reality will ever be known.

Our prakriti is everything, overshadowing our experience of the Self as consciousness. It overwhelms our real state and makes us identify with its kaleidoscopic changes. What must we do? We cannot get rid of it, anymore than God can rid himself of the universe. Rather, we must refine and develop our prakriti-nature until it no longer covers the Self, but reveals it. Yoga is the only means to accomplish this, but unhappily a lot that is called yoga today is only superstition and delusion. So our task is to find real yoga and obtain real realization.

Part of our prakriti is our mind which is a field of vibrating energy. When the mind's energy waves are disturbed or choppy, the individual's perceptions are also disturbed or choppy. When the mental waves subside and are still, then the yogi sees clearly without distortion of any kind.

Cause and effect originate in the Atman-Self. There never really is anything but the Self, both cosmic and individual, the Paramatman and the jivatman. This being so, to not be centered in the Self is to be lost in delusion, which is why yoga is the sole remedy for those lost and drowned in samsara.

The subtler the experience, the closer it is to the fundamental reality of the Self. This is especially true of meditation. Correct meditation practice leads to subtler and subtler levels of the mind (manas) and intelligence (buddhi). If it does not then something is not right.

Chidakasha, conscious (chid) ether (akasha), is the "element" in which perfect realization is attained. Although it is always present, only after the yogi purifies and refines his inner sense will it be perceived and experienced. Just as the eyes become used to dim light, so the mind of the yogi becomes capable of perceiving what before seemed to be nonexistent and only an idea, not a reality. The mind of the yogi is a precious thing indeed and must be constantly and vigilantly guarded.

The Self is in the highest realms of consciousness completely beyond the material world in which the material body exists. This is why it is important to understand the five general levels or bodies (koshas), particularly the fact that the etheric, anandamaya kosha actually touches the pure consciousness that is our true nature. The anandamaya kosha by its nature frees us from itself and enables us to enter into awareness of the Self.

Any yoga that does not begin with the etheric levels of the yogi is not yoga at all. This is a cardinal principle. A practice that does not center us right away in the etheric/anandamaya kosha cannot lead us to the enlightenment that is realization: atma-vidya and Brahma-vidya. And the essential faculty of the etheric body is mentally generated sound (shabda). Therefore mantra is the essence of liberating yoga.

Sattwa, the quality of light and enlightenment, is within every single person, but only yoga sadhana can so clarify the mind that the character of sattwa will pervade it and give divine sight (divya chakshu).

A selfish mind is unsteady because it is fixed on things that are themselves in constant flux: ego, emotions, sense-experience, and the world itself. Being projections of ignorance they are unreal, and there is certainly no stability in dreams and mirages.

Steadiness is only possible when our awareness is centered in that which is unchanging: the Self and the Supreme Self. To do this we must be able to enter the subtle levels of our existence and to literally live there. This requires refinement on all levels of our being.

Purification is the first step: purification of body and mind through thought, behavior, and diet. Then the actual refinement occurs in and through meditation, and is continued through japa outside meditation. In this way we are enabled to maintain the process of meditation continually, and that is the subtle steadiness in which liberation is experienced.

Only the most subtle yoga produces enlightenment. But yogis in India have spent lifetimes engaging in very physical and sometimes violent disciplines, all outward-turned and external. Of course they attained nothing, because the Self is the most subtle thing in existence. Therefore the yogi's meditation must be completely inward and increasingly subtle until he reaches the most subtle, his Self.

A yoga that does not right away begin producing subtle awareness is not yoga at all, but mere physical and psychic gymnastics. It is very much like these words from *The Way of a Pilgrim*: "It's like those fanatics in India and Bokhara who sit down and blow themselves out trying to get a sort of tickling in their hearts, and in their stupidity take this bodily feeling for prayer, and look upon it as the gift of God." Substitute "awakening of Kundalini" for "a sort of tickling in their hearts" and you have the whole picture. Elder Joseph the Hesychast of Mount Athos died of the asthmatic heart disorder which he incurred from strenuous practices to "enter the heart."

I have an edition of Swami Dayananda's *Satyarth Prakash* that is dedicated to a man who died from the strain of trying "to raise the pranas into the head." There is a color photo of him, and his eyes are bloodshot and his entire face a picture of stress and strain. He killed himself thinking the material could produce the spiritual. In the Yoga Boom of the sixties and seventies America was filled with supposed yogis from India who went on and on about energies (shakti) and kundalini but never spoke of Consciousness, which is the essence of the Self–both Atman and Paramatman.

The Chandogya Upanishad (6.5.1-2, 4) tells us that the subtle energies of food become the energies of our mind. This being so, we must be careful of what we eat. Cooked food becomes very susceptible to the bio-energies of those who prepare and serve it, so in India there are various rules regarding the eating of food cooked by others. (Many yogis will not eat in restaurants.) This is not superstition.

My friend, Dr. A. K. Bhattacharya, a pioneer in the field of radionics and homeopathy, told me that he would only eat food cooked by his wife or daughter. One time, though, he accepted an invitation to visit an old school friend who had become warden of a major prison in Bengal, the invitation including lunch. He decided to break his rule and ate the remarkable food that was cooked by one of the inmates who was famous for his cuisine before he went to jail. However, that afternoon Dr. Bhattacharya become unreasonably angry and shouted at everyone around him, something utterly alien to his nature. Shocked at this, he tried to figure out the cause. It did not take long to realize that it might be the food eaten at the prison. He phoned his warden friend and asked if anyone had experienced strange effects after eating there. The warden said that he had received other calls about this and been told that everyone who had eaten the lunch had experienced outbursts of anger and violent impulses, including himself. Dr. Bhattacharya asked him to investigate the background of the cook. He did, and found out that the prisoner was a homicidal maniac, put in the prison because there was no mental institution that could cope with him! He had been taken out of solitary confinement to do the cooking. So he was not just violent, he was murderous, as the effect proved.

Unfortunately there is spiritual snobbery just as there is social snobbery, and often the spiritual is worse than the social. Countless times I have heard people say that since inquirers could not possibly understand, or would not put forth the effort if informed, they either refused to discuss the yoga life with them or gave them some simplistic answer rather than get entangled with questions and discussions.

I must admit I understood their attitude, having myself spent hours and even days with "seekers" who really had no deep interest and had even less ability to pursue spiritual life to its culmination in divine realization. Even as a Protestant I had passed years watching people come, fail and go—or else remain and be hypocrites. When I became a yogi it was even more dramatic because the philosophy and discipline were so utterly out of phase with Western personality and culture.

In the Gita we read: "Of thousands of human beings scarcely anyone at all strives for perfection, and of those adept in that striving, scarcely anyone knows me in truth" (Bhagavad Gita 7:3). This is certainly true, but it is a mistake to think that we can unerringly tell if a person is really interested or capable of being a yogi.

If there was not some power of spiritual wisdom in a person he would not ask about God and the way to God, even if his inquiry is couched in skeptical words and more of a challenge than an inquiry. (For some people who feel unsure of themselves, a backhanded kind of seeking is all they feel safe with.) What we must do is keep in mind these two verses from the Gita: "He who just desires to know about yoga goes beyond the Vedas. By persevering effort and mastery, the totally purified yogi, perfected through many births, reaches the Supreme Goal" (Bhagavad Gita 6:44-45).

Even if the person listens a bit and then goes away never to be seen again, or even if he overtly rejects what we say, nevertheless something significant has taken place. A seed has been planted that will in time begin to grow, develop, and bear fruit. In my very first conversation with Annie Vickerman, one of Yogananda's early disciples, she told me that several times he told her and her husband Warren (Yogananda's second American disciple): "In three generations' time you will not even know that I came to this country." When they asked why he bothered, then, he answered each time: "I have planted the seed." It can be the same with us, even though we are not masters such as he was.

"As thou knowest not what is the way of the spirit, nor how the bones do grow in the womb of her that is with child: even so thou knowest not the works of God who maketh all. In the morning sow thy seed, and in the evening withhold not thine hand: for thou knowest not whether shall prosper, either this or that, or whether they both shall be alike good" (Ecclesiastes 11:5-6).

Keeping in mind that the body and the self are not the same is not just a matter of holding a philosophical concept. Rather, it is a matter of maintaining spiritual awareness throughout external experience, to center our identity in the Self and not in the body. This is accomplished through yoga. "Knowing thus, the ancient seekers for liberation performed action. Do you, therefore, perform action as did the ancients in earlier times" (Bhagavad Gita 4:15). In the thirteenth chapter of the Bhagavad Gita, Krishna speaks of the difference between the "knower of the field," the Self, and the "field," which is the body, saying: "The knowledge of the Field and the Knower of the Field I consider to be *the* knowledge" (Bhagavad Gita 13:2).

It is our delusive *bhava*, the state of mind, that impels us to body identification. It is a deep conviction and "seeing" ourselves as the body. When this deep-rooted mentality is dispelled then we can realize our true nature as the Self. Reading books and making affirmations will not at all accomplish this. Only experience in meditation will reveal the truth that we are spirit and not matter. Certainly it is possible to have flashes of spiritual insight, but to be established in atmabhava, atmic awareness, we must be adept in yoga.

The all-knowing God "sees" us all, but rare are those that are able to "look at the sun"–to diligently cultivate the inner capacity to directly perceive God as directly as God perceives us.

When one strives to live the truth of the upanishadic philosophy (which includes the Bhagavad Gita), then there is true development of the personality. Before that the personality changes from life to life in a very random manner, being merely temporary shapings and responses to the events of the various lives that have been lived. Yoga, on the other hand, increases awareness of the eternal Self steadily until the revelation of that Self is attained as naturally as the child grows into adulthood.

Yoga works for everyone who will try it and persevere. Faith and disbelief has no effect on it at all. The first time I was taught a yoga practice, I was disgusted. "How can anyone believe that such a silly little thing as this could have any effect?" I griped to myself as I considered walking out. But just then the instructor said: "Now, let's just do this for a few minutes." Well, why not? So I closed my eyes and did it, sure that it would do nothing. But it did!!! When I opened my eyes after those few minutes I was a believer.

Within us is a vast treasure-house and we can open it through yoga, and even through sheer will power. As a child Saint John of Kronstadt was mentally backward, but it was such a torment to him that he prayed fervently until a kind of mental veil fell away, and afterward he was not just normal, he was intellectually brilliant and received many academic honors. I knew a girl whose singing was exceptionally beautiful and who could play several musical instruments with outstanding ability. Her parents told me that formerly she had been completely tone deaf and could not sing a note, though she yearned to be able to sing and play musical instruments in church as a service to God. When she was in her mid-teens she went out in the woods around their house and prayed for hours. When she came back in the house she told them she could sing–and did so beautifully. She sat down at the piano, fiddled around a bit and then played a song! Eventually she taught herself to play several instruments very well. She had unlocked her innate musical abilities through the spirit. Think how much more is liberated within us through yoga!

Yoga, being based on the eternal nature of every human being, can free those who diligently practice it. Yogananda had an alcoholic disciple whom he told to sit with a bottle and take a swig and then meditate for a while and take another swig, and so on. In time there were no swigs, only yoga. Sri Ramakrishna cured several alcoholics in the same way, though his approach was for them to get just barely tipsy and then meditate.

Our eternal nature as the Self is why yoga works for everyone. Yoga, being the science of the Self, is in total conformity with the nature of the Self and therefore unfailingly produces results. But those results must be protected and fostered by the yogi.

Yoga is a true science of the inner being. I assure you that real yoga works for anyone who practices it and follows the principles of yama and niyama.

Yoga is the beginning, middle and end of spiritual life. It ties everything together and makes it work.

Do you see how yoga, the unifier, is the key to everything? Completely intellectual, verbal philosophy is seen to be mere noise. Yoga alone is wisdom, it alone is the very state of liberation which is being sought. It is a matter of revelation of the Real as having become the Unreal, of the Light having become the Darkness, and of Immortality having become Death. Yoga is the most sublime version of the game of Peekaboo we all played as infants. This is why, strange at it might seem to many, Paramhansa Yogananda wrote the following poem entitled, "I Am Here."

Alone I roamed by the ocean's shore,
And watched
The wrestling waves in brawling roar—
Bounding with Thine own restless life.

I saw Thee in Thy angry mood, tossing and foaming
Until the very vastness of Thy wrath made me shiver
And turn away in dread from so much violence and
 strife.

And then I walked inland.
A kindly, spreading, sentinel tree
Waved friendly arms to comfort me—
Consoling me with gentler look sublime,
Its leaves and branches swayed in tender lullaby-rhyme,
Conveying a message that I knew was Thine.

Above me, high,
I saw the gaugeless, mystic sky;
And, childlike, in dim valleys
I sought to pry out Thy secrets,
    and to play with Thee.

In vain, alas, did I seek Thee hiding there,
Cloud-robed, foam-sprayed, leaf-garlanded–
Too elusive for mortal eyes to see or ears to hear.

And yet, I knew that Thou wert always near,
As if playing hide-and-seek with me,
Receding each time when I almost touched Thee.

I groped for Thee in the maddeningly complex folds
Of dark ignorance–as old as time itself is old.

At last–
I ceased my search, almost in despair:
What hope had I of finding Thee,
Thou Royal, Sly Eluder!

Thou art, I know, everywhere–
Yet Thou seemest nowhere:
Lost in unplumbed space,
Where none may clasp Thee or behold Thy face!

Yes, despairing,
I ceased my fruitless search,
Turned huffily away from Thee:
My ploy was unsuccessful!

Still, still no answer from the wrathful sea,
And only whispers from the friendly tree;
Naught but silence from the limitless blue sky—
Silence from valleys low and mountains high!

Like a hurt child, within the depths of me
I hid and sulked—no longer seeking Thee.
And then, lo! suddenly:

Unheralded, an Unseen Hand
Snatched from my eyes that all-black band
Which had blinded me so long with fold on fold.

No longer weary, but filled with strength untold,
I stood, and gazed again:
A laughing sea instead of wrathful roars!
A gay, glad world with mystically opening doors!

With only mists of dreams between,
Someone beside me stood unseen—
And whispered to me, calm and clear:
"Hello, playmate! I am here!"

Here he has revealed the entire journey of the jivatman to the Paramatman. And it is an intensely personal journey by its very nature. In the fall of 1960, I first read his words and was inspired to read the Bhagavad Gita and then his *Autobiography of a Yogi*. I could not begin to count the times since that day when suddenly and wondrously there has been whispered to me: "Hello, playmate! I am here!"

Yoga sadhana alone frees the mind from the delusions and desires of this world so the yogi can live in higher consciousness and eventually be born into higher worlds after the death of the physical body.

The three states of consciousness—waking, dreaming and dreamless sleep—are really just atoms in the ocean of possibilities. They must evaporate and leave in their place the turiya, the pure consciousness of the Self that is the intended heritage of each one of us. Yoga is the means to evaporate the ocean of samsara and find ourselves in Infinite Life. We give up that which is nothing to gain That which is All.

No matter what the interior disposition of a person may be, a bath gets every person as clean as another. And this is one of the wonderful aspects of yoga sadhana. No matter what the personality and mental character of a person may be, prolonged practice of meditation and yogic discipline will bring them all to enlightenment.

The only truly learned person is the one who has learned the secret that he is the jivatman, one with the Paramatman. As the Skanda Upanishad says: "Jiva is Shiva and Shiva is Jiva; when bound by husk it is paddy, unbound it is rice. Thus the bound one is Jiva; released from karma he is eternal Shiva. Bound by ropes, he is Jiva; unbound, Shiva" (6-7).

The school of true education is yoga. We enroll as jiva and graduate as Shiva.

When the yogi engages in any yogic process he is actively altering the character of his various bodies. First he enables them to vibrate in harmony with the Self and then begins transmuting them into perfect reflections of the Self which begin to be revealed as the Self. Nothing can accomplish this but yoga—not philosophy or religion or externalized religious practices. Only the masters of yoga comprehend the actual situation of the human being in the midst of samsara, and only those seers of the yogic science have given to us the way to complete our evolutionary journey in full mastery of our personal shakti.

Just as the cosmos emanates from Brahman the Paramatman, so the individual microcosm emanates from the jivatman. All the good and evil in our immediate life sphere comes from us, or rather has been assumed by us just as we put on layers of clothing each day.

Since good and evil came from the Atman, they must return to the Atman of the yogi in order for him to transform and transmute them and ultimately reassimilate them. Only yoga is the way this can be done.

Yoga is in the destiny of every sentient being, for yoga is the way and the power of moksha (liberation). Truly, as Yogananda said, yoga is the beginning of the end.

The five organs of action, the karmendriyas, are voice, hand, foot, organ of excretion, and the organ of generation. These, along with the mind (our thoughts) create karma. As a result, not only does the earth spin, so do we, almost never coming to rest, and even then for a brief time only. Since they are oriented toward earthly existence, the karmas created through them impel us back to earthly incarnation over and over. Throughout creations cycles we come and go, bewildered and powerless. As the Gita says: "They know the true day and night who know Brahma's Day a thousand yugas long and Brahma's Night a thousand yugas long. At the approach of Brahma's Day, all manifested things come forth from the unmanifest, and then return to that at Brahma's Night. Helpless, the same host of beings being born again and again merge at the approach of the Night and emerge at the dawn of Day" (Bhagavad Gita 8:17-19).

This is a pretty grim picture and would naturally tend toward pessimism, but we have been given one thing that can change all that: the spiritual science of yoga. The West has developed material technology that brings no peace or lasting fulfillment. But the spiritual technology of the East, yoga sadhana, fulfills all and brings unchanging peace.

Just being devoted and devotional gets us nowhere. Sincerity and dedication likewise mean nothing. Only knowledge of the path leading to God-realization and its diligent application can end the terrible cycle of birth and death in this world of samsara. And that path is yoga.

Although the mind (both manas and buddhi) may be a problem, still its basic constitution is the same in all people, which is why the science of yoga is timeless. It has remained supremely relevant and effective throughout the ages.

When we speak of spiritual evolution we do not mean that the Self evolves, but that the gross and subtle bodies must be refined and evolved to the condition where they no longer inhibit the light of the Self, and can eventually become transmuted into that Light altogether. When we are in total darkness we cannot see our hands, and the quest for light is hardly a denial that we possess them. In same way, the practice of yoga is an unveiling and an illumination.

The life of samsara is often likened to being lost in a dense forest: we wander around and around and find no way out, being in danger every moment from the wild animals that live there. Before we die spiritually, we must leave this path of samsara and follow the royal road of yoga. Then we will find out what living really is.

Yogananda said that our practice of yoga is the thing that will keep us on the yogic path. Both Shankara and Vyasa said that yoga itself will in time become our teacher and show us many things about its nature, purpose and practice.

We should understand what ananda really is. It is spiritual joy, having nothing to do with thrills, chills, shakings, or goosebumps. It is a totally inward experience of intelligent, clear, stable, divine joy. This is according to the words of the Gita: "He whose happiness is within, whose delight is within, whose illumination is within: that yogi, identical in being with Brahman, attains Brahmanirvana" (Bhagavad Gita 5:24). This is essential for us to understand, as there are many practices that produce abnormal neurological states, including physical and psychic states of "ecstasy." That is why Buddha spoke of the need for *right* bliss.

Once I was visiting with Durga Mata, one of the advanced disciples of Paramhansa Yogananda. She told me that a man had come to consult her about why his meditations were not producing any results. She carefully went over with him his yogic practices, and all was well. "And you are not getting any effects at all from these practices?" she asked in wonder. "No, nothing at all." Are you sure?" she insisted, "nothing at all?" "Well, nothing but bliss–that happens all the time. But not anything else." "You don't understand," Durga Mata told him, "That bliss is God. Your meditations are resulting in the highest experience!" The man's mistake is understandable, because books and talks on yoga continually emphasize exotic experiences rather than the conscious bliss that is the aim of authentic meditation practice. When we experience bliss in meditation, that is God-experience. Conversely, we cannot experience God without experiencing bliss. The two are really one.

But bliss is not just an enjoyable sensation. It is the elixir of immortality that produces wisdom (jnana) within us. The yogi does not come out of meditation "blissed out" or "stoned." He comes out with increased breadth of consciousness and depth of understanding. Bliss bunnies are not yogis, and yogis are not bliss bunnies. Yet, the nectar of jnana is anandamayi–permeated with joy–and is never dry intellectualism. From spiritual experience we gain both joy and knowledge.

The arising of ananda is a sign that we are nearing God. Ananda is the Light of God that radiates from the Divine Source.

The vision of unity is an interior experience and not external at all. In fact, the distinction of inside-outside no longer exists to the person in non-dual consciousness. Actually, real non-dual experience is a result of the union of jivatma and Paramatma. It is exclusively a matter of yoga: union.

It is easy to get discouraged and think that we will never shake off ignorance and the patterns of ignorant behavior. But all external factors and the delusions of the mind they create are temporary, as destined to dissolve as the truth of our being the Self is destined to manifest and be free. In the Gita we find the following:

"Arjuna said: Then by what is a man impelled to commit evil, against his own will, as if urged by some force?

"The Holy Lord said: This force is desire and anger born of the rajo-guna, the great consumer and of great evil. Know this to be the enemy. As fire is enveloped by smoke, as mirrors are covered by dust, as wombs cover embryos, in the same way Knowledge is covered by this, the constant enemy of the wise, having the form of desire which is like insatiable fire. The senses, mind, and intellect are said to be its abode. With these it deludes the embodied one by veiling his innate wisdom. Therefore, controlling the senses at the outset, kill this evil being, which destroys ordinary knowledge and supreme knowledge. They say that the senses are superior [to the body], the mind is superior to the senses, the intellect (buddhi) is superior to the mind. And much superior to the intellect is the supreme intelligence (param buddhi). Having learned this, sustaining the lower self by the higher Self, kill this difficult-to-encounter enemy which has the form of desire" (Bhagavad Gita 3:36-43).

Yoga and Dharma comprise the spiritual and material psychotherapy that all human beings desperately need. One of the reasons so little comes of people's becoming yogis is their assumption that their life is fundamentally sound and all right, that yoga will be the oil that stops their life-wheels from squeaking so they can be peaceful and "happy."

The real truth is that human beings are spiritually insane–actually not just potentially–and need profound correction and reorientation of intellect and consciousness. But this must not be taken in a mistaken way. Yes, we are "crazy" in the superficial levels of our being, but in our true Self we are always perfect, and it is the discovery/recovery of our Self that is the answer to our dilemma. *And we are the ones that should and can do it.* This is a very important fact, in contrast to the disempowering cult-mentality of "you are a sinner," "you are unworthy," "you do not know what is right or good for you." No: *Thou Art That* is the truth. And you can yourself reclaim your eternal heritage. No one either should or can do it for you, and that includes God, who set up the cosmos so you could evolve within it motivated by your own Self-power. Yoga is a supreme help, but it is your divine will that will effect the spiritual alchemy. So when I say we are crazy it is neither an accusation nor a lament. It is a calm diagnosis–calm because I know that we are only momentarily in trouble, and that we can without doubt awaken into Truth, the Truth that is Us.

Part of our self-correction and self-healing is the internalization of our awareness, the living within the various levels of our being as their possessor and controller. When this is done, and even when going through the process, we begin to perceive the inner world and live more and more therein. Does that mean we withdraw from the outer world and disengage ourselves from it? Not at all. For we come to see that the outer is a projection of the inner, that the better we live inwardly the better we live outwardly. As Sri Ramakrishna said: "If you can weigh salt you can weigh sugar." And we certainly can.

YOGA NIDRA

Yoga nidra, "yogic sleep," has several meanings: 1) a state of half-contemplation and half-sleep; 2) light yogic sleep when the individual retains slight awareness; 3) a state between sleep and wakefulness; 4) the state in which the yogi experiences pure consciousness within the state of dreamless sleep, when he is neither awake nor asleep in the usual sense; 5) the state in which the three states of waking, sleep, and deep sleep have become transmuted into the turiya state of pure consciousness and the yogi remains "asleep" in relation to those three lesser states. This latter is the highest meaning, and the others are not very much. So until he reaches the fifth state, the yogi must not over-congratulate himself when experiencing the lesser four.

In meditation we must consciously sleep in yoga nidra, resting on the mind without it affecting us in any way. We must be the silent witness at all times.

Yoga nidra is the state of being fully conscious in the deep (dreamless) sleep state, or sushupti. But yogis can be in that state even while waking. At first glance this may just seem a bit of exotic trivia, but if we ponder it well we can understand that such ability is no doubt the basis of Krishna's description of an enlightened yogi or one nearing that state. When we read in the Gita about how the yogi is to be unmoved by that which normally greatly affects the individual human being, we think of it being some powerful control and suppression of thought and feeling through conscious will. But actually it is awake yoga nidra. One who rests in the unchanging Self is not agitated by anything.

THE YOGI

Many saints have lived their lives surrounded by great crowds, yet have been a light of peace for those people. How? By being always alone with God in the core of their being. For God dwells always there in the heart of all as the Gita tells us.

"I am the Self abiding in the heart of all beings; I am the beginning, the middle and the end of all beings as well" (10:20).

"Also this [Brahman] is said to be the light of lights, beyond all darkness; knowledge, the to-be-known, the goal of knowledge seated in the heart of all" (13:17).

"Seated within the hearts of all, from me come memory and knowledge and their loss: I alone am to be known by all the Vedas; I am the Author of the Vedanta, and the Knower of the Vedas" (15:15).

"The Lord dwells in the hearts of all beings, causing them by his maya to revolve as if mounted on a machine" (18:61).

It is a mistake to think that when we are in the midst of many people we are with them only and not also with God. We are far more with God than we could ever be with them, since God is in our heart, and has been there from eternity. Living outwardly in duality we can live inwardly in unity. As Patanjali says, japa and meditation is the way.

In the state of realization the yogi is totally "asleep" to all externals, and therefore is not affected by them in any way. His chitta makes no response to anything, though he is keenly aware of all things. This is the state which Patanjali defines as yoga. It is the consciousness of perfect unity, even though diversity may be perceived by the senses. The chitta remains a still, perfect mirror of consciousness that is not conditioned or even touched by outer-caused experience. Such a one is always in Spirit, transcending all relative being and existence.

I grew up hearing mentally and spiritually lazy people protesting to others: "You are so much smarter/more spiritual than I am," considering that a legitimate (and flattering) excuse for their being layabouts in mind or soul. Certainly there are great differences in people's abilities, but on one level people are absolutely equal, no one being more gifted than another. The difference might be in the degree the abilities are being accessed, but everyone has the same potential. This is especially true in matters of the spirit.

Knowing himself as the ever-blissful Self, the yogi is ananda incarnate. "Even here on earth rebirth is conquered by those whose mind is established in evenness" (Bhagavad Gita 5:19). As the Gita assures us: "Be free from the triad of the gunas, indifferent to the pairs of opposites, eternally established in reality,... and established in the Self" (Bhagavad Gita 2:45).

As yogis we should be concerned with consciousness, aware that consciousness alone is real. When the great yogi Gorakhnath asked his teacher Matsyendranath: "What is the home of knowledge [jnana]?" the Master replied: Consciousness [chetana] is the home of knowledge" (Gorakh Bodh 21-22). Our sadhana must be the cultivation of consciousness.

The consciousness of an infant is almost completely inward and it is much more aware in the inner world than the outer world. This changes after six months and its consciousness changes from spiritual to physical.

However, the babies are not jnanis. The Gita says: "The yogi... to whom a lump of clay, a stone and gold are the same, steadfast–is said to be in union (yukta)" (Bhagavad Gita 6:8). But there is a vast difference between the yogi and the infant. It is a long journey from infancy to liberation.

"Behold, thou shalt conceive in thy womb, and bring forth a son" (Luke 1:31). These are the words of the Archangel Gabriel to the Virgin Mary. For years, when I was not a yogi, I used to wonder why the angel would say "conceive in thy womb," for where else would conception take place? But when I understood the Gospels as mystery-dramas symbolizing the Christing of each individual, showing the path from the "conception" to the "resurrection" and "ascension" to Divine Consciousness, then I understood.

It is possible for conception to take place outside the womb. Such a conception is abnormal and cannot lead to birth, but it can occur. I knew a woman who conceived in the fallopian tube and the embryo had to be surgically removed. In the same way "spirituality" can be conceived in the intellect and the person become an avid student of spiritual books and other forms of teaching and talking. Or someone can "conceive" in their emotion and be swept along on a flood of "God loves me; I love God" and externalized and externalizing "devotional" activities.

In India people rhapsodize about Krishna's "restless eyebrows," Lakshmi's pink feet, and Durga's "parrot-beak" nose. I knew a man who was scarred all over from running through thick bramble bushes, thinking he was chasing Krishna. All this is silliness and unworthy of the descendants of the rishis of India. In time those who have wrongly conceived will burn out and get bored with it all, and their subsequent births will be completely unaffected by any of it.

The conception of spirit-consciousness must take place in the core of our being, and grow to "term" in the buddhi illumined by intuition. We must conceive in the "womb" of our own consciousness, otherwise nothing will come of it. We must work with our mind, developing its ability to guide us.

Obsession with an external teacher will not do the needful. All the guru-puja in the world will avail nothing. "Neither shall they say, Lo here! or, lo there! for, behold, the kingdom of God is within you" (Luke 17:21). It all begins, continues, and ends right there in the "womb" of our own mind, our own sadguru.

We must not think that the all-pervading Reality is big or small. Pervading something does not make the pervader take on the characteristics of the pervaded. Consciousness pervades all, but is untouched and unconditioned by it. Therefore It is neither vast nor tiny. Space simply does not exist for it. For example, materially-minded people think a very tall and large person is "a big person" and regard him as such. Conversely, they think a very small person is "a shrimp" and of little consequence. Perhaps this comes from too many lives, animal and human, living in social orders where the biggest are the leaders and the smallest are considered nothing and even left behind. Personhood is simply not taken into consideration by these people.

That which has bounds, though, is inherently limited and "small" both spatially and morally. Thus anything that has boundaries or limited (and limiting) qualities is ultimately of little consequence in the realm of the spirit.

Mistaking the outer for the inner is the besetting flaw of most religious thinking, and even yogis can fall into that trap, becoming absorbed in the outer ways and trappings of yoga and dharma, and thereby completely lose their soul-consciousness and be samsarins like nearly everyone else here on earth.

An example was told to me by Peggy Dietz, one of Yogananda's secretaries. A certain "spiritual light" of Los Angeles would occasionally come to visit the Mount Washington ashram on a Sunday when Yogananda and the residents would often be together in what had been the lobby when the ashram was a resort hotel. Eventually she would begin holding

forth on the virtues of vegetarianism, going on and on, always ending
with: "I have no meat whatsoever in my body. There is no meat in my
astral body, either. I have never eaten meat in this life, and I never ate
meat in all my past lives, either!" After the third or fourth time Peggy
heard this rant (and the others had heard it many more times before she
had come to live there), Yogananda very politely showed her and her
coterie to the door, then turned around and said to everyone there: "My
God, I wish somebody would slip her a ham sandwich. It wouldn't hurt
her a bit, and she would never know the difference!" As Sri Yukteswarji
often said: "Too much of a good thing is no longer good." It is good to
be steady in any discipline, but a craze about something is not good, as
Sri Ramakrishna often said.

A samskara is an impression in the mind, either conscious or subconscious, produced by action or experience in this or previous lives. A
vasana is an aggregate or bundle of samskaras that creates in a person the
tendency toward actions according to the nature of the samskaras. Everything we do creates samskaras which in turn create vasanas. Therefore
a sadhaka in the beginning continually experiences the pull of vasanas
contrary to higher realization. But the persevering yogi who conforms
his life and thought thoroughly to the ideals of spiritual life creates
spiritual, upward-tending vasanas that not only help him in this life, but
in future lives or higher worlds. Such a person will gravitate toward the
spiritual life and the truths the sages have discovered from living that
life themselves. Such people will feel happy and at home with purity
and holiness and unhappy and alien to worldly follies. Nevertheless,
they must apply themselves to sadhana lest they exhaust the power of
those positive vasanas and lapse back into the bondage of ignorance.

As a child and young adult I heard a lot of stories at church about
people who when dying claimed to be feeling the fires of hell and died
in great agony. "Went screaming into a devil's hell!" was the favorite

punch line. But yogis see it differently. At the time of death the vital forces (pranas) begin to withdraw into the chakra from which the subtle bodies will exit the material body. If a chakra is in the lower part of the body they will say that they are being pulled down and assume are sinking into hell. Those whose pranas are obstructed or out of phase they will experience intense burning sensations in the body as they are being pulled "against the grain," so to say. This can be very terrible and frightening to the person. In my teens I heard of a woman who had considered herself "saved" all her life, but when this happened to her as she was dying, she assumed she was going to hell and told a minister I knew that he should preach a sermon on hypocrites at her funeral and tell everyone she was damned. I wonder how many times in church she had sung about "The Old-Time Religion," singing: "It will do when I am dying." Anyhow, this is the truth of the matter.

Any action arising from simple, egoic desire never produces any lasting benefit. Only that inspired by spiritually illumined insight will have a lasting effect even to the end of the present incarnation.

Insecurity and uncertainty is always part of the pursuit of desires, because we subconsciously know that it is in violation of our true nature. There is safety in letting our ego-born desires go unheeded.

Greed in all forms is a trait of the adharmic personality. According to Patanjali, a fundamental characteristic of the yogi is aparigraha: non-possessiveness, non-greed, non-selfishness, and non-acquisitiveness. The human being bound by desire is bound inextricably to the cycle of birth and death. But the Gita teaches us that the ending of desire is the ending of samsara, the ending of rebirth.

There is only one God, but the deluded human being has thousands of "gods" he pursues, suffering four forms of misery: misery from not having what he wants, misery from getting what he wants, misery from fears he will lose it, and misery from getting it and finding it does not live up to his expectations. Only when we seek and find the One and realize our eternal union with that One will we be at peace and in joy.

A master is one that lives in absolute desirelessness. Since it is desire that draws us into birth and expels us through death, desirelessness is a state the yogi must aspire to. Proof of the power of a single desire is given in the life of Sri Brahma Chaitanya. In chapter six of *The Saint of Gondawali* we find the following:

"Shantabai, the Master's daughter, was two years old. The girl was extremely handsome as well as silently playful. The Master, therefore, called her Shanti, which means Peace. She could not yet speak, and so used the language of signs. She showed great inclination towards devotion to God.... She would sit undisturbed for an hour to listen to the Master's discourse on God and His devotion. When the Master asked her, 'Shantabai! Do you follow me?' She replied a 'yes' by her sweet, innocent smile. One day her aunt was worshipping the tulsi plant. The girl was in her arms. Just then the Master happened to come there. He asked the child, 'Would you give me your necklace?' The girl removed the necklace and put it into the Master's hand. He again asked her, 'Don't you like to have the necklace? Shall I have it for me?' The child cut a leaf from the tulsi plant and placed it on the necklace, thereby implying that she had no attachment to it. The Master happily remarked, 'Well, child! God will surely give a lift to you.' Six months later the child died. Her mother and the other ladies felt very sorry to lose her. The cremation took place in the evening. When the Master came back a disciple asked him, 'Master, why do children, particularly gifted children, die so young?'' The Master answered, 'Desire is the cause of birth. Desire again becomes the cause of death. When a child is born, it comes to satisfy some desire. The common man does not know who comes to him as a son or a daughter. The saints know it. Sometimes it happens that some spiritually advanced souls fall a prey to some petty desire. This desire dominates at the time of death during the previous birth. Then it forces them to be born again, preferably in the family of a seeker or a saint. They satisfy the desire and soon depart from this world. That is why many gifted children die young. This girl was such an advanced soul. Hence we should not mourn her death.'"

The single desire for a necklace had brought the girl into birth, and her cutting off of that desire by handing it to her father (the putting of a tulsi leaf on the necklace indicated that it was being given to God, actually) freed her to pass through the gate of death into life.

By conquering desire we conquer birth and death.

The desirelessness of the adept yogi is not the mere absence of desire, but the state of realization which ends all desires and bestows liberation. To just live for material gain and enjoyment is truly to be nothing more than an animal–actually less than an animal, for an animal can live in no other manner, but a human can.

SOME ADVICE TO YOGIS

There is a sharp demarcation between the conscious and subconscious minds. And the distinction is to be kept in mind lest we fall into the folly of those that believe their every dream is a revelation. It is very important that the yogi leaves his dreams in dreamland and does not carry them over into his waking life. For those who do not do this there is very real danger of delusion. Dream experience and waking experience have very different purposes and must be viewed accordingly. Few things are more tiresome than having to listen to someone's previous night's dream-dramas. Their recitation is almost always a sign of foolish self-centeredness.

There is a a certain stage in sadhana where it is very beneficial to eat only the food you have yourself cooked. This phase does not last for years, yet for some time you might want to observe this, but only if your intuition tells you to.

When food is cooked its polarity changes and it absorbs the vibrations of both the cook(s) and the environment where it is cooked. So it is traditional in India that only the cook is in the kitchen during the preparation of food. There was a time when I ate only what I cooked, and my cooking and eating utensils, everything I used or touched when eating, were kept separate. I alone touched them, washed them and put them away. In this way my sadhana shakti was preserved intact. I observed this for several months, and then it was no longer necessary. So you might want to take this into consideration. But remember this: good sense and good manners require a sadhaka to behave at all time with consideration for others.

An essential part of purity (shaucha) is purity of personal magnetism. The yogi must preserve the integrity of his personal vibrations, and this is particularly needed in the matter of food, since the subtle energies of food become our mental energies. Never should food be eaten that is mixed with the vibrations of others. We should not eat from the plate of another, nor let others eat from ours. That includes taking or giving something from our plate to another. And never should we eat something that has been partially eaten by someone else, or allow another to do the same with something we have partially consumed.

A lot of psychic vampires violate these rules so they can steal the vibrations of others and implant their negative energies in the bodies and minds of others. Sometimes it is conscious and sometimes it is not, but the result is the same.

We focus our mind on every place and every thing but where it should be. The correct place for the mind is the center of our existence, our spirit-consciousness, and that is where it should always be established. It can never really be "at home" anywhere else. That is why Jesus said: "The foxes have holes, and the birds of the air have nests; but the Son of man hath not where to lay his head" (Matthew 8:20). We are spiritual beings and have no home but Spirit. There is no place on earth where we can truly come to rest and be at peace. We really do need to cultivate "the sense to come in out of the rain."

A flame both kindles light and gives light. Such is the rarefied viveka that arises in the yogi's consciousness as he engages in sadhana. The yogi who assiduously follows that light progresses steadily and surely, gaining even more light. The yogi who neglects that insight will lapse into his former ignorance, claiming it is light. As Jesus said: "If therefore the light that is in thee be darkness, how great is that darkness!" (Matthew 6:23).

A yogi must keep moving forward in his understanding, leaving behind his former limited insight. This process continues throughout his life and beyond, for Infinity is no quick attainment.

We must be ever open to better understanding and realize that today's understanding may be tomorrow's misunderstanding. Those who do not keep moving on, stagnate. It is true there are shallow and fickle people that flit from teaching to teaching and from teacher to teacher, never really learning or practicing anything to any degree, but they are fools, not yogis.

The sum and substance is this: a true yogi is always ready to move forward, and that requires leaving things behind and knowing they should be left behind.

One of the most horrible things I ever saw was in a restaurant that had a huge aquarium. In the aquarium was a kind of miniature frog. Anyone with sense would have realized that it could not just be dropped into the water but needed a solid area above water so it could breathe and rest. But no one with sense was around, so the miserable little creature would frantically kick itself to the surface of the water, breathe a moment, and then apparently pass out and sink down. In just a matter of seconds it would regain consciousness and again desperately impel itself upward to breathe. This terrible spectacle went on and on, over and over. I have never forgotten that unfortunate frog. So many religious people live in this pendulum manner, swinging back and forth from spiritual high to spiritual low, between pure exalted consciousness and degraded low consciousness. This is not a truly human mode of life.

Most people live in a wandering manner, like people walking their way through a crooked, meandering path in the forest, not seeing where they are going or where they have been, truly "not seeing the forest for the trees." Traveling a great highway is just the opposite. Easily the traveler sees before and behind. Further, instead of moving on a roundabout path of twisting and turnings, every single step carries him in a straight line to his destination. One time while traveling in Turkey I happened to come across a road built by the Romans that was still being used. Even though it went through mountains, there was no doubling back at all—it was a marvel of engineering. In the same way the yogi must think, speak, and live in a completely straight line, ever moving toward the goal.

Never trust the mind completely, because its nature is to change. We must center our thought in our buddhi, in the faculty of discriminative intelligence, and never let feelings or emotions influence our behavior. Through meditation and japa we must elevate our consciousness to increasingly higher levels.

Yoga is not like "getting saved" where the "saved" just sit around and wait to die and go to heaven and be rewarded for "believing." The yogi at every moment must be moving onward, for there is a very long journey to take before we are established in the practice of yoga. And then a further even longer journey is necessary through higher worlds to reach ultimate Self-realization and become permanently free in spirit.

It is very important that the aspiring yogi knows that effort and perseverance are needed, otherwise he will fail and be no better off than if he had never heard of yoga. In some instances he may be actually worse. Those who wish to succeed in yoga must be prepared for difficulties and determined to overcome them.

In this age of easy-come-easy-go "spirituality" in both East and West, it is thought that a person need only learn some yogic technique, practice it and attain liberation. But it does not happen that way. That is why in the Yoga Sutras (2:30-32) Patanjali lists yama-niyama before anything else:

1. Ahimsa: non-violence, non-injury, harmlessness

2. Satya: truthfulness, honesty

3. Asteya: non-stealing, honesty, non-misappropriativeness

4. Brahmacharya: sexual continence in thought, word and deed as well as control of all the senses

5. Aparigraha: non-possessiveness, non-greed, non-selfishness, non-acquisitiveness

6. Shaucha: purity, cleanliness

7. Santosha: contentment, peacefulness

8. Tapas: austerity, practical (i.e., result-producing) spiritual discipline

9. Swadhyaya: introspective self-study, spiritual study

10. Ishwarapranidhana: offering of one's life to God

Every one of these, except for the tenth, are processes of purification, and the yogi needs all nine. Without them, the tenth step, offering of one's life to God, would be a mockery.

The aspiring yogi has to empty himself of all that has gone before and dig out of the mud of past and present lives and start over. His life's motto should be: "Behold I Make All Things New" (Revelation 21:5).

Jesus puts it another way in the Aquarian Gospel: "The man who hears the words of life and does them not is like the man who builds his house upon the sand, which when the floods come on, is washed away and all is lost. But he who hears the words of life and in an honest, sincere heart receives and treasures them and lives the holy life, is like the man who builds the house upon the rock; the floods may come, the winds may blow, the storms may beat upon his house; it is not moved. Go forth and build your life upon the solid rock of truth, and all the powers of the evil one will shake it not" (101:29-32).

We freely talk of karma, but how much do we grasp? We agree with Saint Paul's definition: "Whatsoever a man soweth, that shall he also reap" (Galatians 6:7), but what about the converse: *"Whatsoever a man does not sow, that shall he also not reap"?* Yama and niyama are the seeds that must be sown if we would reap the harvest of liberation through yoga sadhana. Otherwise we are tossing our life into the wind. I have seen it over and over. If sadhana is not based on the necessary foundation the whole thing will collapse.

Right here I could tell you the history of beloved friends with whom I began my study of yoga, friends who meditated faithfully and for a while made the search for God the core of their life until slowly, little by little, their aspiration waned until they were only empty husks with a past but (for this life) no future. Some kept up a pretence of yoga, but most did not. The result was the same.

At the beginning of my yoga search I heard a recording of Yogananda in which he said that his hearers who persevered would find people to their right and left falling away from the search, many of whom would come right to the door of liberation and fall asleep. His concluding words were: "But you go after God." We all sang together, "My Lord, I will be Thine always," but nearly all took back their resolve and turned away.

Yogananda wrote another chant, "They Have Heard Thy Name." It was recommended that we sing it in intercession for those who were in spiritual need. So one day I was singing it for some of my friends who had abandoned the yoga life. When I came to the phrase: "Those who are drowned in sin, to whom will they go? They have no one, Lord, they have no one; do not turn them away," suddenly I realized that I was insulting, even blaspheming, God with these words. Those people I was singing about were not turned away by God. They had deliber-ately, intentionally turned away from God, jumped into the ocean of samsara and drowned themselves! They had rejected God; he had not rejected them. Shame on me! I prayed for forgiveness of my outrageous presumption in singing those words. Yogananda knew what he was doing in composing that chant, but I was misapplying his intention.

I have seen that many yogis fall into the trap of learning all kinds of externalized trivia, but they are only distracting their minds from the One Goal and keeping it on this world.

Those who love the world obsess on the world. As Jesus said: "Where your treasure is, there will your heart be also" (Matthew 6:21). That is why he advised us: "Lay up for yourselves treasures in heaven" (Matthew 6:20). Spiritual insights gained in meditation should be stored in the superconscious levels opened by meditation.

A yogi's conversation and home environment should reveal his spiritual orientation. It should be with us as it was with Saints Peter and John: Those who met them "took knowledge of them, that they had been with Jesus" (Acts 4:13).

There is absolute necessity for sadhana in the form of yoga discipline (yama and niyama) and yoga meditation. There are those who fool themselves into thinking that if their mind is not avidly pursuing the objects of the senses, then they are all right. But if the mind is even capable of being attracted to sense objects things are very much not right. Some people live an entire lifetime in unbroken abstinence and in their next life spend their life indulging themselves. The very capacity for enjoyment of material and sensual things is a threat that must be eliminated from the yogi's mind, both conscious and subconscious.

An ancient occult maxim is: "Know, Will, Dare–and Keep Silence." This is very much the case with the yogi. The yogi's practice should be deeply personal and deeply interiorized. Sri Ramakrishna said: "A devotee meditates on God in absolute secret, perhaps inside his mosquito net [while others are sleeping and unaware he is meditating]. Others think he is asleep." To a disciple who was building a small kutir on the bank of the Ganges for the practice of spiritual discipline, he said: "Let me tell you that the less people know of your spiritual life, the better it will be for you. Devotees endowed with sattwa meditate in a secluded corner or in a forest, or withdraw into the mind. Sometimes they meditate inside the mosquito net."

A lot of tiresome people with what Yogananda called "intellectual indigestion" talk on and on about unity and non-duality, their incessant conversation (even lecturing) being an act of confirmed duality in consciousness. A friend of mine once commented about a man who talked constantly on spiritual topics: "If you could get to God by talking about God he would have been Self-realized years ago." But it does not work that way.

When we enter the One we do not keep talking about the One, we become the One, and then who is there to talk to about it, or even talk to? As Sri Ramakrishna often said: "A salt doll went to sound the ocean but it melted away no sooner had it descended into it. It turned into the same form. Who then was to surface and tell how deep the ocean was?... The sign of perfect wisdom is that a person becomes silent upon its attainment. Then the salt doll of the form of the ego melts in the ocean of Satchidananda (existence-consciousness-bliss) and becomes one with it and not a trace of the feeling of distinction remains."

One of my acquaintances in India had lived there for a little over fifty years. Since he was European, when Arthur Koestler (hardly known to anyone now, but he was famous then) came to the ashram where he was living, he was asked to speak to him. At one point in the conversation Koestler, who considered himself quite a philosopher, asked Vijayananda if after attaining liberation he would then help others to also attain liberation. Vijayananda asked him: "If you are asleep and dreaming you are in prison, do you say to yourself: 'When I wake up I am going to come back and set these people free'?"

It is very crucial that the yogi should internalize his practice and keep it to himself, only speaking about it to qualified teachers or yogis who have years of experience behind them.

Do not dissipate the calmness and centering gained through meditation by talking about it to others. Experiences in meditation are not only subtle, they are fragile, as delicate as spun glass, and speaking about them can shatter their beneficial effects. Bragging, eulogizing, and swapping notes about meditation experiences is a very harmful activity. Avoid it. Otherwise you or others may be tempted to force things or imitate one another.

Do not satisfy any curiosity about your personal yogic experiences or benefits except in the most general terms. Naturally you can tell people that meditation helps you, but do so in only a general way.

Missionarying is one of the first delusions that strikes spiritual aspirants when they finally find how worthwhile spiritual teaching and practice really are. Happy at their new discovery and wishing well to others, their motivation is positive and even laudable, so why do I call it a delusion? Their delusion is the assumption that others have the same qualifications and levels of dedication that they possess. They start thinking of all their relatives and friends (especially best friends from school) that are so "spiritual" or "looking for something real," often stating that "they are really ahead of me," and remembering how close they were to each other and how inspiring and worthy of respect they were, etc. So they set about writing letters or making phone calls, often spending a good bit of money buying books they are sure will "light the fire." And they are right: the fire gets lit; but it's the fire of contempt, rejection, and resentment. In all my many years I have never seen even one such person react in a courteous manner, much less with interest. The poor missionary is ultimately hurt and bewildered, finding that his old friends are no longer friends at all but spiteful and angry at being pestered.

One of my friends received a hate-filled letter in the form of a long satire which charged her with being fanatical, pushy, hateful (!) and alienating her friends. "But we even promised each other that if we ever found anything real we would let the other one know," she told me, in profound shock. "We used to talk about spiritual life for hours...." Others of my yogi friends were accused of becoming Satanists and perhaps even drug addicts.

If someone is not truly spiritually hungry (whatever claims they may make), they will react negatively when being faced with genuine spiritual opportunity. For having a mind and heart full of the ego and the world, the suggestion of authentic spiritual life repulses and even offends them. All their "aspiration" is an act, though they often do not know that.

The yogi can never let any thing or situation inhibit his wise discrimination (viveka). The "marriage" of the intellect and mind are not a matter of give and take as earthly marriage must be. Rather, it must be the constant ascendency of the buddhi and the complete subjection of the manas. This is no easy condition to attain, and is certainly a tremendous accomplishment to continually maintain it. The mind is needed, but it must serve the intellect at all times.

The buddhi is the etheric level, the anandamaya kosha which is composed of the element of akasha, whose property is sound (shabda). Consequently, the conquest of mind and the mastery of intellect can be accomplished solely by sound—by mantra. Through sound the yogi comes to know well the truth of the final Brahma Sutra (4.4.22): "By sound one becomes liberated [*Anavrittih shabdai*]."

The sun does not move, but the movement of air causes the water in which the sun is reflected to ripple, and a child or foolish person may conclude that the sun is moving. If the mind is responsive to external stimuli and loses itself in the phenomena that are only appearances, not actualities, it develops an affinity for them that is incredibly hard to control and banish. We become enamored of maya; in love with it and therefore enslaved by something that does not even really exist.

Once things start getting serious in his practice, the yogi begins finding out that his mind is incorrigible in its infatuation with even the silliest and most obvious illusions of the mind. Knowing that his addiction is to something that is nonexistent, he yet finds himself reflexively involved with the mirage and seeking for even more involvement with what he knows is nothing. Like a child he prefers Pretend to Reality; he knows it, yet does not rebel against it.

This is an incredibly dangerous situation. Its very obvious foolishness is its power. Nothing will arise against it to dispel it. A yogi can lose everything by indulgent inaction. I grew up with people who continually lied to themselves, declaring that deadly elements in their lives were of no real harm. I never saw them shake off that illusion. But this which I am describing is something infinitely worse. "Oh, that is nothing" is the seal of death for the yogi. This is why sadhana must become an inseparable part of his life. If it continues, it will of itself dissolve the mirage.

Wealth often makes someone very small, even petty. Money is life energy, the life energy of those who earn it and those who spend it. It takes a very strong personality indeed to not be overwhelmed by the possession of great wealth. Wealth has the power to sap the life- and mind-force from those who think they possess it. Many of us have known wealthy people, especially "rich kids," who were just walking shells, servants of money without any real personality or will power. It does not matter if they behave in eccentric ways such as dressing shabbily and being cheap in their daily life. After all, in this way they are hoarding their wealth and gaining more. Making money can be an unbreakable habit. I once met a very dynamic minister who in conversation told me: "Any fool can make money and stack it up and hold on to it. It takes a wise man to have no use for money beyond his basic needs."

When we draw near to God and begin to experience the true, eternal life, we attain unshakeable peace. It cools our mind and manifests as inner and outer content and tranquility. Life will still have ups and downs and backwards and forwards, but the sadhaka will be steady and optimistic about his spiritual future. In this condition his mind becomes increasingly refined and purified. For it is an absolute law: the pure in heart do see God, and those who hunger and thirst for that vision become filled with the divine.

Spiritual life is a fully positive thing. Virtue is not an absence of vice but the presence of positive goodness. Fundamentalist Protestants love to brag about all the "sinful" things they do not do anymore, or never did do. They boast of all they have been "delivered from." But it is not enough to turn from darkness; we must enter and live in the Light.

This perspective is essential for us. To decide to not be selfish is insufficient. We must decide to be generous. It is of little worth to resolve to not think negatively. We must think positively. Instead of thinking of all kinds of things to not do, we must make a list of positives that we will do. For example, instead of thinking: "I must quit thinking of X," we should think: "I must always do japa and fix my mind on God." Then we will not think of wrong things.

To "hate" sin is to love it, for we always think of that which we love. The wise thing is to love goodness and the highest good: God.

"To the good all things are good." I heard this a great deal in India, but never outside India. Yet it is true. I saw it as an actualization, not just an ideal, in Swami Sivananda, who saw not just the good, but the God in everyone. Of course, if we ponder the matter, we can conclude that taken to its furthest reach, Good and God are synonymous. That is truly good which reflects God. There is no good outside God, but since all things are in God, they, too, are good. This is not an easy state of awareness to attain or maintain, but it is certainly a worthy goal for all sadhakas. Those who strive for union with God cannot help but become good, and then in time become God. "Therefore be a yogi" (Bhagavad Gita 6:46).

Samadarshana is the state of mind in which one sees all things as the One, making no differentiation in the sense of liking or disliking. It also implies perfect equanimity in all situations and toward all things. This is actually a divine trait, for in the Gita Krishna says: "I am the same to all beings. There is no one who is disliked or dear to me" (Bhagavad Gita 9:29). It is also a trait of the illumined, for Krishna further says: "He is preeminent among men who is impartial to friend, associate and enemy, neutral among enemies and kinsmen, impartial also among the righteous and the unrighteous" (Bhagavad Gita 6:9). And: "Absorbed in Brahman, with Self serene, he grieves not nor desires, the same to all beings, he attains supreme devotion unto me" (Bhagavad Gita 18:54).

An infant regards all with the same attitude, but that is no virtue for it is based on ignorance and inexperience. Tamasic people have a knack for not caring what or who comes and goes, but that is the samadarshana of stupidity and moral torpidity. Real samadarshana is the result of Self-realization, a state of clarity of perception united with absolute stability of consciousness.

The true yogi is not a juggler of intellectual words, but maintains awareness of his true nature as the Self—not intellectually, but through yogic application. "With mind absorbed in me, practicing yoga, taking refuge in me, hear how without doubt you shall know me completely. To you I shall explain in full this knowledge, along with realization, which being known, nothing further remains to be known in this world" (Bhagavad Gita 7:1-2).

It is crucial that we understand the Self cannot be perceived by the senses. Because of not realizing this yogis can be deceived into thinking that they experience the Self when they have only had a sensory experience, even though it might have been a very subtle experience centered in the subtle bodies. Many have been deluded through this error.

The Upanishads tell us that when we experience any object, that cannot be experience of the Self or Brahman, for the Self and Brahman are beyond subject-object consciousness. Yogis must be very wary of any experience, for true spiritual experience is not in the senses, mind or intellect, but in the consciousness of Consciousness itself.

"One acts according to one's prakriti. Even the wise man does so. Beings follow their own prakriti; what will restraint accomplish?" (Bhagavad Gita 3:33). At the moment we are experiencing two "selves." One is pure consciousness, our true Self, the witness of the various energy bodies which go to make up the relative part of "us." The other is those levels of our being we are witnessing and which seem to have an independent existence of their own, and with which we usually identify.

In actuality, it is only the consciousness-spirit that is our real, permanent and eternal Self. The energy bodies are just koshas (coverings) of the Self. Intellectually understanding that this is true accomplishes very little. We must be able to experience that for ourselves and prove its truth by will, by applying the yogic practices which enable us to experience (also at will) the nature of the Self.

In the beginning Self-experience is an involuntary coming and going very much like the ocean tides. But in time we should become proficient enough to produce the state of genuine Self-awareness at will. This matter of being able to reproduce or enter into yogic states at will is very crucial. Few people can do it because they simply do not know the necessary processes. And they do not know them because their teachers did not know them, which is why such teachers cover up the true state of things by telling their followers that they will do everything for them (or already have) and all they need do is "surrender" or "just love," and that will do everything. It will not, as the disciples will learn, even though it be at the time of death.

So until the yogi becomes able to not just distinguish between his spirit and prakriti, but to experience and direct them at will, he will indeed be subject to his prakriti. But with right practice in time it will certainly be gained by him.

Many people are seeking God in various ways, but now many will find God? Not many. Why? Because they run after the unattainable, not truly understanding that since God and our true Self are one, we must seek our Self alone. And when we find our Self we shall have found God.

What is the practical side of all this? To get to our Self we must master all the bodies in which our Self is now encased (imprisoned, actually). In the Indian scriptures, horses always represent prana, the energies of which all the bodies are made. If we master and "ride" those energies through the breath, we will not vaguely "seek" God, rather we shall go to God step-by-step in a precise, methodical manner as masters of yoga sadhana. This is the only way. Others may achieve some kind of higher states, but it will only be temporary and they will eventually revert to their original condition, or fall lower than they were when they began yoga. (This happens to many.) Only the yogi who knows and applies the real science of yoga will attain and retain.

The yogi must thoroughly master the energy (shakti) of the various bodies and ascend to the Self. And he must do so quickly, not dallying or delaying. Otherwise that itself creates karma which will put obstacles in his way. The yogi does not meander on the path, but runs as fast as he can lest he fall asleep by the wayside and not reach the goal.

A person may not be speaking outwardly, but chattering away in his mind. Anandamayi Ma was very definite about this, even saying that not speaking and keeping silence were two completely different things. Satya Sai Baba said: "Avoid those who while not speaking make gestures and write notes," because that is hypocrisy. In India I became acquainted with a brahmacharini who would pester people to show her their watch. When she saw that it was time for her "silence" she would purse her lips together in a very determined way. Nothing would make her open them! But she would gyrate around and flail her arms and make "mmm-mmm" sounds and carry on like she was having a seizure to get her message across. Then, ironically, the moment she saw that her silence time was past, she would walk away and not speak a word to anyone. When I was living next door to the Hollywood SRF center I was surprised at the number of people who would come into the restaurant or wander around the grounds with a piece of paper pinned on them that read: "This is my day of silence." I knew a yogini in New York City who would spend a great deal of her "day of silence" leaning out the window and looking at what was going on up and down the street.

On the other hand I have known yogis in India who lived in interior silence no matter whether they spoke or not. Their very presence was a blessing.

At first the mind is our major problem, an incorrigible obstacle. Then we become yogis and learn to use the mind to tame, purify and refine itself. It is truly a miracle. First we see its errant ways, but through sadhana we come to understand its potential, and by persevering in sadhana we transmute it into spirit. "Therefore be a yogi" (Bhagavad Gita 6:46).

The yogi's mind is his primary teacher, for it is his applied will that ultimately delivers him. The external teacher is only secondary, and can never replace the mind-guru. The Self is the guru of the student's mind. (Mind here includes buddhi as well as manas.)

We seek God because we intuit the reality of finding God. As Saint Paul said: "He that cometh to God must believe that he is, and that he is a rewarder of them that diligently seek him" (Hebrews 11:6). This is a function of our own mind alone; no external force can bring it about or cause us to intuit these truths.

The mind in virtually everyone is gripped by the world of the senses and takes it to be the ultimate reality. But when the mind begins to lose its grip on the world and begins to be transformed into the buddhi and the atman through yoga sadhana, it sees that the world is completely without stability, that it whirls around constantly and that the yogi has been whirling too, dragged along by it, though he did not realize it. More and more the delusive nature of the world becomes clear and the yogi's response to it less and less. Then truly, the yogi's mind is free of the habitual waves and it sees only spirit and truth.

Viveka—discrimination between the Real and the unreal, between the Self and the non-Self, between the permanent and the impermanent—is a prime necessity for the yogi. At first it is a matter of intellectual analysis, but in time it ripens into a subtle intuition which enables the sadhaka to perfectly understand the objects to which he subjects his discrimination. It is meditation that refines and sharpens the buddhi, bringing about this subtle viveka. Such discrimination is a side effect of sadhana, a faculty that is produced by prolonged tapasya. It is not an independent faculty and therefore cannot be sought on its own. Rather, it appears automatically in the mind as a consequence of diligent meditation. There is no way to develop it specifically; it arises spontaneously from meditation. We do not even need to aspire to it. Nevertheless, we must first apply ourselves to the intellectual discrimination which prepares us for the subtle form.

"Dharana is the confining [fixing] of the mind within a point or area" (Yoga Sutras 3:1). When the purified mind is totally fixed on something then its true nature is revealed. The yogi must live in a continual state of discriminative dharana, focused on the truth of a person, situation or thing rather than the external appearance. Such insight is very close to the Self and can in time lead to realization of the Self.

For success in spiritual life we must get ourselves "sorted out" and have all our levels of being integrated and working together, not over-lapping or usurping each other. People are not just mentally confused, their outer and inner bodies are confused and in conflict. A prime example of this is people who deal with emotions by eating. Feeling and digestion are worlds apart, and to mix them up is very unfortunate. To feel inwardly small because we are physically very slight or short is to confuse the mind with the body. You get the idea.

Paramhansa Nityananda said: "One becomes bad by oneself; one becomes good by oneself." This is a principle that should have great impact on the spiritual aspirant. In the West it is believed that environ-ment is the major factor in our development. In the East it is believed that heredity, especially as a manifestation of personal karma, is the major factor in all the forms of sentient life. So the West says we are a product of external forces that shape our psychology and therefore our behavior. Inside and out we are a bundle of responses to external factors. The East says the opposite: we are a product of inner impulses and perceptions that determine our outer behavior. Actually we have physical, psychic and spiritual "genetics."

In Western religion everyone and everything is considered responsible for the individual's behavior and troubles but themselves. "The devil made me do it" is employed in many variations. The sin of Adam, evil spirits and bad people are completely at fault—not us. This is of course utterly sociopathic. Western psychology only reinforces the erroneous views of Western religion, even if it considers itself an adversary of religion since it is a rival in the control and shaping of others' minds. Both Western religion and Western psychology attribute every bit of our psychic existence to factors other than ourself. This of course implies that we have no moral responsibility whatsoever, even though Western religion tells us that God is going to send us to hell for our wrong actions, that it is everybody's fault but ours, yet a just deity is going to punish us for behavior which is no fault of our own.

Nityananda is stating the Eastern position: we and we alone are responsible for our actions; no one else can be blamed. As the Theravada Buddhist monks recite every day: "I have nothing but my actions. I shall never have anything but my actions." We engage in thoughts, attitudes, emotions and deeds that lead us astray and corrupt our hearts and result in negative outlook and behavior. We made the mess and no one else can clean it up. Religion offers "saviors" that supposedly can do it for us, but it is a lie: we alone have the power to save ourselves from the misery and distortion we have created. In the East it is understood that all things in our life are a result of previous action (karma) done by no one but us. We act and experience the karmic reaction. Everything in our inner and outer life are reactions to our prior actions. We are at the center of the entire thing.

We harm ourselves, but we also have the power to heal ourselves. The very fact that we dug the pit we now find ourselves in tells us that we have the ability to climb out and be free. So whereas the Western view is totally pessimistic (and useless), the Eastern view is thoroughly optimistic and practical. The West only offers religious dogmas and rules of behavior that accomplish nothing but more confusion in our minds. The East offers Yoga, the science of knowledge and freedom. "Even a little of this dharma protects from great fear" (Bhagavad Gita 2:40).

A yogi continually advances in jnana. Just as a child grows continually, outgrowing his prior conditions physically and mentally, so does the yogi. People like to tell a child: "My, how you've grown and changed! I hardly knew you." It should be the same for a yogi. He should continually expand and deepen his understanding, progressing beyond his prior views, sometimes by seeing them more clearly or more fully, and sometimes by seeing that he was mistaken, that the truth is more, less, or completely different from his earlier opinion.

The inner bodies, including the buddhi (the faculty of intellect), are refined by right yoga practice and thus they are evolved, for the impulse to evolution is inherent in every atom. The yogi in time has everything, but the non-yogi never really has anything at any time. How few realize this!

When the yogi begins his practice, he will encounter all kinds of strange sensations as the subtle energy passages, known as nadis, in the subtle bodies are activated and purified. This often puzzles and even frightens the beginning yogi, but if he ignores them and keeps intent on his practice, all will be well.

The yogi is introducing himself into a totally different world, a totally different dimension, from that of his past experiencing. As Sri Ramakrishna often pointed out, there is no drastic physical change in his appearance, but he is stepping into another world altogether. It is a fact that a devoted yogi only minimally lives in this world. Rather, he becomes a citizen of higher realms right now. He must be prepared for this. The stronger his practice the more he unfolds aspects of interior life that he could never have believed existed beforehand.

On occasion the yogi can feel as though he is viewing life and those around him in a very detached manner. Often it seems as though he is watching a drama going on in which he has little if any part. Odd as it is, if he remains calm and observant and keeps a mantra the center of his attention, all will come out very well indeed.

Sometimes the yogi sees very ugly and disturbing things, usually rooted in his past lives. If he remains calm and keeps on meditating, in time these things will evaporate and not recur. If the yogi dealt with negative spirits in past lives, especially in magical or occult practices, those spirits may come to him hoping for continuing association. At such times he must ignore them completely and fix his mind on the mantric vibrations. If ignored, after a while they will go away and never return. Some foolish, troubled or evil spirits are just wandering around, and when they see someone sitting for meditation they try to distract him and stop his spiritual practice. Indifference to them is the way. Just stay with God in the form of the mantra. Then you will experience the truth of Saint John's statement: "Ye are of God, little children, and have overcome them: because greater is he that is in you, than he that is in the world" (I John 4:4).

A yogi is the savior of his personal world, for he changes everything about himself and his life sphere as well, purifying his karma and his consciousness. All yogis are embryonic sages, and meditation on God is the most sagely of all activities. Even if we are beginners in yoga, we are moving into territory that will eventually open before us into infinity.

All caterpillars are destined to be butterflies, and no butterfly should disrespect a caterpillar, for that is what he once was and they in time will be, too. Realizing that he was once where all those around him are at present, how can the yogi feel superior to anyone? Wishing them well, he should keep on diligently walking the path.

There is no place in the yogi's heart for pride and arrogance, for even an adept yogi is just on the first rung of the ladder. The quest for godhead is a long, high road indeed.

Honor and dishonor are not realities, but only the opinions of fallible human beings. We are never what people think or say we are; we are what we are—which is the Atman-Self. So we also need not bother with what we think about ourselves if it is based on externals and our ego-centered ideas. Basically, we should ignore our ego and the egos of others and pursue the Self.

When surrounded by many people we are susceptible to the influence of the vibrations emitted by their auras. To resist being influenced and perhaps even controlled by group vibration is a matter of great strength. Only those who have cultivated their inner strength through meditation and constant japa will have a chance of completely resisting external influences. And they will take no chances.

One of my university professors told us that just before America entered the Second World War, one of her very good friends had visited relatives in Germany. She wanted a see Hitler in action for herself, so her relatives took her to a rally at which he was to speak. At first she was disgusted at the insanity of it all, and when Hitler began to speak felt real aversion to him. Then something shifted in her mind and the next thing she knew she was standing up with tears flowing down her face and her throat sore from shouting *Sieg Heil* with the crowd over and over again. It was as though she had gone into a trance and awoke yelling and weeping hysterically along with the rest of the mob. She got out of there and left Germany the next day, utterly horrified at her experience.

The same professor told us that at the time of the second World War it was common for businesses that sold radios to have a speaker outside on the street relaying the sound of a broadcast to attract customers. One day as she was walking downtown, at a distance she saw a crowd gathered around one such store and hurried to see what the attraction was. As she came near she heard the voice of Hitler screaming and screeching in his usual manner. "The thing that shocked me," she told us, "was that many of the people were standing there as though hypnotized, and not one of them moved away until the broadcast was over. And these were Americans who could not even understand German. That day I learned the power of speech itself, even if its meaning would be unknown."

Yogananda said that when Jesus said: "Out of the abundance of the heart the mouth speaketh" (Matthew 12:34), he was referring to the vibrations of the mind that are projected through our voice whenever we speak. So we can be influenced by both the silent and verbal presence of others. Our aura, then, must be kept strong by japa and meditation.

Having told two ugly instances, I want to tell you one quite wonderful incident that demonstrates this principle. An Indian acquaintance of mine during his university years went on vacation to Calcutta. He was riding in a car with several friends when suddenly he demanded that the car be stopped. He listened intently and heard a sound so faint it was almost like he was imagining it. No one else could hear it. "We have to follow that sound!" he insisted, and since the driver was a good friend, on they went with him hanging out the car window, listening. Several times he lost the sound and they had to backtrack, but after a while the sound became stronger and the others could hear it, too. The more my friend heard the sound, the more it drew him. "I felt that it was a matter of life or death to find the source of that sound," he told me. So they followed that sound through all kinds of streets and lanes and finally could tell that it was the sound of a man's voice over a loudspeaker. My friend felt as though in another world altogether. Finally they came to a vast open space in which literally thousands were gathered. At the front, speaking into the microphone was Jagadguru Shankaracharya Brahmananda Saraswati, the head of Joshi Math in the Himalayas. When the speech was over my friend pushed his way onto the platform and saluted the Shankaracharya, who immediately asked him to visit him at Joshi Math. My friend did so right away and became his disciple and a monk there. Such is the power of sound, which is why the final verse of the Brahma Sutras states that liberation is attained through sound.

Paramhansa Yogananda often said: "Company is greater than will power." There is no doubt that we are influenced by the people we associate with. If we are fortunate they will strengthen our good qualities, but usually they either infect us with negative ones or strengthen the negative ones we already have.

It is very significant that Sri Ramana Maharshi said that two things are essential for the seeker of enlightenment: a vegetarian diet and satsang. Both shape our mind. To keep ourselves always oriented toward the Self and its realization we must be very careful about the company we keep. We must actively seek out positive company and we must actively avoid negative company. Often positive company is very difficult to find. In that case, "You must not mix with others" should be the rule of life for us.

Even an adept yogi must consciously hold on to his inner state of peace when he approaches contact with worldly people, for they are in the belly of the tiger of samsara, of material, egoic consciousness, and it can be catching, for it is a spiritual malady. Yogananda often cautioned his disciples about this danger. Those who heeded it were able to help themselves and others. Those who did not were eaten by the tiger, however much they may have rationalized and pretended they were not. I was blessed to meet holy, angelic disciples of the Master who had remained true to his ideals. But I also met utter spiritual ruins who had not remained true to his ideals and were clutching to themselves the spiritual rags of a compromised and wasted life in hope of covering up their condition: "Thou sayest, I am rich, and increased with goods, and have need of nothing; and knowest not that thou art wretched, and miserable, and poor, and blind, and naked" (Revelation 3:17). But they did know.

We must learn how to be in the water of samsara and not sink and drown. In India they use two similes: a lotus leaf and butter. They float in water and never absorb it. The yogi is able to be in the water of external experience and yet not wet. All those who seek peace must learn how to swim in the ocean of this world (samsara). Then they can be delivered from it and pass to better worlds.

Because we project our ignorance onto the external world we attribute ignorance to it and speak frequently of "maya" and so forth, but creation is divine manifestation.

"He who agitates not the world, and whom the world agitates not, who is freed from joy, envy, fear and distress [anxiety]–he is dear to me" (Bhagavad Gita 12:15). Keeping this in mind, we realize that the adept yogi finds the world an abode of peace because he experiences being the witness, and is not caught in its ever-changing appearances. The universe is really wisdom embodied, but when misused by the unwise it becomes a source of pain and confusion. The yogi, whose buddhi has become subtle (refined), is not pained or confused, but moves through the world in perfect knowing and therefore perfect peace, making an instrument of his enlightened will.

There is a contentment that is pathological, arising from a false sense of egoic security. But those of subtle mind are at ease in the wisdom of discrimination which protects them from falling into the traps of suffering. They are safe and at peace in a dangerous and agitating world. Why? Because they are really living in the Self, untouched by the world. Through enlightened discrimination, through perfect viveka, we cultivate the seed of liberation until it comes to fruition in our perfect freedom.

There are very many fake "hermits" who live off to themselves, supported by others who trust their motives, and yet are no more than bums with a fixed abode. There are many of these in the Himalayas. When Swami Ramdas was wandering in the north of India he visited the famous Vashishtha Cave where Rama's guru had done tapasya. He found there a retired merchant who was just living off the kindness of devotees who assumed he was a real yogi. But later a great saint, Swami Purushottamananda, lived there, and after his mahasamadhi one of his advanced disciples Swami Shantanandaji lived there. So all "hermits" are not equal.

If a yogi lives in solitude and does real sadhana, he benefits the whole world, for all is contained in the One.

"Save yourself and you will save thousands," Yogananda often said. But first we must save ourselves. There are hundred of thousands (if not millions) of people who want to change the world, but they do not change themselves, so nothing happens. I knew two men who were thoroughly addicted to alcohol and drugs. They could blather for hours about profound philosophy while swilling beer and smoking marijuana. When one was dying the other came to see him. The dying man said: "Billy, I thought we were going to make a difference." A difference in *what?* Yet this delusion persists in human beings. No telling how many people right now are confident that they are going to be major factors in "bringing in the (Newer) New Age."

Half a century ago I knew just such a person. Alcoholic and drug-addicted, he clung to some psychic revelations he had had in which he was told that he was going to have a large role to play in bringing in the New Age. Meanwhile he was a parasite, living off of anyone he could, if they would provide him nightly with a gallon of Gallo wine to drink. Once that was consumed he would pass out and urinate on himself. Yet he said to me more than once: "My 'forces' tell me that I must wait a few years and then my powers will awaken and my work will begin. I think it is likely going to be in Brazil." He did not have fare for a Los Angeles bus, but he would be going to Brazil.

On the other hand, those who do light their lamp can help others to light their way. Consider the holy ones of the past. Even if gone from this world for hundreds or thousands of years, they still inspire and empower many to find the Goal. I have met people who facilitated the awakening of untold thousands, some of them by staying in one place and others by traveling. Some wrote books and others did not. Some kept silence and others spoke freely. Some were considered geniuses and others were thought to be retarded or crazy. God apparently likes variety in his garden of saints. As Nagendranath Bhaduri said in *Autobiography of a Yogi*: "God plants his saints sometimes in unexpected soil, lest we think we may reduce Him to a rule!" But they had one thing in common: the ability to light lamps like themselves. As Swami Kebalananda said, also in *Autobiography of a Yogi*, "The numerous bodies which were spectacularly healed through Lahiri Mahasaya eventually had to feed the flames of cremation. But the silent spiritual awakenings he effected, the Christlike disciples he fashioned, are his imperishable miracles."

Purushartha in the ordinary sense means the four goals of human life: wealth (artha), desire (kama), righteousness (dharma), and liberation (moksha). But for the yogi whose mind and intellect are free from the three gunas, it means spiritual attainment, fulfillment of spiritual aspiration, perfection in righteousness and liberation from ignorance and rebirth. For him the ordinary goals are impossible to desire any longer, for he possesses something much better: awakened consciousness.

QUALITIES OF A YOGI

Being without doubt is the mark of true yogi. How does he become free from doubts? By diligent sadhana, for sadhana eventually removes all doubts and establishes us in true spiritual insight. Then we know the unknowable and understand the incomprehensible. Without this preparation we will never free our minds from the patterns of samsara and attain Brahmajnana. Those who have no doubt find that this doubt-lessness is the path to one-pointedness of mind, to perfection in yoga.

It is completely normal to want to avoid pain and even discomfort, but that can be a real mistake for the yogi. The more we shield and pamper ourselves the more we will feel pain and discomfort when it comes.

Many people who have no warm clothing in time find that they have become inured to the cold. I saw a sadhu from Gangotri (the source of the Ganges) who lived on the ice much of the time. He was absolutely naked, but he said that in the bitter Delhi winter weather he was feeling miserably hot! Those of us who came for his darshan used to shiver as we stood out in a bare field where he was sitting on a bit of straw on the ground. None of us managed to stand there for even an hour.

A great saint of the Eastern Christian Church once had a dream-vision in which a dish containing a shining white substance was placed before him. It seemed as though made of light, and he immediately tasted it. Never in his life had he tasted such intense sweetness and flavor! Without delay he ate it all up and called for more. A dish was then set before him in which there was a substance as black as the former had been white. This must be another treat! Thinking so, he literally dug right in. It was

as horridly disgusting as the other had been delectable. He was nause-
ated, and felt that he might be poisoned. Retching, he tried to expel
the awful taste from his mouth. When he turned to protest, he found
another dish of the white substance set by the side of the unfinished
dish of black material. A voice said to him: "You can have all you want
to eat, but you must eat an equal amount of both. There is no gaining
of the sweet dish without eating the other."

We become addicted to the sweet and insist on having it always.
This is impossible, so we are even more miserable when we experience
the bitter. The nature of relative existence is the continual alternation
between opposites. Those who accept it are on the way to even-mind-
edness, which is a requisite for peace and happiness.

Fearlessness (abhaya) is another trait of the yogi. Fear is a conditioned
reflex in the human being, first because it is a survival mechanism and
second because of lifetimes of fear caused by threatening situations.
Consequently fear is one of the main tools of false religion because it
appeals directly to the ego principle. Fear is a predisposition to weakness.
Often negative people think they fear what they are really attracted to
and hoping for. Negative energies almost always generate a fear response
in those that feel them. Manipulative people usually try to instill fear in
some manner before they begin their intellectual and emotional coercion.

The yogi must never fear if he is to survive. This is directly opposite to
the instinctive reactions of samsarins. It must be realized that to succeed
a yogi must be going utterly against the current of things and must be
striving to become a completely different order of being than he is at
the present. That is a matter of evolutionary development.

Adept yogis are fearless, for they know the dream nature of the
world and life in the world. An example of their fearlessness and the

harmlessness of animals, even the humans one, in their presence is given by Yogananda in the twelfth chapter of *Autobiography of a Yogi*.

"It so happened that I never saw Master at close quarters with a leopard or a tiger. But a deadly cobra once confronted him, only to be conquered by my guru's love. This variety of snake is much feared in India, where it causes more than five thousand deaths annually. The dangerous encounter took place at Puri, where Sri Yukteswar had a second hermitage, charmingly situated near the Bay of Bengal. Prafulla, a young disciple of later years, was with Master on this occasion.

"'We were seated outdoors near the ashram,' Prafulla told me. 'A cobra appeared near-by, a four-foot length of sheer terror. Its hood was angrily expanded as it raced toward us. My guru gave a welcoming chuckle, as though to a child. I was beside myself with consternation to see Master engage in a rhythmical clapping of hands. [The cobra swiftly strikes at any moving object within its range. Complete immobility is usually one's sole hope of safety.] He was entertaining the dread visitor! I remained absolutely quiet, inwardly ejaculating what fervent prayers I could muster. The serpent, very close to my guru, was now motionless, seemingly magnetized by his caressing attitude. The frightful hood gradually contracted; the snake slithered between Master's feet and disappeared into the bushes.

"'Why my guru would move his hands, and why the cobra would not strike them, were inexplicable to me then,' Prafulla concluded. 'I have since come to realize that my divine master is beyond fear of hurt from any living creature.'"

We usually have very mistaken ideas about the nature of humility. It is not having a low opinion of yourself, rather it is having no opinion of yourself, because in true humility you are absorbed in your opinion of, and desire for, God alone. If you try to get rid of the ego, you just obsess on the ego and thereby strengthen your ties with it. But if you seek and find God, the ego will melt away naturally like mist before the rising sun.

Certainly no one becomes a real spiritual teacher by adopting all kinds of external paraphernalia, but a lot of fakes do, and make money at it. They put on different kinds of unusual clothes—vivid red, orange, and yellow—and wear a load of huge beads looped everywhere, and have elaborate tilak (sectarian marks) on their foreheads, and sometimes on other parts of their bodies, as well. This is the way of people who foolishly think that outward signs will produce the inward state, and who egotistically desire to be thought of as great yogis and fervent devotees. Swami Sri Yukteswar, Yogananda's guru, detested this behavior, and sternly rebuked those who came to his ashram decked out in them. If anyone (even among his own disciples) protested his "bad manners" in doing so, he would firmly say: "Too much of a good thing is no longer good!"

On the other hand, real yogis have a simple appearance with no show or interest in gaining attention. There is a video of Swami Sivananda showing him with various well-known religious figures. Nearly all of them have some kind of theatrical get-up, but there is Sivananda dressed so simply, without beads, tilak, or any such. He did not need them, for those with inner vision could see his glory. He did not need to make an impression on anyone, for he possessed Infinity.

Most of us think that if we are sincerely mistaken about something it is no moral defect. But a false principle is an anti-truth and vibrates contrary to the universe, to life itself. This is demonstrated by the lie detector which registers abnormal and unhealthy conditions produced in the body when someone lies. A lie detector is actually a kind of dowsing device, a kind of backhanded truth detector.

The problem is that if we believe a lie we will perpetuate it by both word and deed. In this way we weaken the fabric of the cosmos and our own life sphere. Unawareness of the real situation does not make things right. We are harming ourselves and others and even the universe by believing and speaking lies, even though in sincerity and innocence. Any breach of truth, whatever the reason, is harmful and produces mind- and soul-deadening karma.

Truth has the exact opposite effect of falsehood. Truth strengthens our mind, body, life sphere and even the universe itself. Truth is Life. This is why Truth (Satya) is a cardinal principle of yoga philosophy. Truth is purifying, healing, empowering and uplifting.

Habitual liars have nothing of truth about them, but are incarnations of falsehood. Such people are sociopathic, and should be avoided by anyone, especially those who seek higher consciousness.

There no white lies or positive lies. All are destructive.

Vyasa writes in the sixteenth chapter of the Bhagavad Gita that truthfulness is a trait of the divine personality and falsehood is a trait of the demonic personality.

Without truthfulness in word and deed the spiritual path cannot even be entered, nor can this principle ever be abandoned on the way. Those who violate this principle are not on the Way of Truth at all. No exceptions are ever made to this rule.

Those who engage in sadhana will steadily gain in inner strength, or virya. It is that accumulated power which fuels our flight to the infinite. Unhappily, "getting and spending we lay waste our powers" by involvement in the world, as Wordsworth said. But the yogi is like a wise bee, distilling his yogic experience and insight into practical means for furthering his realization.

It is not enough to know mere words or theory. We must be able to manifest those words. We must know how to live what we know. Internal knowledge is not enough, external skill must be its proof.

We have been conditioned for lifetimes by exoteric religion to consider that we have no ability to direct ourselves in our life, but must be told what to do by scriptures and "spiritual authorities." But the very word for liberation, Kaivalya, means Independence. Authentic yoga gives us the experience we need to carry on our practice and to evaluate it, as well. And authentic yogis are not scripture- or guru-driven robots. Because of the negative conditioning of Western religion many yogis are afraid to rely on their own experience, though of course still respecting the words of the wise. But it has to be done.

Certainly when we have experienced the highest states of consciousness we will not be made to doubt by those that disagree with us, nor will we let them influence us. But along the way it is hard to practice self-reliance. Yet once we know for ourselves, we must not let anyone deflect us from our chosen course. As Jesus said in Revelation: "Hold that fast which thou hast, that no man take thy crown" (Revelation 3:11).

We sometimes have a regrettable propensity or inclination to let others tell us what we have and have not experienced, or what we are or are not. Humility is a cardinal virtue, but humility is not letting ourselves be bullied by others, including supposedly holy people.

I well remember a yogi speaking to a group of Westerners and expressing his amazement at the number of people that would say to him: "I read it in a book" as though that settled the matter and it must be true because it was in a book. Laughing, he said: "So I am going to have to write a book for them to read and believe!" But even that would not work. What everyone needs is experience for themselves. Then there will be no doubts.

We like to think that we are helpless victims, that we are tossed about by the ocean of samsara against our will. But the truth is otherwise. Only those who turn inward through yoga and perceive the truth of their inner being will begin to understand that it is their will alone that is causing the entire drama of their external life.

Once we become proficient in yogic practice, everything tends toward realization and manifestation of the One. The mind and heart must become one-pointed both in and out of meditation. For that is our real nature.

Those who cannot persevere and remember that Plod Rhymes With God will not produce inner spiritual realization. Yoga is a lifetime commitment, not just an additive to an already crowded life where little time can be spared for its practice. Yoga is many things, but never cheap and casual.

THIS AND THAT

One of the fundamental problems of religion is its continual attempt to limit God rather than to free its adherents from limitation so they can become one with God.

Consistency is essential in spiritual life. The inner and the outer must be the same. Mere words and mere deeds are not enough; they must match the interior condition.

Activating just part of us is not sufficient for genuine spiritual progress. Our total being must be engaged in sadhana according to the dictates of the Upanishads, the Gita and the Yoga Sutras. Otherwise it is little more than fantasy.

Through his intuition developed by intense and prolonged sadhana the yogi will come to see the hand of God in all that he has undergone in his life.

In the company of a true sadhu the mind is definitely uplifted. Therefore sadhu-sanga is a wonderful thing if it can be found.

The conditionings and flaws of the mind are eliminated when the yogi's consciousness merges with that of God, and it is revealed as spirit itself.

To know God is the fruit of yoga. It is also the knowledge of time and destiny—to look back at all our incarnations in relative existence and to comprehend them as steps leading to liberation.

See the world in, through and as God. The inner eye of Consciousness, of Shiva, must be opened through yoga, which should be the central fact and interest of our life. Then the jiva will be revealed as Shiva.

The greater the degree of spiritual aspiration, the greater will be the aspirant's spiritual discipline and sadhana, and the greater will be the resulting realization.

The conviction that God is real and all else is unreal is the faith (shraddha) that fuels our search for God.

Anybody can believe anything and not have it produce any effect in their life.

It is evident that jnana yoga, the yoga of wisdom and intelligence, alone culminates in complete liberation.

We must be intent on the purpose and nature of everything. What a thing really is should determine our reaction to it and the way we handle or relate to it.

The dynamic power of the universe is accessible to all, and that power eventually makes all equal by lifting them up to spiritual perfection in which there is no longer any difference.

The realization of God is the fundamental drive of the human being, no matter how deeply buried it may be.

A person's religion is worthless if he does not see the divine value of all sentient beings and their Divine Origin.

Those people who keep drawing lines of difference everywhere to separate themselves and somehow make themselves superior to others are the real outcastes.

Being the most subtle, non-dual realization is the rarest; nevertheless it must come to us all.

Advaita is not a mere philosophical proposition, it is a realization which frees from all rebirth.

Sometimes the world appears completely unreal, and at other times we realize that we are seeing God manifesting as the world. That is the experience of the yogi.

The sole duty or purpose of all sentient beings is the realization of God. So the master yogis have told us.

We need not die to gain "eternal peace," but live the yoga life to gain it.

God is both the cause and the goal of life.

Those who have no spiritual realization or even intellectual wisdom from life to life will be consumed by the fires of this world, attaining nothing but their eventual death.

Having no freedom, a bound person cannot be at rest or peace because the world to which they are bound is the source of all misery and frustration.

"Remember that finding God will mean the funeral of all sorrows," said Swami Sri Yukteswar.

TOUCH NOT

"Come out from among them, and be ye separate, saith the Lord, and touch not the unclean thing; and I will receive you" (II Corinthians 6:17). The yogi is not intended to be a pharisee or a snob, nevertheless he is called out from the delusions of samsara, much of which are part of ordinary daily life. The yoga life is separation on all levels, for body, mind and soul are in constant interchange in a kind of "chicken or the egg?" situation. And as Saint John has told us: "Beloved, now are we the sons of God, and it doth not yet appear what we shall be: but we know that, when he shall appear, we shall be like him; for we shall see him as he is. *And every man that hath this hope in him purifieth himself, even as he is pure*" (I John 3:1,2).

Purity is a matter of vibration, and so also is impurity. It is a matter of magnetism; when we encounter or touch an object, its vibrations begin to influence our own vibrations. Objects, places, and persons can elevate or degrade our personal vibrations. That is why Yogananda often told people: "Environment is stronger than will power."

One of Yogananda's monastic disciples, Brother Anandamoy, told me that Yoganandaji would insist that brooms and other cleaning equipment be kept stored and never left out in the open. "They have dirty vibrations," he would say. So a yogi should be very careful about what he touches or keeps near him.

It is significant that in the Bible the Hebrew word for pure is *taher*, which means "to be bright." Purity is that which reveals and conveys the divine light. The Greek word *katharos* used in the New Testament means "to be clear" like a crystal. Here, too, is the idea of receiving and even magnifying light. By this we can see that purity is a state of being, which includes vibrations of spiritual, divine Light.

The two major factors for purity are meditation and diet. That is obvious. People are a third very major factor. Just being in their aura affects us. Therefore we have to be careful of all associations, even casual ones.

To keep this simple, I will just list here the impure things that must be carefully avoided by us. This is part of the successful yoga life.

Money from an impure source:

given us by a negative person,

earned by working for a negative person or business,

earned by not purely honest or moral means.

Employment by a negative, corrupt, or dishonest person or business, or that necessitates close contact with people of low vibrations.

Things given us by morally corrupt people, or received undeservingly.

Anything, including clothing, made of impure elements such as leather, fur, bone (bone china, for example), etc.

Anything given us dishonestly or with the intention to influence us in any way.

Food prepared by an impure or negative person. Cooked food especially picks up the vibrations around it as well as those of the cooks.

Water is extremely susceptible to vibrations. We must be very careful about the water we wash with and drink. It is absolutely unclean to swim in swimming pools with other people.

Anything derived from animal sources, especially those that entail the death, suffering, or imprisonment of the animals.

Music written or performed by impure or ignorant people, especially "pop" music of all kinds. Music itself is pure vibration and directly goes into our subtle bodies and mind and shapes them. Music is an effective tool for both negative and positive influence.

Books written by or about impure persons or subjects. Books embody the mind-vibrations of the authors, therefore a person who reads a book takes into himself the mental vibration of the author. Books on occultism can particularly be sources of negative vibrations. There are some books that simply have to go—and not into a used book store to infect others, but into the garbage and on to the dump.

The touch of living beings imparts their biomagnetic energies directly into our physical and subtle bodies. Be extremely careful whom you touch and whom you allow to touch you—even slightly. Assiduously avoid chronic huggers, touchers and kissers. They are psychic invaders and vampires.

We are profoundly affected by what we see, because the experience of sight shapes our mental energies into the visual impressions we are receiving. All visual images are inside us, even if the objects are outside us. We psychically touch whatever we look at fixedly. Pictures and visual images directly influence us. Motion pictures and television broadcasts directly feed into our mind the underlying vibrations of the producers and the actors. And the sound tracks.

Not only do we not touch or keep the unclean—unbalanced or neg-ative—thing, we do not allow it to touch us.

Most of the things listed above have positive counterparts that will be uplifting to the yogi. Consequently we should be sure to surround ourselves with such beneficial influences.

It is like this: "The kingdom of heaven is like unto a net, that was cast into the sea, and gathered of every kind: which, when it was full, they drew to shore, and sat down, and gathered the good into vessels, but cast the bad away" (Matthew 13:47, 48). We need to go through the net of our life and keep the good and toss away the bad. Then we will make spiritual progress unhindered by any outside influences.

THE GITA SPEAKS TO THE YOGI

The wise yogi reads the Bhagavad Gita daily and ponders its truths. The more he does so, the more he will understand as his buddhi (intellect/intelligence) is being continually purified and enlightened through daily meditation.

The entire scripture is directed to the yogi, so all seven hundred verses speak to him, but I would like to present those that are specific about the principles of the Yoga Life.

"In this yoga, even the abortive attempt is not wasted. Nor can it produce a contrary result. Even a little practice of this yoga will save you from the terrible wheel of rebirth and death" (2:40).

"The scriptures declare that merit can be acquired by studying the Vedas, performing ritualistic sacrifices, practicing austerities and giving alms. But the yogi who has understood this teaching of mine will gain more than any who do these things. He will reach that universal source, which is the uttermost abode of God" (8:28).

"In this yoga, the will is directed singly toward one ideal" (2:41). "When can a man be said to have achieved union with Brahman? When his mind is under perfect control and freed from all desires, so that he becomes absorbed in the Atman, and nothing else" (6:18).

"Great is that yogi who seeks to be with Brahman, greater than those who mortify the body, greater than the learned, greater than the doers of good works: therefore become a yogi" (6:46).

"How hard to break through is this, my Maya, made of the gunas! But he who takes refuge within me only shall pass beyond Maya: he, and no other" (7:14).

"Strive without ceasing to know the Atman, seek this knowledge and comprehend clearly why you should seek it: such, it is said, are the roots of true wisdom: ignorance, merely, is all that denies them" (13:11).

"The Lord lives in the heart of every creature. He turns them round and round upon the wheel of his Maya. Take refuge utterly in him. By his grace you will find supreme peace, and the state which is beyond all change" (18:61, 62).

"Give me your whole heart, love and adore me, worship me always, bow to me only, and you shall find me: this is my promise who love you dearly. Lay down all duties in me, your refuge. Fear no longer, for I will save you from sin and from bondage" (18:65, 66).

"Only that yogi whose joy is inward, inward his peace, and his vision inward shall come to Brahman and know Nirvana" (5:24).

"The yogi should retire into a solitary place, and live alone" (6:10).

"Adore me only with heart undistracted; turn all your thought toward solitude, spurning the noise of the crowd, its fruitless commotion" (13:10).

"He must exercise control over his mind and body" (6:10).

"He must free himself from the hopes and possessions of this world" (6:10).

"He should meditate on the Atman unceasingly" (6:10).

"Make a habit of practicing meditation, and do not let your mind be distracted. In this way you will come finally to the Lord, who is the light-giver, the highest of the high" (8:8).

"When a yogi has meditated upon me unceasingly for many years, with an undistracted mind, I am easy of access to him, because he is always absorbed in me" (8:14).

"If a man will worship me, and meditate upon me with an undistracted mind, devoting every moment to me, I shall supply all his needs, and protect his possessions from loss" (9:22).

"He who flouts the commandments of the scriptures, and acts on the impulse of his desires, cannot reach perfection, or happiness, or the highest goal. Let the scriptures be your guide, therefore, in deciding what you must do, and what you must abstain from. First learn the path of action, as the scriptures teach it. Then act accordingly" (16:23, 24).

"Yoga is not for the man who overeats, or for him who fasts excessively. It is not for him who sleeps too much, or for the keeper of exaggerated vigils. Let a man be moderate in his eating and his recreation, moderately active, moderate in sleep and in wakefulness. He will find that yoga takes away all his unhappiness" (6:16, 17).

"Who burns with the bliss and suffers the sorrow of every creature within his own heart, making his own each bliss and each sorrow: him I hold highest of all the yogis" (6:32). This is most important. Many sincere yogis think that unattachment means to be indifferent to others. I have known some yogis who tried to cultivate indifference to their children, showing them no love or affection. This is a terrible misunderstanding.
"A man should not hate any living creature. Let him be friendly and compassionate to all" (12:13).

"He gives me all his heart, he worships me in faith and love: that yogi, above every other, I call my very own" (6:47).
"Devote your whole mind to me, and practice yoga. Take me for your only refuge. By doing this, you can know me in my total reality, without any shadow of doubt" (7:1).
"Great in soul are they who become what is godlike: they alone know me, the origin, the deathless: they offer me the homage of an unwavering

mind. Praising my might with heart and lips for ever, striving for the virtue that wins me, and steadfast in all their vows, they worship adoring, one with me always" (9:13, 14).

"Whatever your action, food or worship; whatever the gift that you give to another; whatever you vow to the work of the spirit: O son of Kunti, lay these also as offerings before Me. Thus you will free yourself from both the good and the evil effects of your actions. Offer up everything to me. If your heart is united with me, you will be set free from karma even in this life, and come to me at the last. My face is equal to all creation, loving no one nor hating any. Nevertheless, my devotees dwell within me always: I also show forth and am seen within them. Though a man be soiled with the sins of a lifetime, let him but love me, rightly resolved, in utter devotion: I see no sinner, that man is holy. Holiness soon shall refashion his nature to peace eternal; O son of Kunti, of this be certain: the man that loves me, he shall not perish" (9:27-31).

"Those whose minds are fixed on me in steadfast love, worshipping me with absolute faith, I consider them to have the greater understanding of yoga…Quickly I come to those who offer me every action, worship me only, their dearest delight, with devotion undaunted. Because they love me these are my bondsmen and I shall save them from mortal sorrow and all the waves of Life's deathly ocean" (12:2, 6, 7).

"He who is free from delusion, and knows me as the supreme Reality, knows all that can be known. Therefore he adores me with his whole heart" (15:19).

"At the hour of death, when a man leaves his body, he must depart with his consciousness absorbed in me. Then he will be united with me. Be certain of that. Whatever a man remembers at the last, when he is leaving the body, will be realized by him in the hereafter; because that will be what his mind has most constantly dwelt on, during this life. Therefore you must remember me at all times, and do your duty. If your mind and heart are set upon me constantly, you will come to me. Never doubt this" (8:5-7).

"On Him let man meditate always, for then at the last hour of going hence from his body he will be strong in the strength of this yoga, faithfully followed: the mind is firm, and the heart so full, it hardly holds its love. Thus he will take his leave: and now, with the life-force indrawn utterly, held fast between the eyebrows, he goes forth to find his Lord, that light-giver, who is greatest" (8:10).

"You find yourself in this transient, joyless world. Turn from it, and take your delight in me. Fill your heart and mind with me, adore me, make all your acts an offering to me, bow down to me in self-surrender. If you set your heart upon me thus, and take me for your ideal above all others, you will come into my Being" (9:33-34).

"Be absorbed in me, lodge your mind in me: thus you shall dwell in me, do not doubt it, here and hereafter" (12:8).

"Who sees his Lord, within every creature, deathlessly dwelling amidst the mortal: that man sees truly. Thus ever aware of the Omnipresent always about him, he offers no outrage to his own Atman, hides the face of God beneath ego no longer: therefore he reaches that bliss which is highest. Who sees the separate lives of all creatures united in Brahman brought forth from Brahman, himself finds Brahman" (13:27-28, 30).

"He must free himself from the delusion of 'I' and 'mine.' He must accept pleasure and pain with equal tranquility. He must be forgiving, ever-contented, self-controlled, united constantly with me in his meditation. His resolve must be unshakable. He must be dedicated to me in intellect and in mind. Such a devotee is dear to me. He neither molests his fellow men, nor allows himself to become disturbed by the world. He is no longer swayed by joy and envy, anxiety and fear. Therefore he is dear to me. He is pure, and independent of the body's desire. He is able to deal with the unexpected: prepared for everything, unperturbed by anything. He is neither vain nor anxious about the results of his actions. Such a devotee is dear to me. He does not desire or rejoice in what is pleasant. He does not dread what is unpleasant, or grieve over it. He remains unmoved by good or evil fortune. Such a devotee is dear to me. His attitude is the same toward friend and foe. He is indifferent to honor and insult, heat and cold, pleasure and pain. He is free from attachment. He values praise and blame equally. He can control his speech. He is content with whatever he gets. His home is everywhere and nowhere. His mind is fixed upon me, and his heart is full of devotion. He is dear to me. This true wisdom I have taught will lead you to immortality. The faithful practice it with devotion, taking me for their highest aim. To me they surrender heart and mind. They are exceedingly dear to me" (12:13-20).

"Be humble, be harmless, have no pretension, be upright, forbearing, serve your teacher in true obedience, keeping the mind and the body in cleanness, tranquil, steadfast, master of ego, standing apart from the things of the senses, free from self; aware of the weakness in mortal nature, its bondage to birth, age, suffering, dying; to nothing be slave, nor desire possession of man-child or wife, of home or of household; calmly encounter the painful, the pleasant" (13:7-9).

"Yogis who have gained tranquility through the practice of spiritual disciplines, behold him in their own consciousness" (15:11).

"A man who is born with tendencies toward the Divine, is fearless and pure in heart. He perseveres in that path to union with Brahman which the scriptures and his teacher have taught him. He is charitable. He can control his passions. He studies the scriptures regularly, and obeys their directions. He practices spiritual disciplines. He is straightforward, truthful, and of an even temper. He harms no one. He renounces the things of this world. He has a tranquil mind and an unmalicious tongue. He is compassionate toward all. He is not greedy. He is gentle and modest. He abstains from useless activity. He has faith in the strength of his higher nature. He can forgive and endure. He is clean in thought and act. He is free from hatred and from pride. Such qualities are his birthright" (16:1-3).

"Learn from me now how man made perfect is one with Brahman, the goal of wisdom. When the mind and the heart are freed from delusion, united with Brahman, when steady will has subdued the senses, when sight and taste and sound are abandoned without regretting, without aversion; when a man seeks solitude, eats but little, curbing his speech, his mind and his body, ever engaged in his meditation on Brahman the truth, and full of compassion; when he casts from him vanity, violence, pride, lust, anger and all his possessions, totally free from the sense of ego and tranquil of heart: that man is ready for oneness with Brahman. And he who dwells united with Brahman, calm in mind, not grieving, not craving, regarding all men with equal acceptance: he loves me most dearly. To love is to know me, my innermost nature, the truth that I am: through this knowledge he enters at once to my Being. All that he does is offered before me in utter surrender: my grace is upon him, he finds the eternal, the place unchanging. Mentally resign all your action to me. Regard me as your dearest loved one. Know me to be your only refuge. Be united always in heart and consciousness with me. United with me, you shall overcome all difficulties by my grace" (18:50-58).

"By your grace, O Lord, my delusions have been dispelled. My mind stands firm. Its doubts are ended. I will do your bidding" (18:73).

The translation of the Bhagavad Gita cited in this section is The Song of God: Bhagavad Gita, *translated by Swami Prabhavananda and published by the Vedanta Press.*

LIVING THE YOGA LIFE

"The kingdom of heaven is like unto treasure hid in a field; the which when a man hath found, he hideth, and for joy thereof goeth and selleth all that he hath, and buyeth that field" (Matthew 13:44). The kingdom of heaven is our eternal spirit-self. It is hidden in the "field" of the body according to the thirteenth chapter of the Bhagavad Gita, and we must "buy" that field through the disciplines and practices of yoga. And the price of purchase is ALL that we have. It is the same for everyone: our entire life must be dedicated to the attainment of liberation.

"The yogi should retire into a solitary place, and live alone" (Bhagavad Gita 6:10). It is not enough to live in a solitary place, the yogi should live alone. Why? "Adore me only with heart undistracted; turn all your thought toward solitude, spurning the noise of the crowd, its fruitless commotion" (Bhagavad Gita 13:10). Solitude is necessary so we can live "with heart undistracted."

The greatest monk of the Christian church was Saint Arsenios the Great who lived in the Egyptian desert. At the beginning of his spiritual search he prayed for guidance from God. A voice sounded from heaven, saying: "Arsenios: Flee men"–which he did, and became "an earthly angel and a heavenly man" as a result.

This holy solitude is an ideal to be striven for. It need not involve living miles from others. Location is the key. For example, I am writing this in a house located on the side of a tree-covered mountain. When I look out the window I see at the foot of the mountain a neighborhood which includes a campground, but no noise is ever heard from there at any time. I can also see a minor highway at the foot of the mountains across the valley that is also silent. But the important thing is that the atmosphere is totally solitary. It feels as though this property is many miles from other habitations. Having lived far out in the countryside away from all others, I know the feeling and it is the same here. The windows are kept open much of the year and the only sounds usually heard are birds and breezes.

A yogi living in a tranquil neighborhood can turn his home into a spiritual haven and live there alone with God. I knew two yogis who lived in Beverly Hills in a sound-proofed apartment in splendid solitude. Again, location is the key–and the yogi's sincere intention.

It was said of an ancient Christian hermit who lived in the desert of Israel: "He went into the desert and took the whole world with him." So living in quiet solitude while having the mind filled with worldly clamor is defeating the purpose. It is crucial to control the telephone, not let others invade your quiet, and not bring in the world through newspapers, news magazines, or news programs on radio and television.

What if you have a family or unavoidably live with others? Then you can follow the advice of Ram Gopal Mazumdar, the Sleepless Saint of *Autobiography of a Yogi*. "Are you able to have a little room where you can close the door and be alone?... That is your cave.... That is your sacred mountain. That is where you will find the kingdom of God." I knew a nun who used to climb up into a tree so she could be alone, hidden by the leaves from being disturbed by others. At the same time you must find the right balance between being alone and being with those you live with.

For those that live with others, going into solitude occasionally was one of the major spiritual practices advocated by Sri Ramakrishna. Here are some of the things he said about it.

"The mind cannot dwell on God if it is immersed day and night in worldliness, in worldly duties and responsibilities; it is most necessary to go into solitude now and then and think of God. To fix the mind on God is very difficult, in the beginning, unless one practices meditation in solitude. When a tree is young it should be fenced all around; otherwise it may be destroyed by cattle.

"To meditate, you should withdraw within yourself or retire to a secluded corner or to the forest. And you should always discriminate between the Real and the unreal. God alone is real, the Eternal Substance; all else is unreal, that is, impermanent. By discriminating thus, one should shake off impermanent objects from the mind."

"One must go into solitude to attain this divine love. To get butter from milk you must let it set into curd in a secluded spot: if it is too much disturbed, milk won't turn into curd. Next, you must put aside all other duties, sit in a quiet spot, and churn the curd. Only then do you get butter.

"Further, by meditating on God in solitude the mind acquires knowledge, dispassion, and devotion. But the very same mind goes downward if it dwells in the world....

"The world is water and the mind milk. If you pour milk into water they become one; you cannot find the pure milk any more. But turn the milk into curd and churn it into butter. Then, when that butter is placed in water, it will float. So, practice spiritual discipline in solitude and obtain the butter of knowledge and love. Even if you keep that butter in the water of the world the two will not mix. The butter will float."

It is essential that you spend some time each day alone, but as often as you can it is good to go away to a solitary place for meditation and spiritual study. But it should be a personal retreat, not in some place where you can get pulled into their routine. (Some retreat facilities have individual houses for retreatants to live alone.)

I am not speaking of being anti-social, but of being a serious yogi.

The great Master Yogananda said that when we are alone we should be truly alone, forgetting the world and everything in it, including all that is dear to us, but when we are with others, we must really be with them. He was the perfect example of this. When he was alone and withdrawn the awesome atmosphere around him bespoke of his total absorption in God, and when he was with people they felt his entire heart was with them, that he was their very own. Yet, he was never over-familiar or "folksy." His was the perfect balance, and we must seek the same.

Many people think that "keeping silence" is a good thing, and it is if it is silence of mind and heart, but if it is nothing more than not speaking, it is of little worth. So do not waste your time "in silence" around other people–that is just ego display and an annoyance to others. Instead, seek solitude, for when there is no one to speak to that is the best silence.

Whether a yogi is alone or with others, he should always be relaxed, cheerful, and thoughtful of others.

When you are with people and it seems you are wasting your time sitting and listening to inane and silly talk, you will not be wasting your time if you calmly sit and meditate with open eyes. Never "go into meditation" around others–that is just holy show and escapism. If it does not look odd, there is nothing wrong in looking downward or at some blank surface as you continue to be what one spiritual writer called an "interior soul." But the moment your attention is needed, give it wholeheartedly and enter into things as long as there is no harm in them. And please do not go slinking off for a meditation fix like some addict sneaking a cigarette. Stay put and keep on with the cultivation of consciousness through your inner yoga process. The spiritual vibrations will help everyone around you.

What I have written above should be followed in moderation. Whenever you can, be alone and quiet. Please do not caught in the net of "good works" and "helping others." These kind of activities are good for those who have not yet learned to cultivate the inner life, but believe me, your solitary life and meditation will help more people than any external acts ever could. Every moment of your practice makes it easier for other yogis to maintain their practice and contributes to the awakening of those who do not yet know yoga.

Absolutely avoid the opposite sex. (If you are attracted to your own sex, then avoid everybody.) Do not fall into the trap of "just good friends" or think that disparity of age matters. Past life impressions are ready to rise and disrupt the spiritual life of the unwary. And truly have nothing to do with those that tell you: "I am your mother"—or father. I have never known a one of those who said that who were not defiled in thought and intention. Remember: to the yogi there should be no "special people" or "exceptions to the rule" in these matters. You may have to put up with emotional blackmail from these "offended" and "hurt" people, but their attempts to accuse and make you feel guilty are the proof of their negative and destructive nature.

By the way: Learn to become totally deaf to those who say to you: "I only want you to be happy." They NEVER really want any such thing. They want to manipulate you into making *them* happy.

Be prepared for opposition, ridicule, and even vicious reaction to your aspirations to the yoga life. If you cannot stand up to outer pressures, how will you stand up to the delusions of your ego-mind? Another thing: Never think that you have to justify your beliefs and way of life. Do not get snagged into "discussions" with those who oppose your life and think you need prove anything to them. They are blind and deaf, and will remain so for a long time. As Yogananda told aspirants in reference to such people: "You go after God" and leave them far behind. Change your vibrations, and those people will disappear from you life, even if only after they make a lot of fuss.

Here is a conversation Mahendranath Gupta, "Master Mahasaya the Blissful Devotee" in *Autobiography of a Yogi*, had with Sri Ramakrishna (referred to here as "M" and "Master.")

"M. (to the Master): What should one do if one's wife says: 'You are neglecting me. I shall commit suicide'?

"MASTER (in a serious tone): Give up such a wife if she proves an obstacle in the way of spiritual life. Let her commit suicide or anything else she likes. The wife that hampers her husband's spiritual life is an ungodly wife.

"Immersed in deep thought, M. stood leaning against the wall. ... suddenly going to M., he [Sri Ramakrishna] whispered in his ear: But if a man has sincere love for God, then all come under his control–the king, wicked persons, and his wife. Sincere love of God on the husband's part may eventually help the wife to lead a spiritual life. If the husband is good, then through the grace of God the wife may also follow his example.

"This had a most soothing effect on M.'s worried mind. All the while he had been thinking: Let her commit suicide. What can I do?

"M. (to the Master): This world is a terrible place indeed.

"MASTER (to the devotees): That is the reason Chaitanya said to his companion Nityananda, 'Listen, brother, there is no hope of salvation for the worldly-minded.'"

Now I am going to give you a piece of advice regarding associations that may seem severe, but it is very necessary and based on practical experience: Do not keep animals either in or outside your home. Animal slavery for our amusement and "love" is morally wrong. Animals were not intended to be captured and bred away from their true nature for human amusement and obsession. One of the effects of this is the harm to the health of humans who live in close contact with animals. Many times it has been found that pets were the source of their owner's illnesses. Children are especially susceptible to picking up problems from animals.

It is ridiculous to avoid contact with human beings who at least have human vibrations, and yet keep the company of an animal which will be a distraction and a source of animal vibrations. I have observed that people of low consciousness and development, however well they may hide it, absolutely need to keep an animal around so they can associate with subhuman consciousness and have someone inferior to them that they literally own and from whom they claim to get "unconditional love." And of course they continually say that animals are better than people.

It is also absurd to abstain from eating meat in order to observe ahimsa, yet feed it to animals.

Sri Ramakrishna said that when a man or woman gets old and is obviously heading for death, instead of preparing for the end of their life they get and keep a cat, becoming very attached to it. I expect we all know people who refer to their animals as little girls or little boys and call themselves mommy or daddy in relation to them. And then there are the people who think they are being cute when they speak of being "owned" by their pets. But it is a sad truth.

Please avoid this shameless exploitation of animals and willful taking on of what can only be a distraction from spiritual life and a lowering of your consciousness. A yogi must take on disciplines far beyond those of ordinary people who are samsarins slated for future births in ignorance.

As Yogananda pointed out, St. Francis de Sales used to say: "A saint that is sad is a sad saint!" and we are saints in training. A sense of humor is indispensable to the yogi—especially about himself. The good ashrams in India are what Sri Ramakrishna called "a mart of joy." Those who live there freely laugh and enjoy jokes and even pranks. Swami Sivananda was known for his lively sense of humor, and Yogananda loved to tell funny things that had happened to him and also played pranks. (His favorite was dropping bags of water out of windows or spraying people with a hose. It was really a blessing with holy water!) Sometimes, because of his accent and hearty laughing in the telling of a story, people would say: "I could hardly understand a word, but I never laughed so much in my life."

When I met Swami Satyananda Giri, the author of *Yogananda Sanga*, in 1963, I asked him to tell me about Sri Yukteswar, Yogananda's guru, since Satyananda had lived for many years with him and was the first person Yogananda took to meet him after becoming his disciple. Since it is usual for people to have a perception of Sri Yukteswar as severe and exacting, I was surprised to hear his first words: "In his entire life he never hurt the feelings of anyone, but was always gentle and kind." (This does not mean he did not discipline those who asked for it, for discipline only "hurts" the sore ego.) But the most impressive thing he told me was his quotation of Sri Yukteswar's often-said words: "He is a real man who can sing his life through!"

Since God is bliss, the yogi's life should be joyful, based on optimism about his future in God and reflecting the divine experience that comes in meditation—and later all the time. Frankly, the yogi alone can really enjoy himself without needing the frantic "fun" and distractions prized by those who live in a world of unreality, darkness, and mortality. So when I urge you to enjoy yourself I mean it in the perspective of yoga.

There is a story of a serious man who was shocked when he saw some very ascetic monks joking and laughing. Noticing this, one of the monks later on asked him: "Can you shoot a bow?" When the man said he could, the monk asked: "Do you always keep the bow strung tightly?" "No," said the man, "If I did, the bow would loose its tone and become slack and useless." "In the same way," replied the monk, "it is good to relax the mind through innocent enjoyment and even laughter. A mind held in tension will either snap or go slack." However there is a great difference between relaxing and being lax, and we should act accordingly.

It is good to do things just for the enjoyment, not insisting that all we do be "useful," "constructive," or "educational," though the principles of yama-niyama can never be ignored or laid aside for even a moment.

God gave us a brain so we would use it. As a child I noticed that people turned off their mind when they entered the church door and turned it back on when they left. Considering the idiocy of what they saw, did and heard there, it was no doubt a good idea, but it would have been better if they had recognized foolish religion for what it was and searched for something better. So I was very disappointed when after becoming a yogi I constantly saw people agreeing with stupidity, arrogance, and misinformation dispensed by teachers and other authority figures of the yoga world. No matter how moronic the "reasoning" handed them, they just looked bright-eyed and noble and said: "O yes!" Nothing can come of this pious acquiescence to ignorance and falsehood.

Here it is in a nutshell: Spot The Looney. And acknowledge the looney as being a looney and their looniness as being looniness. Forget the hype, the miracle stories, the accounts of great yoga feats, the list of what "big" people revere them, the prophecies of supposed saints about how great they were going to be or are. A fool is a fool and none more vicious than a religious/spiritual fool. Some are not fools but heartless frauds. So look closely and long and make your own conclusion about the teachers, gurus, and avatars that abound now they have found the wealth of the West. And that includes the ones in India waiting like spiders for you to come fall into their web.

In East and West people have a reputation for holiness and avatarness that are really foolish or crazy. Some are senile in varying degrees. The same applies to yoga. If you notice that the practicers of a yoga are either duds or falling apart mentally and physically, then get away and stay away. Ignore their rhapsodies about how beneficial it has been to them—this only proves the depth of their delusion.

Trust your own experience. If a yoga is not delivering the goods, drop it. Do not be fooled by the old nonsense about not digging in a number of places rather than sticking to one. When professionals drill for water or oil, if they do not find any after some days or weeks they have the sense to abandon the site and drill elsewhere. Drill a thousand "holes" if necessary until you find one that gives real results. How will you know? Right away you will begin seeing the positive spiritual effects, which will keep on developing from your practice.

Here is the wisdom of Swami Vivekananda about much of supposed yoga and the supposed gurus who peddle it: "They exercise a singular control for the time being over sensitive persons, alas! often, in the long run, to degenerate whole races. Ay, it is healthier for the individual or the race to remain wicked than be made apparently good by such morbid extraneous control. One's heart sinks to think of the amount of injury done to humanity by such irresponsible yet well-meaning religious fanatics. They little know that the minds which attain to sudden spiritual upheaval under their suggestions, with music and prayers, are simply making themselves passive, morbid, and powerless, and opening themselves to any other suggestion, be it ever so evil. Little do these ignorant, deluded persons dream that whilst they are congratulating themselves upon their miraculous power to transform human hearts, which power they think was poured upon them by some Being above the clouds, they are sowing the seeds of future decay, of crime, of lunacy, and of death. Therefore, beware of everything that takes away your freedom. Know that it is dangerous, and avoid it by all the means in your power."

Never take vows to a guru or institution, and especially not before being given the "secret techniques." Nobody with an operating mind would buy something they had never seen, making non-refundable payment in advance. No worthy spiritual teacher would require this, either. How can you reasonably declare loyalty and adherence to something or someone you do not know? As Sri Ramakrishna said: "Be a devotee, but why a fool?"

Furthermore, wherever there is secrecy there is usually charlatanry. A lot of egotists like to think they know something others do not. Remember the children in your childhood that liked to sing-song: "I know something you don't know!"? Yogis immersed in secrets and secrecy are both immature and false. One time we met a "light of yoga" after he had given a slide lecture on India, throughout which he had expressed contempt for the land and the people. When told we had associated many years with one of the best-known teachers of modern India, he asked eagerly: "Did you learn any secret techniques?" because he and his organization trafficked in such phony spiritual currency. Why it did not occur to him that once a secret is told it is no longer a secret is beyond me.

Swami Vivekananda had this to say about secrecy in yoga: "In India, for various reasons, it [yoga] fell into the hands of persons who destroyed ninety per cent of the knowledge, and tried to make a great secret of the remainder....Anything that is secret and mysterious in these systems of Yoga should be at once rejected. The best guide in life is strength. In religion, as in all other matters, discard everything that weakens you, have nothing to do with it. Mystery-mongering weakens the human brain. It has well-nigh destroyed Yoga—one of the grandest of sciences. From the time it was discovered, more than four thousand years ago, Yoga was perfectly delineated, formulated, and preached in India. It is a striking fact that the more modern the commentator the greater the mistakes he makes, while the more ancient the writer the more rational he is. Most of the modern writers talk of all sorts of mystery. Thus Yoga fell into the hands of a few persons who made it a secret, instead of letting the full blaze of daylight and reason fall upon it. They did so that they might have the powers to themselves."

There are some things it is wise to avoid. Here are some.

Avoid the merely religious—the more religious, the more they should be avoided. Remember that crazy religion makes crazies, lying religions make liars and hypocrites, and ignorant religion makes ignoramuses.

Avoid those whose religion is nothing more than believing in some book or doing merely external observances.

Avoid spiritual dabblers and followers of fake gurus or false religions. Sincerity counts for nothing when a person is sincerely ignorant.

Avoid vows of any kind, and that includes any of your own making. Do not vow: Do it. Live it.

Avoid health crazes, but do learn about alternative therapies, especially vibrational medicine and those that deal with bio-energy. They are the most suitable for a yogi, though other modes of medicine should not be ignored or rejected.

Avoid proselytizers of all sorts, whatever their philosophy.

Avoid all supposed yogis and gurus that make annual tours around the world.

Avoid shallow people of all types.

Avoid those who do not respect your spiritual orientation and life.

Avoid those that claim to be "spiritual but not religious." They are not. True religion is the science of the spirit, and that alone opens the path to spirituality.

Avoid the impure and the materialistic.

Avoid people who are hell-bent on making themselves and others "nice."

Avoid those who cannot take a stand on anything.

Avoid those who advertise themselves (and their religion if they have any) as "inclusive" and "non-judgmental." They are morally and spiritually bankrupt, and usually immoral.

As said previously, avoid women that want to be your "mother" and men that want to be your "father." Even in India this is always a prelude to attempted sexual impropriety. And remember: old people can have very "young" ideas about you-know-what.

Avoid those that are "offended" when your ideas do not suit them and "hurt" when they cannot bully or blackmail you into conforming to their ways or get you to do what they want. HOLD TO YOUR PRINCIPLES. Once you lose them you have nothing at all—and are nothing at all.

Avoid those that have no sense of humor—especially about themselves.

Avoid all political entanglements.

Avoid all "good deeds" and social activism—and those addicted to them.

Avoid all Western "advaita teachers" and most of the Eastern ones, too.

Avoid all religious and spiritual teachers and teachings that are not based on yoga and spiritual experience. (I use "yoga" here in the broad sense of any consciousness-opening methodology.)

Avoid like poison those who use any kind of mind-altering substance, pretending it "opens" them to higher consciousness and perceptions.

Avoid all addicts of any kind: they are next to demons.

Avoid becoming addicted to anything yourself, material, intellectual, or spiritual (God excepted).

Avoid thinking you can help others when they will not help themselves. You have to do it alone, and so do they. Point them to your sources of wisdom and let them go for it on their own steam. Otherwise you are just churning water in hope of getting milk and trying to dig a hole in the sky—it will never happen.

Avoid those that are not willing to "go it alone" just as you are doing.

Avoid those that always "need to talk to someone."

Avoid people who have to be consoled and cajoled to keep up spiritual life.

Avoid those who continually claim to be "disturbed," "worried," and "confused"—especially in relation to you and your ideals and way of life.

Avoid those who claim to be liberal or broad-minded. They never are.

Avoid those who claim they need spiritual "help." God truly does only help those that help themselves.

Avoid anyone who habitually says: "I am a 'doubting Thomas.'" They are not doubters, but deniers who will become very unhappy with you if you prove to be true the things they pretend to doubt.

Avoid monotonous and boring people. As a wonderful American saint once said to me in reference to man I knew: "Why carry around empty space?"

Avoid useless thought and talk about "getting rid of the ego." Meditate and the ego will vanish like the ghost it really is.

Avoid compromise like the death-bearing evil it is.

Avoid food-faddism and be very wary of what the "experts" say about diet. In fact, pay very little attention to "scholars," "experts," and (especially) "scientists" and "science."

Avoid thinking there is anything you cannot live without–except God.

Avoid the world of men and live in the world of God.

And there are things that we should definitely do and have in our life, such as the following.

Make your house a personal spiritual haven and your heart a hermitage, as Paramhansa Yogananda continually advised.

Watch and take care of your health, getting a medical and dental checkup at least once or twice a year. The moment a problem arises, get professional help. It is very unlikely you can cure yourself on your limited knowledge. Without health any form of life is difficult, including the yoga life. Do not be like a "yogi" friend of mine who decided she could cure diabetes with ginseng and other "natural cures." She ended up in a coma, nearly dying, and spent the rest of her life an invalid on dialysis.

Swami Sri Yukteswar told all his students to only be close friends with other yogis.

Keep holy depictions or imagery throughout your home, especially the photographs of saints and masters.

Follow a diet that is healthy and appetizing. No food that is repulsive or boring is good for you. (Yogananda really insisted on this, as more than one of his disciples told me.)

Acquire an extensive Sanskrit vocabulary, but do not study Sanskrit itself unless you feel you must, for it is a years-long process in which you might have done better by reading good translations.

Meditation will expand your consciousness, but the mind–manas and buddhi–must also be cultivated and expanded by spiritual study.

As a yogi you will become very sensitive to the spiritual effects of sound. Especially seek out good religious music of both East and West.

Unfortunately a lot of contemporary recordings of Indian music are sung in a raucous or phony style and loaded with silly sound effects and instruments–the worse being the vibraphone. Look for traditional Indian music played on traditional instruments. Avoid recordings that have heavy jungle-beat drumming–another curse of modern Indian bad taste. The recordings of Yogananda's chants sung by the monks and nuns of Self-Realization Fellowship are very good, Brahmacharini Meera's recordings being at the top, for she was a true saint. Do not forget Buddhist and Taoist music.

If, however, oriental music sounds too peculiar to your ears, do not bother with it. The Christian music of both East and West holds great potential for upliftment and calm. Whatever the style, acapella singing is almost always best. Recordings of Eastern Orthodox Greek and Russian liturgical music can be extraordinarily beautiful, as well as that of other Slavic countries. If Gregorian chant appeals, good, but if not it is just fine. Gregorian was originally intended to be sung with a holding note or ison, and not monophonically. Also it was sung much faster and did not sound like the singers were heavily sedated all the time. (Both these defects are modern aberrations stemming from the French monastery of Solesme.) Do not disdain ordinary church hymns, some of which have a profound message when heard with a yogi's perspective. Remember: Yogananda's favorite hymn was *In The Garden* which, when looked upon as a description of meditation, is really inspiring.

Never listen to a piece of music like it is medicine–if it does not really appeal to you, listen to something else or enjoy outer silence.

SPIRITUAL READING

I want to assure you of the necessity for spiritual reading. It is a great source of mental purification when engaged in as an extension of meditation by maintaining inner awareness through japa while reading.

The yogi need not be an intellectual–perhaps even should not be–but he must be intelligent and informed–not so he can burden others with revelations of his knowledge (which must not be confused with wisdom), but so he can attune himself to the departed masters of the spiritual life who have infused their writings with their own state of realization. Also, he needs to dialogue with himself inwardly about those ideas, engaging in an intellectual version of chewing the cud. If he does not think about these high things, what will he think about?

At the beginning of my yoga search I was in a harshly anti-intellectual group (yoga cult) who wanted the members to read nothing but their own publications which were very few and very feeble intellectually. I was always rebuked when others saw my "big" library of not even two dozen books! One leader expressed chagrin when he learned I had read the *Gospel of Sri Ramakrishna*. Why? Because their teachings were so minimal and inconsequential, as well as without any basis in authentic Indian texts, they were terrified that their members might encounter other, better and more sensible ideas. They were right... I did and I quit. Such a mentality is one sign of a destructive cult. A yogi should not hesitate to look into any philosophy or spiritual inquiry. He should be very informed about the various religions and philosophies of the world.

Although I am going to recommend some books to read it is just a hint. There is a big world out there and since we are living in it we should take advantage of it. There are not only books out there, there are immense resources on the internet, including many websites which are actual libraries of online texts, including our own ocoy.org.

There are five books whose value cannot be estimated. They are foundation stones of understanding spiritual life and spiritual philosophy. They should be read through many times carefully and reflectively. I think they should be made the yogi's lifetime companions and guides.

1. The Bhagavad Gita. There are many translations, but my favorite is: *The Song of God: Bhagavad Gita*, translated by Swami Prabhavananda of the Vedanta Society of Southern California. It is remarkably beautiful language, yet accurate. In many places the translation is interpretive, but according to the commentary of Shankaracharya and other authorities. I recommend you also get the translations of Swamis Swarupananda and Sivananda, and that of Winthrop Sargeant. My commentary, *The Bhagavad Gita For Awakening*, might be useful.

2. *The Upanishads, Breath of the Eternal,* by Swami Prabhavananda. The Upanishads are the basis of the Bhagavad Gita and contain thrilling expositions of the nature of the Self and its realization. My commentary, *The Upanishads For Awakening*, might also be useful.

3. *Meditation and Spiritual Life*, by Swami Yatiswarananda of the Ramakrishna Mission of India (in America: the Vedanta Society). This book is immensely practical and insightful. It covers virtually every aspect of the yogi's spiritual life.

4. *The Philosophy of Gorakhnath*, Akshaya Kumar Banerjea, Motilal Banarsidass. This is a masterful exposition of the teachings of India's greatest yogi.

These are treasures beyond evaluation. The Gita should be read daily, and it is still supplying me with new insights. I am sure it will do the same for you.

The books of Paramhansa Yogananda are extremely valuable. I especially recommend:

Man's Eternal Quest (collection of talks).

The Divine Romance (collection of talks).

Journey to Self-realization (collection of talks).

The Science of Religion.

Sayings of Paramahansa Yogananda (originally *The Master Said*).

God Talks With Arjuna, (commentary on the Bhagavad Gita).

The Second Coming of Christ, (commentary on the Gospels).

I also highly recommend these books about Yogananda: *The New Path* and *Paramhansa Yogananda*; both by Swami Kriyananda. And *The Life of Yogananda: The Story of the Yogi Who Became the First Modern Guru,* by Philip Goldberg.

Conversations With Yogananda by Kriyananda is an absolute treasure.

In addition you need some Sanskrit dictionaries. I recommend: *A Concise Dictionary of Indian Philosophy* by John Grimes, *The Yoga-Vedanta Dictionary* of Swami Sivananda, *Sanskrit Glossary of Yogic Terms* by Swami Yogakanti and *A Sanskrit Dictionary* by John M. Denton. My own endeavor, *A Brief Sanskrit Glossary,* is certainly helpful, and definitely complements them.

The Gospel of Sri Ramakrishna, translated by Swami Nikhilananda, is a remarkable treasury of spiritual philosophy. It consists of of conversations with Sri Ramakrishna spanning several years. It was set down by Mahendranath Gupta, who next to Sri Yukteswar was the most important influence in Yogananda's spiritual development. (He is written about in Yogananda's autobiography as "Master Mahasaya the Blissful Devotee.") It is good to read it straight through the first time, but you can also simply open it at random and read amazing things, including the words of truly spiritual songs.

For the authentic teachings of Christ I heartily recommend *The Aquarian Gospel of Jesus the Christ,* by Levi H. Dowling. This is a transcription of the psychic investigations into the life of Christ made by Dowling in what is popularly known as "the akashic records" and I believe contains the authentic teachings of Jesus, but makes no claim to infallibility or absolute accuracy.

I also urge you to get *The Complete Mystical Works of Meister Eckhart* translated by Maurice O'C Walshe. It is expensive but you will use it the rest of your life. *Meister Eckhart: A Modern Translation* by Raymond Blakney will do if your budget is limited. But do not forget the *Complete Works* for the future.

For the facts about diet, I recommend *Diet For a New America* by John Robbins, *What's Wrong With Eating Meat?* by Vistara Parham, the books of Dr. Neal Barnard, particularly *Food for Life: How the New Four Food Groups Can Save Your Life*. The best researched and most informative book on nutrition and health is Dr. Michael Greger's *How Not To Die*. For vegetarian and vegan recipes the cookbooks of Robin Robertson are very good.

GORAKHNATH SPEAKS TO THE YOGI

In conclusion here are the immortal words of Gorakhnath which he addressed to all yogis in the *Gokakh Bani*:

O Yogi, die; die to the world. Such death is sweet. Die in the manner of Goraksha who "died" and then saw the Invisible.

Speak not in haste, walk not in haste. Take slow cautious steps. Let not pride overtake you. Lead a simple life, says Gorakshanath.

Goraksha says: Listen, O Avadhuta, this is how you should lead your life in this world. See with your eyes, hear with your ears but never speak. Just be a dispassionate witness to the happenings around you. Do not react.

Goraksha says one who remains steadfast in observing his sadhana keeping his spiritual practice, food habits and sleeping habits under strict yogic discipline neither grows old nor dies.

Goraksha says he who meditates, controls the five senses [withdrawing] from their pleasures and burns his body in the holy fire of Brahman finds the Great God [Mahadeva].

The mind is dull and fails to comprehend the secret of the yogamarga [path of yoga]. It is very capricious and is always engaged in mischief, thus causing a man to drift away from the true path.

The mind itself is the abode of the good as well as of the evil. One may either let the good prevail or may allow free play to the evil instincts. This mind is pure and pious only when it lets the good in it prosper.

If the mind promotes the evil instincts residing in it then it becomes impure and impious. Yogamarga is the means by which the mind can be trained to promote and sustain the good instincts.

And from the *Goraksha Sataka*:

O excellent men! Practice Yoga, the fruit of the wish-fulfilling tree [kalpataru], which brings to an end the misery of the world (6).

[The yogi should be] chaste, one who eats little, an abstainer from worldly pleasures, a practicer of Yoga (54).

In the *Gorakh Bodha*: Gorakhnath: How should one sit and how walk, how speak and how meet [others]; how should one deal with one's body? Matsyendranath: He should sit, walk, speak and meet *awake and aware*; with his attention and discrimination thus handled, he should live fearlessly (91-92).

AND A FINAL WORD FROM ME

In yoga, practice combined with right thinking and living is everything.

It is the matter of perseverance that usually presents the greatest difficulty to the meditator. It is essential in yoga, as in ordinary matters, to realize that all goes according to precise laws. Wishing, wanting, hoping, praying, believing–or their opposites–have no effect at all. When speaking of meditation, Patanjali says: "Its application is by stages" (Yoga Sutras 3:6). That is, meditation keeps moving onward in its effect *when regularly practiced*, just like the taking of a journey. It all goes in an exact sequence. Therefore we cannot expect that meditation will produce enlightenment in a random way like a slot machine in its payoffs. Meditation produces steady growth if there is steady practice.

The secret of success is regularity in meditation. "A diamond is a piece of coal that never gave up." Paramhansa Yogananda formulated a more spiritual version: "A saint is a sinner who never gave up." If you meditate regularly, every day, great will be the result. Water, though the softest substance known, can wear through the hardest stone by means of a steady dripping. In the old story of the tortoise and the hare, the tortoise won the race because he kept at it steadily, whereas the hare ran in spurts. He ran much faster then the tortoise, but the irregularity of his running made him lose the race. Meditation keeps moving onward in its effect when regularly practiced, producing steady growth through steady practice. The more we walk the farther we travel; the more we meditate the nearer and quicker we draw to the goal.

Yoga, the spiritual state, is produced by yoga the practice. Those who persevere in their yoga practice find unfailing and abundant happiness, peace, and fulfillment. Certainly the goal is not reached without much practice through the years, but every step of the way is blessed and brings rejoicing to the yogi's heart. Then at last no more steps are needed, and he enters the ocean of Satchidananda. "A tiny bubble of laughter, I am become the Sea of Mirth Itself," wrote Yogananda.

DID YOU ENJOY
READING THIS BOOK?

Thank you for taking the time to read *Living the Yoga Life*. If you enjoyed it, please consider telling your friends or posting a short review at Amazon.com, Goodreads, or the site of your choice.

Word of mouth is an author's best friend and much appreciated.

GET YOUR FREE MEDITATION GUIDE

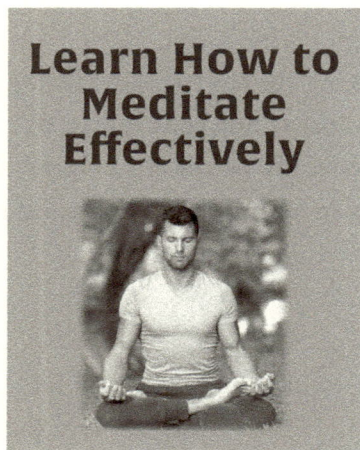

Sign up for the Light of the Spirit Newsletter and get
Learn How to Meditate Effectively.

Get free updates: newsletters, blog posts, and podcasts, plus exclusive
content from Light of the Spirit Monastery.

Visit: http://ocoy.org/newsletter-registration

GLOSSARY

Abhaya(m): "Without fear;" fearlessness; a state of steadfastness in which one is not swayed by fear of any kind.

Abhyasa: Sustained (constant) spiritual practice.

Abhyasa Yoga: Yoga, or union with God, through sustained spiritual practice.

Adharma: Unrighteousness; demerit, failure to perform one's proper duty; unrighteous action; lawlessness; absence of virtue; all that is contrary to righteousness (dharma).

Advaita: Non-dualism; non-duality; literally: not [a] two [dvaita].

Agni: Fire; Vedic god of fire.

Ahankara: Ego; egoism or self-conceit; the self-arrogating principle "I," "I" am-ness; self-consciousness.

Ahata: Natural sound.

Ajapa Gayatri: So'ham Mantra.

Ajna chakra: "Command Wheel." Energy center located at the point between the eyebrows, the "third eye." The seat of the mind. The medulla center opposite the point between the eyebrows, having two "petals" or rays.

Ajnana: Ignorance; nescience.

Ajnani: One who is ignorant, devoid of knowledge and wisdom.

Akasha: Ether; space; sky; literally: "not visible." The subtlest of the five elements (panchabhuta), from which the other four arise. It is all-pervading, and is sometimes identified with consciousness–chidakasha. It is the basis of sound (shabda), which is its particular property.

Akhanda: Unbroken (literally: "not broken"); indivisible; undivided; whole.

Amrita: That which makes one immortal. The nectar of immortality that emerged from the ocean of milk when the gods churned it.

Ananda: Bliss; happiness; joy. A fundamental attribute of Brahman, which is Satchidananda: Existence, Consciousness, Bliss.

Anandamaya kosha: "The sheath of bliss (ananda)." The causal body (karana sharira). The borderline of the Self (atman).

Ashtanga Yoga: The "eight-limbed" Yoga of Patanjali consisting of yama, niyama, asana, pranayama, pratyahara, dharana, dhyana, and samadhi (see separate entries for each "limb").

Amrita: That which makes one immortal. The nectar of immortality that emerged from the ocean of milk when the gods churned it.

Anahata: "Unstruck;" "unbeaten." Continuous bell-like inner resonance; the heart; the heart chakra; the inner divine melody (mystic sounds heard by the Yogis); supernatural sound; So'ham.

Anandamayi Ma: One of the major spiritual figures in twentieth-century India, first made known to the West by Paramhansa Yogananda in his *Autobiography of a Yogi.*

Annamaya kosha: "The sheath of food (anna)." The physical—or gross—body, made of food.

Anubhava: Perception; direct personal experience; identity of the Jiva with Brahman; spiritual experience; intuitive consciousness and knowledge.

Apah: Water.

Arani: Sacrificial wood stick for creating fire through friction.

Artha: Wealth; object; thing; meaning; sense; purpose; an object of desire. It is the secular value which is both desired and desirable. It satisfies the acquisitive tendency in individuals. It is the economic value.

Arya(n): One who is an Arya—literally, "one who strives upward." Both Arya and Aryan are exclusively psychological terms having nothing whatsoever to do with birth, race, or nationality. In his teachings Buddha habitually referred to spiritually qualified people as "the Aryas." Although in English translations we find the expressions: "The

Four Noble Truths," and "The Noble Eightfold Path," Buddha actually said: "The Four Aryan Truths," and "The Eightfold Aryan Path."

Ashram(a): A place for spiritual discipline and study, usually a monastic residence. Also a stage of life. In Hinduism life is divided ideally into four stages (ashramas): 1) the celibate student life (brahmacharya); 2) the married household life (grihasta); 3) the life of retirement (seclusion) and contemplation (vanaprastha); 4) the life of total renunciation (sannyasa).

Asura: Demon; evil being (a-sura: without the light).

Asuric: Of demonic character.

Atma(n): The individual spirit or Self that is one with Brahman. The true nature or identity.

Atma-bhava: The nature of the Self; awareness of the self; feeling: "I am the Self."

Atmajnana: Direct knowledge of the Self; Brahma-Jnana.

Atmarama: Satisfied–delighted–in the Self.

Atmavichara: Enquiry into the Self.

Avadhuta: "Cast off" (one who has cast off the world utterly). A supreme ascetic and jnani who has renounced all worldly attachments and connections and lives in a state beyond body consciousness, whose behavior is not bound by ordinary social conventions. Usually they wear no (or virtually no) clothing. They embody the highest state of asceticism or tapas.

Avatar(a): A fully liberated spirit (jiva) who is born into a world below Satya Loka to help others attain liberation. Though commonly referred to as a divine incarnation, an avatar actually is totally one with God, and therefore an incarnation of God-Consciousness.

Bandha: "Lock;" bond; bondage; tie or knot; a Hatha Yoga exercise.

Baul or Bauls: A group of mystic minstrels from Bangladesh. There are also some people in the Indian states of West Bengal, Tripura and Assam's Barak Valley, who came from Bangladesh. Bauls constitute both a syncretic religious sect and a musical tradition. Bauls are a very heterogeneous group, with many sects, but their membership mainly consists of Vaishnava Hindus and Sufi Muslims. They can often be identified by their distinctive clothes and musical instruments. Although Bauls comprise only a small fraction of the Bengali population, their influence on the culture of Bengal is considerable.

Bhagavad Gita: "The Song of God." The sacred philosophical text often called "the Hindu Bible," part of the epic Mahabharata by Vyasa; the most popular sacred text in Hinduism.

Bhagavan: The Lord; the One endowed with the six attributes, viz. infinite treasures, strength, glory, splendor knowledge, and renunciation; the Personal God.

Bhakta: Devotee; votary; a follower of the path of bhakti, divine love; a worshipper of the Personal God.

Bhakti: Devotion; dedication; love (of God).

Bhava: Subjective state of being (existence); attitude of mind; mental attitude or feeling; state of realization in the heart or mind.

Bhuta: What has come into being; an entity as opposed to the unmanifested; any of the five elementary constituents of the universe; element.

Bindu: Point; dot; seed; source; the creative potency of anything where all energies are focused; the point from which the subtle Omkara arises that is experienced in meditation.

Brahmajnana: Direct, transcendental knowledge of Brahman; Self-realization.

Brahmajnani: One who possess Brahmajnana.

Brahman: The Absolute Reality; the Truth proclaimed in the Upanishads; the Supreme Reality that is one and indivisible, infinite, and eternal; all-pervading, changeless Existence; Existence-knowledge-bliss Absolute (Satchidananda); Absolute Consciousness; it is not only all-powerful but all-power itself; not only all-knowing and blissful but all-knowledge and all-bliss itself.

Brahmananda: The bliss of communion with Brahman.

Brahmarandhra: "The hole of Brahman," the subtle (astral) aperture in the crown of the head. Said to be the gateway to the Absolute (Brahman) in the thousand-petaled lotus (sahasrara) in the crown of the head. Liberated beings are said to exit the physical body through this aperture at death.

Brahmavidya: Science of Brahman; knowledge of Brahman; learning pertaining to Brahman or the Absolute Reality.

Brahmin (Brahmana): A knower of Brahman; a member of the highest Hindu caste consisting of priests, pandits, philosophers, and religious leaders.

Buddhi: Intellect; intelligence; understanding; reason; the thinking mind; the higher mind, which is the seat of wisdom; the discriminating faculty.

Buddhi Yoga: The Yoga of Intelligence spoken of in the Bhagavad Gita which later came to be called Jnana Yoga, the Yoga of Knowledge.

Chaitanya: Consciousness; intelligence; awareness; the consciousness that knows itself and knows others; Pure Consciousness.

Chakra: Wheel. Plexus; center of psychic energy in the human system, particularly in the spine or head.

Chidakasha: "The Space (Ether) of Consciousness." The infinite, all-pervading expanse of Consciousness from which all "things" proceed; the subtle space of Consciousness in the Sahasrara (Thousand-petalled Lotus). The true "heart" of all things. Brahman in Its aspect as limitless knowledge; unbounded intelligence. This is a familiar concept of the Upanishads. It is not meant that the physical ether is consciousness. The Pure Consciousness (Cit) is like the ether (Akasa), an all-pervading continuum.

Chit: Consciousness (that is spirit or purusha); "to perceive, observe, think, be aware, know;" pure unitary Consciousness. The principle of universal intelligence or consciousness.

Chitta: The subtle energy that is the substance of the mind, and therefore the mind itself; mind in all its aspects; the field of the mind; the field of consciousness; consciousness itself; the subconscious mind.

Dharana: Concentration of mind; fixing the mind upon a single thing or point. "Dharana is the confining [fixing] of the mind within a point or area" (Yoga Sutras 3:1).

Dharma: The righteous way of living, as enjoined by the sacred scriptures and the spiritually illumined; law; lawfulness; virtue; righteousness; norm.

Dharma shastras: Scriptures which set forth the rules for society and individuals, including spiritual observances. Manu Smriti is the most authoritative–and the foundation–of all the dharmashastras of India.

Divya: Divine; divine nature; heavenly; celestial; sacred; luminous; supernatural.

Divyachakshu: Divine eye.

Durga: "Incomprehensible One;" "Difficult to reach;" the Universal Mother; she rides a lion (or tiger) and carries a weapon in each of her eight arms symbolizing the powers of the Self against ignorance and evil. She is invoked against all forms of evil–physical and metaphysical. Considered the consort, the shakti, of Shiva.

Dwandwa(s): The pairs of opposites inherent in nature (prakriti) such as pleasure and pain, hot and cold, light and darkness, gain and loss, victory and defeat, love and hatred.

Dwesha: Aversion/avoidance for something, implying a dislike for it. This can be emotional (instinctual) or intellectual. It may range from simple non-preference to intense repulsion, antipathy and even hatred. See Raga.

Ekadashi: "The eleventh." The eleventh day of each half of the lunar month (that is, the eleventh day after the new and full moons) that is devoted to the worship of Vishnu and his avataras.

Ekadashi Vrata: Observing ekadhashi (the eleventh day after the new and full moons, sacred to Vishnu) by fasting–through abstinence from grains and other staples and eating much less than usual, oftentimes fasting from food (and sometimes water) until after sundown.

Gayatri Mantra: A Rig Vedic mantra in the gayatri meter invoking the solar powers of evolution and enlightenment, recited at sunrise and sunset.

Gerua: The brownish-orange mud used to dye the clothing of Hindu monastics; the color produced by dyeing with gerua is also itself called gerua.

Gita: Song; The Bhagavad Gita.

Govinda: "Cowherd"–a title of Krishna.

Grihastha: One who is living in the second stage (ashrama) of Hindu social life; married householder's life.

Guna: Quality, attribute, or characteristic arising from nature (Prakriti) itself; a mode of energy behavior. As a rule, when "guna" is used it is in reference to the three qualities of Prakriti, the three modes of energy behavior that are the basic qualities of nature, and which determine the inherent characteristics of all created things. They are: 1) sattwa–purity, light, harmony; 2) rajas–activity, passion; and 3) tamas–dullness, inertia, and ignorance.

Guru: Teacher; preceptor; spiritual teacher or acharya.

Hardwar: "The Gateway to Hari," a holy city in north-central India where the Ganges river flows into the plains.

Hatha Yoga: A system consisting of physical exercises, postures, and breathing exercises for gaining control over the physical body and prana.

Hridaya: Heart; essential center or core of something; essence; the Self.

Ida: The subtle channel that extends from the base of the spine to the medulla on the left side of the spine.

Indra: King of the lesser "gods" (demigods); the ruler of heaven (Surendra Loka); the rain-god.

Isha: The Lord; Ishwara.

Ishwara: "God" or "Lord" in the sense of the Supreme Power, Ruler, Master, or Controller of the cosmos. "Ishwara" implies the powers of omnipotence, omnipresence, and omniscience.

Jagadguru: World guru; world teacher.

Japa: Repetition of a mantra.

Jiva: Individual spirit.

Jivanmukta: One who is liberated here and now in this present life.

Jivanmukti: Liberation in this life.

Jivatma(n): Individual spirit; individual consciousness.

Jnana: Knowledge; knowledge of Reality–of Brahman, the Absolute; also denotes the process of reasoning by which the Ultimate Truth is attained. The word is generally used to denote the knowledge by which one is aware of one's identity with Brahman.

Jnanamaya kosha: "The sheath of intellect (buddhi)." The level of intelligent thought and conceptualization. Sometimes called the Vijnanamaya kosha. The astral-causal body.

Jnanendriyas: The five organs of perception: ear, skin, eye, tongue, and nose.

Jnani: A follower of the path of knowledge (jnana); one who has realized–who knows–the Truth (Brahman).

Kaivalya: Transcendental state of Absolute Independence; state of absolute freedom from conditioned existence; moksha; isolation; final beatitude; emancipation.

Kama: Desire; passion; lust.

Kamandalu: A water vessel carried by a traveling sannyasi; usually made of a gourd or coconut shell, it may also be earthenware. The kamandalu and staff (danda) are considered the insignia of the sannyasi along with gerua clothing.

Karma: Karma, derived from the Sanskrit root *kri*, which means to act, do, or make, means any kind of action, including thought and feeling. It also means the effects of action. Karma is both action and reaction, the metaphysical equivalent of the principle: "For every action there is an equal and opposite reaction." "Whatsoever a man soweth, that shall he also reap" (Galatians 6:7). It is karma operating through the law of cause and effect that binds the jiva or the individual soul to the wheel of birth and death. There are three forms of karma: sanchita, agami, and prarabdha. Sanchita karma is the vast store of accumulated actions done in the past, the fruits of which have not yet been reaped. Agami karma is the action that will be done by the individual in the future. Prarabdha karma is the action that has begun to fructify, the fruit of which is being reaped in this life.

Karma Yoga: The Yoga of selfless (unattached) action; performance of one's own duty; service of humanity.

Karmendriyas: The five organs of action: voice, hand, foot, organ of excretion, and the organ of generation.

Karmic: Having to do with karma.

Kaupina: A small strip of cloth used to cover one's private parts. Also called a langoti.

Kirtan(a): Singing the names and praises of God; devotional chanting.

Krishna: An avatar born in India about three thousand years ago, Whose teachings to His disciple Arjuna on the eve of the Great India (Mahabharata) War comprise the Bhagavad Gita.

Krodha: Anger, wrath; fury.

Kundalini: The primordial cosmic conscious/energy located in the individual; it is usually thought of as lying coiled up like a serpent at the base of the spine.

Lahiri Mahasaya: Shyama Charan Lahiri, one of the greatest yogis of nineteenth-century India, written about extensively in *Autobiography of a Yogi* by Paramhansa Yogananda.

Lakshmana: The brother of Rama whom he accompanied into exile.

Lakshmi: The consort of Vishnu; the goddess of wealth and prosperity.

Lila: Play; sport; divine play; the cosmic play. The concept that creation is a play of the divine, existing for no other reason than for the mere joy of it. The life of an avatar is often spoken of as lila.

Lobha: Greed; covetousness.

Mada: Pride; arrogance.

Mahaprana: The undifferentiated, intelligent cosmic life-force that becomes the five pranas; all things contain the mahaprana and are manifestations of the mahaprana; the dynamic aspect of universal Consciousness; the superconscious Divine Life in all things.

Maharaj(a): "Great king;" lord; master; a title of respect used to address holy men.

Mahashakti: The Great Power; the divine creative energy.

Mahat Tattwa: The Great Principle; the first product from Prakriti in evolution; intellect. The principle of Cosmic Intelligence or Buddhi; universal Christ Consciousness, the "Son of God," the "Only Begotten of the Father," "the firstborn of every creature."

Mahatma: Literally: "a great soul [atma]." Usually a designation for a sannyasi, sage or saint.

Mahima (1): Greatness; glory; magnification; extensive magnitude; miracle.

Manas(a): The sensory mind; the perceiving faculty that receives the messages of the senses.

Manava: Man; a human being; a descendant of Manu.

Manava dharma: The essential nature of man; religion of man; the duties of man.

Manomaya kosha: "The sheath of the mind (manas–mental substance)." The level (kosha) of the sensory mind. The astral body.

Manu: The ancient lawgiver, whose code, The Laws of Manu (Manu Smriti) is the foundation of Hindu religious and social conduct.

Math: A monastery.

Mati: Thought; view; opinion; faith; religion; doctrine; tradition; conviction; mind rightly directed towards knowledge revealed and practice enjoined by the shastras.

Matsarya: jealousy.

Maya: The illusive power of Brahman; the veiling and the projecting power of the universe, the power of Cosmic Illusion. "The Measurer"–a reference to the two delusive "measures," Time and Space.

Moha: Delusion–in relation to something, usually producing delusive attachment or infatuation based on a completely false perception and evaluation of the object.

Moksha: Release; liberation; the term is particularly applied to the liberation from the bondage of karma and the wheel of birth and death; Absolute Experience.

Mukti: Moksha; liberation.

Muladhara chakra: "Seat of the root." Energy center located at the base of the spine. Seat of the Earth element.

Mulaprakriti: Avyaktam; the Root [Basic] Energy from which all things are formed. The Divine Prakriti or Energy of God.

Nadi: A channel in the subtle (astral) body through which subtle prana (psychic energy) flows; a physical nerve. Yoga treatises say that there are seventy-two thousand nadis in the energy system of the human being.

Nirguna: Without attributes or qualities (gunas).

Nirguna Brahman: The impersonal, attributeless Absolute beyond all description or designation.

Nirvikalpa: Indeterminate; non-conceptual; without the modifications of the mind; beyond all duality.

Nirvikalpa samadhi: Samadhi in which there is no objective experience or experience of "qualities" whatsoever, and in which the triad of knower, knowledge and known does not exist; purely subjective experience of the formless and qualitiless and unconditioned Absolute. The highest state of samadhi, beyond all thought, attribute, and description.

Nitya: Eternal; permanent; unchanging; the ultimate Reality; the eternal Absolute. Secondarily: daily or obligatory (nitya karma–that which must be done every day).

Nityananda (Paramhansa): A great Master of the nineteenth and twentieth centuries, and the most renowned Nath Yogi of our times. His *Chidakasha Gita* contains some of the most profound statements on philosophy and yoga.

Niyama: Observance; the five Do's of Yoga: 1) shaucha–purity, cleanliness; 2) santosha–contentment, peacefulness; 3) tapas–austerity, practical (i.e., result-producing) spiritual discipline; 4) swadhyaya–self-study, spiritual study; 5) Ishwarapranidhana–offering of one's life to God.

Paramananda: Supreme (param) bliss (ananda).

Paramatma(n): The Supreme Self, God.

Paramhansa: Literally: Supreme Swan, a person of the highest spiritual realization, from the fact that a swan can separate milk from water and is therefore an apt symbol for one who has discarded the unreal for the Real, the darkness for the Light, and mortality for the Immortal, having separated himself fully from all that is not God and joined himself totally to the Divine, becoming a veritable embodiment of Divinity manifested in humanity.

Parampurusha: The Supreme Spirit; Supreme Person.

Patanjali: A yogi of ancient India, a Nath Yogi and the author of the Yoga Sutras.

Pingala: The subtle channel that extends from the base of the spine to the medulla on the right side of the spine.

Pradhana: Prakriti; causal matter.

Prajapati: Progenitor; the Creator; a title of Brahma the Creator.

Prakriti: Causal matter; the fundamental power (shakti) of God from which the entire cosmos is formed; the root base of all elements; undifferentiated matter; the material cause of the world. Also known as Pradhana. Prakriti can also mean the entire range of vibratory existence (energy).

Prana: Life; vital energy; life-breath; life-force; inhalation. In the human body the prana is divided into five forms: 1) Prana, the prana that moves upward; 2) Apana: The prana that moves downward, producing the excretory functions in general. 3) Vyana: The prana that holds prana and apana together and produces circulation in the body. 4) Samana: The prana that carries the grosser material of food to the apana and brings the subtler material to each limb; the general force of digestion. 5) Udana: The prana which brings up or carries down what has been drunk or eaten; the general force of assimilation.

Pranamaya kosha: "The sheath of vital air (prana)." The sheath consisting of vital forces and the (psychic) nervous system, including the karmendriyas.

Pranayama: Control of the subtle life forces, often by means of special modes of breathing. Therefore breath control or breathing exercises are usually mistaken for pranayama. It also means the refining (making subtle) of the breath, and its lengthening through spontaneous slowing down of the respiratory rate.

Prithivi: The element of earth with density and fragrance as its characteristic features.

Prithivitattva: Principle of earth-element.

Purana: Literally "The Ancient." The Puranas are a number of scriptures attributed to the sage Vyasa that teach spiritual principles and practices through stories about sacred historical personages which often include their teachings given in conversations.

Purusha: "Person" in the sense of a conscious spirit. Both God and the individual spirits are purushas, but God is the Adi (Original, Archetypal) Purusha, Parama (Highest) Purusha, and the Purushottama (Highest or Best of the Purushas).

Purushartha: The four goals (artha) of human life: wealth (artha), desire (kama), righteousness (dharma), and liberation (moksha). The first is the economic value, the second is the psychological value, the third is the moral value, and the fourth is the spiritual value. Human effort; individual exertion; right exertion.

Raga: Blind love; attraction; attachment that binds the soul to the universe. Attachment/affinity for something, implying a desire for it. This can be emotional (instinctual) or intellectual. It may range from simple liking or preference to intense desire and attraction. Greed; passion. See Dwesha.

Raja Yoga: See Ashtanga Yoga.

Rajas: Activity, passion, desire for an object or goal.

Rakshasa: There are two kinds of rakshasas: 1) semidivine, benevolent beings, or 2) cannibal demons or goblins, enemies of the gods. Meat-eating human beings are sometimes classed as rakshasas.

Rama: An incarnation of God–the king of ancient Ayodhya in north-central India. His life is recorded in the ancient epic Ramayana.

Ramakrishna, Sri: Sri Ramakrishna lived in India in the second half of the nineteenth century, and is regarded by all India as a perfectly enlightened person–and by many as an Incarnation of God.

Ramana: Enjoyer; one who enjoys or delights in something.

Ramana Maharshi: A great twentieth-century sage from Tamil Nadu, who lived most of his life at or on the sacred mountain of Arunachala in the town of Tiruvannamalai.

Rasa: Taste; essence; savor; juice; nectar of delight.

Ravana: The demon king of Lanka, who kidnapped Sita and was subsequently slain by Rama.

Rudraksha: "The Eye of Shiva;" a tree seed considered sacred to Shiva and worn by worshippers of Shiva, Shakti, and Ganesha, and by yogis, usually in a strand of 108 seeds. Also used as a rosary to count the number of mantras repeated in japa.

Sadguru: True guru, or the guru who reveals the Real (Sat–God).

Sadhaka: One who practices spiritual discipline–sadhana–particularly meditation.

Sadhana: Spiritual practice.

Sadhu: Seeker for truth (sat); a person who is practicing spiritual disciplines; a good or virtuous or honest man, a holy man, saint, sage, seer. Usually this term is applied only to monastics.

Saguna: Possessing attributes or qualities (gunas).

Saguna Brahman: Brahman with attributes, such as mercy, omnipotence, omniscience, etc.; the Absolute conceived as the Creator, Preserver, and Destroyer of the universe; also the Personal God according to the Vedanta.

Sahaja: Natural; innate; spontaneous; inborn.

Sahaja Nirvikalpa Samadhi: Natural, non-dual state of Brahmic Consciousness.

Sahaja samadhi: See Sahaja Nirvikalpa Samadhi.

Sahasrara: The "thousand-petalled lotus" of the brain. The highest center of consciousness, the point at which the spirit (atma) and the bodies (koshas) are integrated and from which they are disengaged.

Samadarshana: Equal vision; seeing all things equally; equal-sightedness; equanimity.

Samadhi: The state of superconsciousness where Absoluteness is experienced attended with all-knowledge and joy; Oneness; here the mind becomes identified with the object of meditation; the meditator and the meditated, thinker and thought become one in perfect absorption of the mind.

Samsara: Life through repeated births and deaths; the wheel of birth and death; the process of earthly life.

Samsari: The transmigrating soul.

Samsaric: Having to do with samsara; involved with samsara; partaking of the traits or qualities of samsara.

Samsarin: One who is subject to samsara–repeated births and deaths–and who is deluded by its appearances, immersed in ignorance.

Samskara: Impression in the mind, either conscious or subconscious, produced by action or experience in this or previous lives; propensities of the mental residue of impressions; subliminal activators; prenatal tendency. See Vasana.

Sanatana Dharma: "The Eternal Religion," also known as "Arya Dharma," "the religion of those who strive upward [Aryas]." Hinduism.

Sanatana Dharmi: One who follows Sanatana Dharma.

Sankalpa: A life-changing wish, desire, volition, resolution, will, determination, or intention—not a mere momentary aspiration, but an empowering act of will that persists until the intention is fully realized. It is an act of spiritual, divine creative will inherent in each person as a power of the Atma.

Sannyas(a): Renunciation; monastic life. Sannyasa literally means "total throwing away," in the sense of absolute rejection of worldly life, ways and attitudes. True sannyas is based on viveka and vairagya. It is not just a mode of external life, but a profound insight and indifference to the things of the world and the world itself—not the world of God's creation, but the world of human ignorance, illusion, folly and suffering which binds all sentient beings to the wheel of continual birth and death. The sannyasi's one goal is liberation through total purification and enlightenment. His creed is Shankara's renowned Vedanta in Half a Verse: "Brahman is real. The world is illusion. The jiva is none other than Brahman."

Sannyasi(n): A renunciate; a monk.

Sat: Existence; reality; truth; being; a title of Brahman, the Absolute or Pure Being.

Sat Chakras: The six chakras: Muladhara, Swadhishthana, Manipura, Anahata, Vishuddha and Ajna, located at the base of the spine, in the spine a little less than midway between the base of the spine and the area opposite the navel in the spine, the point in the spine opposite the navel, the point in the spine opposite the midpoint of the sternum bone, the point in the spine opposite the hollow of the throat, and the point between the eyebrows, respectively.

Satsang(a): Literally: "company with Truth." Association with god-ly-minded persons. The company of saints and devotees.

Sanskrit: The language of the ancient sages of India and therefore of the Indian scriptures and yoga treatises.

Satchidananda: Existence-Knowledge-Bliss Absolute; Brahman.

Sattwa: Light; purity; harmony, goodness, reality.

Sattwa Guna: Quality of light, purity, harmony, and goodness.

Satya(m): Truth; the Real; Brahman, or the Absolute; truthfulness; honesty.

Savikalpa Samadhi: Samadhi in which there is objective experience or experience of "qualities" and with the triad of knower, knowledge and known; lesser samadhi; cognitive samadhi; samadhi of wisdom; meditation with limited external awareness.

Shabda: Sound; word.

Shadripu: The six enemies to realization of the Self: desire (kama), anger (krodha), greed (lobha), arrogance (mada), delusive attachment (moha) and jealousy (matsarya).

Shakti: Power; energy; force; the Divine Power of becoming; the apparent dynamic aspect of Eternal Being; the Absolute Power or Cosmic Energy; the Divine Feminine.

Shankara: Shankaracharya; Adi (the first) Shankaracharya: The great reformer and re-establisher of Vedic Religion in India around 500 B.C. He is the unparalleled exponent of Advaita (Non-Dual) Vedanta. He also reformed the mode of monastic life and founded (or regenerated) the ancient Swami Order.

Shastra: Scripture; spiritual treatise.

Shiva: A name of God meaning "One Who is all Bliss and the giver of happiness to all." Although classically applied to the Absolute Brahman, Shiva can also refer to God (Ishwara) in His aspect of Dissolver and Liberator (often mistakenly thought of as "destroyer").

Shraddha: Faith; confidence or assurance that arises from personal experience.

Shyama Charan Lahiri: See Lahiri Mahasaya.

Siddha: A perfected–liberated–being, an adept, a seer, a perfect yogi.

Siddha Purusha: A perfectly enlightened being.

Siddhi: Spiritual perfection; psychic power; power; modes of success; attainment; accomplishment; achievement; mastery; supernatural power attained through mantra, meditation, or other yogic practices. From the verb root sidh–to attain.

Sita: The consort of Rama, an avatara of the Divine Mother aspect of God.

Sivananda (Swami): A great twentieth-century Master, founder of the world-wide Divine Life Society, whose books on spiritual life and religion are widely circulated in the West as well as in India.

Soham: "That am I;" the ultimate Atma mantra, the mantra of the Self; the Ajapa Gayatri formula of meditation in which "So" is intoned mentally during natural inhalation and "Ham" is intoned mentally during natural exhalation.

So'ham Bhava: The state of being and awareness: "THAT I am." Gorakhnath says that So'ham Bhava includes total Self-comprehension (ahamta), total Self-mastery (akhanda aishwarya), unbroken awareness of the unity of the Self (swatmata), awareness of the unity of the Self with all phenomenal existence–as the Self (vishwanubhava), knowledge of all within and without the Self–united in the Self (sarvajñatwa).

Sri Yukteswar Giri, Swami: The guru of Paramhansa Yogananda.

Sthira: Fixed; firm; still; steady; stable; enduring.

Sthitaprajna: One who is established in the divine Consciousness or superconsciousness.

Sthiti: Steadiness; condition or state; existence; being; subsistence; preservation.

Sukshma: Fine; subtle; invisible; belonging to a subtler order of existence than the physical.

Sushumna: A subtle passage in the midst of the spinal column, corresponding to the spinal cord, that extends from the base of the spine to the medulla oblongata in the head.

Sushupti: The dreamless sleep state.

Sutra: Literally: a thread; an aphorism with minimum words and maximum sense; a terse sentence; in Buddhism, an entire scripture.

Sutratma: "The thread-Self;" immanent deity of the totality of the subtle bodies, referring to the Gita verse: "All this creation is strung on me like pearls on a thread" (7:7).

Swabhava: One's own inherent disposition, nature, or potentiality; inherent state of mind; state of inner being.

Swadharma: One's own natural (innate) duty (dharma, based on their karma and samskara. One's own prescribed duty in life according to the eternal law (ritam).

Swayambhu: Self-existent or self-generated.

Swayamprakash(a): Self-luminous; self-illumined.

Tamas: Dullness, darkness, inertia, folly, and ignorance.

Tamasic: Possessed of the qualities of the tamo guna (tamas). Ignorant; dull; inert; and dark.

Tapasya: Austerity; practical (i.e., result-producing) spiritual discipline; spiritual force. Literally it means the generation of heat or energy, but is always used in a symbolic manner, referring to spiritual practice and its effect, especially the roasting of karmic seeds, the burning up of karma.

Tattwa: "Thatness." Principle; element; the essence of things; truth; reality.

Tilak: A sacred mark made on the forehead or between the eyebrows denoting what form of God the person worships.

Turiya: The state of pure consciousness. *A Ramakrishna-Vedanta Wordbook* defines it as: "The superconscious; lit., 'the Fourth,' in relation to the three ordinary states of consciousness—waking, dreaming, and dreamless sleep—which it transcends."

Upadhi: Adjunct; association; superimposed thing or attribute that veils and gives a colored view of the substance beneath it; limiting adjunct; instrument; vehicle; body; a technical term used in Vedanta philosophy for any superimposition that gives a limited view of the Absolute and makes It appear as the relative.

Upanayana(m): Investure with the sacred thread (yajnopavita) and initiation into the Gayatri mantra.

Upanishads: Books (of varying lengths) of the philosophical teachings of the ancient sages of India on the knowledge of Absolute Reality. The upanishads contain two major themes: (1) the individual self (atman) and the Supreme Self (Paramatman) are one in essence, and (2) the goal of life is the realization/manifestation of this unity, the realization of God (Brahman). There are eleven principal upanishads: Isha, Kena, Katha, Prashna, Mundaka, Mandukya, Taittiriya, Aitareya, Chandogya, Brihadaranyaka, and Shvetashvatara, all of which were commented on by Shankara, Ramanuja and Madhavacharya, thus setting the seal of authenticity on them.

Urdhvareta yogi: A yogi in whom the subtle (including sexual) energies flow upwards.

Urdhvareta(s): The state of being an urdhvareta yogi; one who is an urdhvareta yogi.

Vairagya: Non-attachment; detachment; dispassion; absence of desire; disinterest; or indifference. Indifference towards and disgust for all worldly things and enjoyments.

Vaishnava: A devotee of Vishnu.

Vaishnavism: A religious sect of Hinduism, whose members follow the path of devotion to God as Vishnu or one of Vishnu's avatars—especially Sri Rama, Sri Krishna, and (in Bengal) Sri Chaitanya.

Vaishwanara: Universal Being; the Self of the waking state; the sum-total of the created beings; Brahman in the form of the universe; Cosmic Fire; the god of fire; the digestive fire; the gastric fire; the sum-total of the created beings; Brahma in the form of the universe; Virat-purusha.

Vasana: Subtle desire; a tendency created in a person by the doing of an action or by experience; it induces the person to repeat the action or to seek a repetition of the experience; the subtle impression in the mind capable of developing itself into action; it is the cause of birth and experience in general; an aggregate or bundle of samskaras–the impressions of actions that remain unconsciously in the mind.

Vasana(s): A bundle or aggregate of such samskaras.

Vayu: Air; vital breath; prana.

Vijnana: The highest knowledge, beyond mere theoretical knowledge (jnana); transcendental knowledge or knowing; experiential knowledge; a high state of spiritual realization–intimate knowledge of God in which all is seen as manifestations of Brahman; knowledge of the Self.

Vikshepa: The projecting power of the mind, causing external involvement; the movement of pushing outward or away; the projecting power of ignorance; mental restlessness resulting from the awareness moving out from the center that is the Self; Distractions; causes of distractions; projection; false projection; the tossing of the mind which obstructs concentration.

Virya: Strength; power; energy; courage; seminal energy.

Vishwaprana: The universal life force (prana).

Vishnu: "The all-pervading;" God as the Preserver.

Vishuddha: Supremely pure; totally pure.

Viveka: Discrimination between the Real and the unreal, between the Self and the non-Self, between the permanent and the impermanent; right intuitive discrimination.

Vivekananda (Swami): The chief disciple of Sri Ramakrishna, who brought the message of Vedanta to the West at the end of the nineteenth century.

Vritti: Thought-wave; mental modification; mental whirlpool; a ripple in the chitta (mind substance).

Vyasa: One of the greatest sages of India, commentator on the Yoga Sutras, author of the Mahabharata (which includes the Bhagavad Gita), the Brahma Sutras, and the codifier of the Vedas.

Yajnopavita: Sacred thread. A triple thread worn by the twice-born (dwijas) that represents the threefold Brahman. It is essential for the performance of all the rites of the twice-born. Usually worn only by Brahmins, originally it was worn by Kshatriyas and Vaishyas as well.

Yama: Restraint; the five Don'ts of Yoga: 1) ahimsa—non-violence, non-injury, harmlessness; 2) satya—truthfulness, honesty; 3) asteya—non-stealing, honesty, non-misappropriativeness; 4) brahmacharya—continence; 5) aparigraha—non-possessiveness, non-greed, non-selfishness, non-acquisitiveness. These five are called the Great Vow (Observance, Mahavrata) in the Yoga Sutras.

Yoga: Literally, "joining" or "union" from the Sanskrit root yuj. Union with the Supreme Being, or any practice that makes for such union. Meditation that unites the individual spirit with God, the Supreme Spirit. The name of the philosophy expounded by the sage Patanjali, teaching the process of union of the individual with the Universal Soul.

Yoga Nidra/Yoganidra: A state of half-contemplation and half-sleep; light yogic sleep when the individual retains slight awareness; state between sleep and wakefulness.

Yoga Sutras: The oldest known writing on the subject of yoga, written by the sage Patanjali, a yogi of ancient India, and considered the most authoritative text on yoga. Also known as Yoga Darshana, it is the basis of the Yoga Philosophy which is based on the philosophical system known as Sankhya.

Yoga Vashishtha: A classical treatise on Yoga, containing the instructions of the Rishi Vashishta to Lord Rama on meditation and spiritual life.

Yogananda (Paramhansa): The most influential yogi of the twentieth century in the West, author of *Autobiography of a Yogi* and founder of Self-Realization Fellowship in America.

Yogeshwara: Lord of Yoga; a title of both Shiva and Lord Krishna.

Yogiraj: "King of Yogis," a title often given to an advanced yogi, especially a teacher of yogi.

Yukti: Reasoning (about something); skill; cleverness; device.

ABOUT THE AUTHOR

Swami Nirmalananda Giri (Abbot George Burke) is the founder and director of the Light of the Spirit Monastery (Atma Jyoti Ashram) in Cedar Crest, New Mexico, USA.

In his many pilgrimages to India, he had the opportunity of meeting some of India's greatest spiritual figures, including Swami Sivananda of Rishikesh and Anandamayi Ma. During his first trip to India he was made a member of the ancient Swami Order by Swami Vidyananda Giri, a direct disciple of Paramhansa Yogananda, who had himself been given sannyas by the Shankaracharya of Puri, Jagadguru Bharati Krishna Tirtha.

In the United States he also encountered various Christian saints, including Saint John Maximovich of San Francisco and Saint Philaret Voznesensky of New York.

For many years Swami Nirmalananda has researched the identity of Jesus Christ and his teachings with India and Sanatana Dharma, including Yoga. It is his conclusion that Jesus lived in India for most of his life, and was a yogi and Sanatana Dharma missionary to the West. After his resurrection he returned to India and lived the rest of his life in the Himalayas.

He has written extensively on these and other topics, many of which are posted at OCOY.org.

ATMA JYOTI ASHRAM
(LIGHT OF THE SPIRIT MONASTERY)

Atma Jyoti Ashram (Light of the Spirit Monastery) is a monastic community for those men who seek direct experience of the Spirit through yoga meditation, traditional yogic discipline, Sanatana Dharma and the life of the sannyasi in the tradition of the Order of Shankara. Our lineage is in the Giri branch of the Order.

The public outreach of the monastery is through its website, OCOY.org (Original Christianity and Original Yoga). There you will find many articles on Original Christianity and Original Yoga, including *The Christ of India*. *Foundations of Yoga* and *How to Be a Yogi* are practical guides for anyone seriously interested in living the Yoga Life.

You will also discover many other articles on leading an effective spiritual life, including *Soham Yoga: The Yoga of the Self* and *Spiritual Benefits of a Vegetarian Diet*, as well as the "Dharma for Awakening" series—in-depth commentaries on these spiritual classics: the Bhagavad Gita, the Upanishads, the Dhammapada, the Tao Teh King and more.

You can listen to podcasts by Swami Nirmalananda on meditation, the Yoga Life, and remarkable spiritual people he has met in India and elsewhere, at http://ocoy.org/podcasts/

You can watch over 100 videos on these topics and more, including recordings of online satsangs where Swami Nirmalananda answers various questions on practical aspects of spiritual life.

Visit our Youtube channel here:
Youtube.com/@lightofthespirit

Reading for Awakening

Light of the Spirit Press presents books on spiritual wisdom and
Original Christianity and Original Yoga. From our "Dharma for
Awakening" series (practical commentaries on the world's scriptures) to
books on how to meditate and live a successful spiritual life, you will
find books that are informative, helpful, and even entertaining.

Light of the Spirit Press is the publishing house of Light of the Spirit
Monastery (Atma Jyoti Ashram) in Cedar Crest, New Mexico, USA. Our
books feature the writings of the founder and director of the monastery,
Swami Nirmalananda Giri (Abbot George Burke) which are also found
on the monastery's website, OCOY.org.

We invite you to explore our publications in the following pages.

Find out more about our publications at
lightofthespiritpress.com

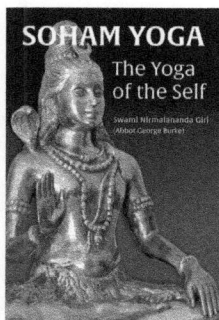

Soham Yoga
The Yoga of the Self

A complete and in-depth guide to effective meditation and the life that supports it, this important book explains with clarity and insight what real yoga is, and why and how to practice Soham Yoga meditation.

Discovered centuries ago by the Nath yogis, this simple and classic approach to self-realization has no "secrets," requires no "initiation," and is easily accessible to the serious modern yogi.

Includes helpful, practical advice on leading an effective spiritual life and many Illuminating quotes on Soham from Indian scriptures and great yogis.

"This book is a complete spiritual path." –Arnold Van Wie

Light of Soham
The Life and Teachings of Sri Gajanana Maharaj of Nashik

Gajanan Murlidhar Gupte, later known as Gajanana Maharaj, led an unassuming life, to all appearances a normal unmarried man of contemporary society. Crediting his personal transformation to the practice of the Soham mantra, he freely shared this practice with a small number of disciples, whom he simply called his friends. Strictly avoiding the trap of gurudom, he insisted that his friends be self-reliant and not be dependent on him for their spiritual progress. Yet he was uniquely able to assist them in their inner development.

The Inspired Wisdom of Gajanana Maharaj
A Practical Commentary on Leading an Effectual Spiritual Life

Presents the teachings and sayings of the great twentieth-century Soham yogi Gajanana Maharaj, with a commentary by Swami Nirmalananda.

The author writes: "In reading about Gajanana Maharaj I encountered a holy personality that eclipsed all others for me. In his words I found a unique wisdom that altered my perspective on what yoga, yogis, and gurus should be.

"But I realized that through no fault of their own, many Western readers need a clarification and expansion of Maharaj's meaning to get the right understanding of his words. This commentary is meant to help my friends who, like me have found his words 'a light in the darkness.'"

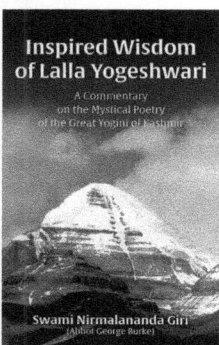

Inspired Wisdom of Lalla Yogeshwari
A Commentary on the Mystical Poetry
of the Great Yogini of Kashmir

Lalla Yogeshwari was a great fourteenth-century yogini and wandering ascetic of Kashmir, whose mystic poetry were the earliest compositions in the Kashmiri language. She was in the tradition of the Nath Yogi Sampradaya whose meditation practice is that of Soham Sadhana: the joining of the mental repetition of Soham Mantra with the natural breath.

Swami Nirmalananda's commentary mines the treasures of Lalleshwari's mystic poems and presents his reflections in an easily intelligible fashion for those wishing to put these priceless teachings on the path of yogic self-transformation into practice.

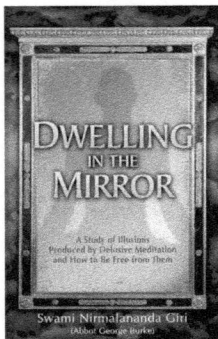

Dwelling in the Mirror

A Study of Illusions Produced By Delusive Meditation
And How to Be Free from Them

Swami Nirmalananda says of this book:

"Over and over people have mistaken trivial and pathological conditions for enlightenment, written books, given seminars and gained a devoted following.

"Most of these unfortunate people were completely unreachable with reason. Yet there are those who can have an experience and realize that it really cannot be real, but a vagary of their mind. Some may not understand that on their own, but can be shown by others the truth about it. For them and those that may one day be in danger of meditation-produced delusions I have written this brief study."

BOOKS ON YOGA & SPIRITUAL LIFE

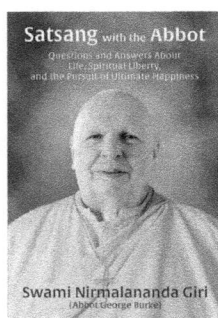

Satsang with the Abbot

Questions and Answers about Life, Spiritual Liberty,
and the Pursuit of Ultimate Happiness

The questions in this book range from the most sublime to the most practical. "How can I attain samadhi?" "I am married with children. How can I lead a spiritual life?" "What is Self-realization?" "How important is belief in karma and reincarnation?"

In Swami Nirmalananda's replies to these questions the reader will discover common sense, helpful information, and a guiding light for their journey through and beyond the forest of cliches, contradictions, and confusion of yoga, Hinduism, Christianity, and metaphysical thought.

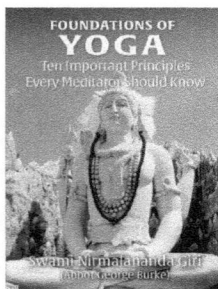

Foundations of Yoga

Ten Important Principles Every Meditator Should Know

An introduction to the important foundation principles of Patanjali's Yoga: Yama and Niyama

Yama and Niyama are often called the Ten Commandments of Yoga, but they have nothing to do with the ideas of sin and virtue or good and evil as dictated by some cosmic potentate. Rather they are determined by a thoroughly practical, pragmatic basis: that which strengthens and facilitates our yoga practice should be observed and that which weakens or hinders it should be avoided.

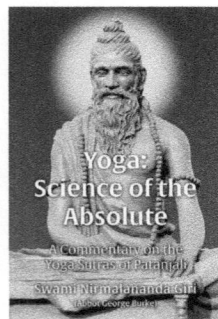

Yoga: Science of the Absolute

A Commentary on the Yoga Sutras of Patanjali

The Yoga Sutras of Patanjali is the most authoritative text on Yoga as a practice. It is also known as the Yoga Darshana because it is the fundamental text of Yoga as a philosophy.

In this commentary, Swami Nirmalananda draws on the age-long tradition regarding this essential text, including the commentaries of Vyasa and Shankara, the most highly regarded writers on Indian philosophy and practice, as well as I. K. Taimni and other authoritative commentators, and adds his own ideas based on half a century of study and practice. Serious students of yoga will find this an essential addition to their spiritual studies.

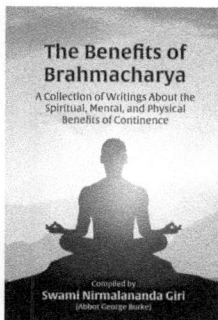

The Benefits of Brahmacharya

A Collection of Writings About the Spiritual, Mental, and Physical Benefits of Continence

"Brahmacharya is the basis for morality. It is the basis for eternal life. It is a spring flower that exhales immortality from its petals." Swami Sivananda

This collection of articles from a variety of authorities including Mahatma Gandhi, Sri Ramakrishna, Swami Vivekananda. Swamis Sivananda and Chidananda of the Divine Life Society, Swami Nirmalananda, and medical experts, presents many facets of brahmacharya and will prove of immense value to all who wish to grow spiritually.

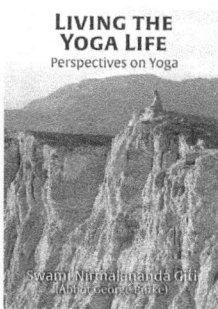

Living the Yoga Life

Perspectives on Yoga

"Dive deep; otherwise you cannot get the gems at the bottom of the ocean. You cannot pick up the gems if you only float on the surface." Sri Ramakrishna

In *Living the Yoga Life* Swami Nirmalananda shares the gems he has found from a lifetime of "diving deep." This collection of reflections and short essays addresses the key concepts of yoga philosophy that are so easy to take for granted. Never content with the accepted cliches about yoga sadhana, the yoga life, the place of a guru, the nature of Brahman and our unity with It, Swami Nirmalananda's insights on these and other facets of the yoga life will inspire, provoke, enlighten, and even entertain.

Spiritual Benefits of a Vegetarian Diet

The health benefits of a vegetarian diet are well known, as are the ethical aspects. But the spiritual advantages should be studied by anyone involved in meditation, yoga, or any type of spiritual practice.

Diet is a crucial aspect of emotional, intellectual, and spiritual development as well. For diet and consciousness are interrelated, and purity of diet is an effective aid to purity and clarity of consciousness.

The major thing to keep in mind when considering the subject of vegetarianism is its relevancy in relation to our explorations of consciousness. We need only ask: Does it facilitate my spiritual growth–the development and expansion of my consciousness? The answer is Yes.

BOOKS ON THE SACRED SCRIPTURES OF INDIA

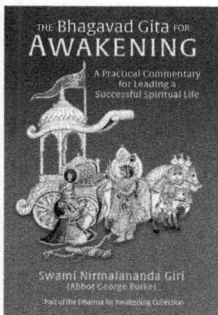

The Bhagavad Gita for Awakening

A Practical Commentary for Leading a Successful Spiritual Life

Drawing from the teachings of Sri Ramakrishna, Jesus, Paramhansa Yogananda, Ramana Maharshi, Swami Vivekananda, Swami Sivananda of Rishikesh, Papa Ramdas, and other spiritual masters and teachers, as well as his own experiences, Swami Nirmalananda illustrates the teachings of the Gita with stories which make the teachings of Krishna in the Gita vibrant and living.

From *Publisher's Weekly*: "[The author] enthusiastically explores the story as a means for knowing oneself, the cosmos, and one's calling within it. His plainspoken insights often distill complex lessons with simplicity and sagacity. Those with a deep interest in the Gita will find much wisdom here."

The Upanishads for Awakening
A Practical Commentary on India's Classical Scriptures

The sacred scriptures of India are vast. Yet they are only different ways of seeing the same thing, the One Thing which makes them both valid and ultimately harmonious. That unifying subject is Brahman: God the Absolute, beyond and besides whom there is no "other" whatsoever. The thirteen major Upanishads are the fountainhead of all expositions of Brahman.

Swamiji illumines the Upanishads' value for spiritual seekers from the unique perspective of a lifetime of study and practice of both Eastern and Western spirituality.

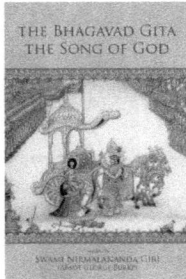

The Bhagavad Gita–The Song of God

Often called the "Bible" of Hinduism, the Bhagavad Gita is found in households throughout India and has been translated into every major language of the world. Literally billions of copies have been handwritten or printed.

The clarity of this translation by Swami Nirmalananda makes for easy reading, while the rich content makes this the ideal "study" Gita. As the original Sanskrit language is so rich, often there are several accurate translations for the same word, which are noted in the text, giving the spiritual student the needed understanding of the fullness of the Gita.

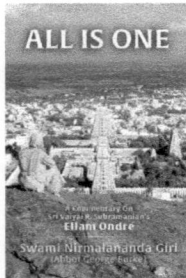

All Is One
A Commentary On Sri Vaiyai R. Subramanian's Ellam Ondre

Swami Nirmalananda's insightful commentary brings even further light to Ellam Ondre's refreshing perspective on what Unity signifies, and the path to its realization.

Written in the colorful and well-informed style typical of his other commentaries, it is a timely and important contribution to Advaitic literature that explains Unity as the fruit of yoga sadhana, rather than mere wishful thinking or some vague intellectual gymnastic, as is so commonly taught by the modern "Advaita gurus."

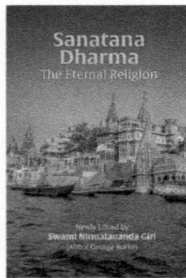

Sanatana Dharma
The Eternal Religion

Sanatana Dharma, commonly called Hinduism, is not just beautiful temples, colorful festivals, gurus and unusual beliefs. It is, simply put, "The Way Things Are" on a cosmic scale. It is the facts of existence and transcendence.

Swami Nirmalananda has edited for the modern reader a book originally printed nearly one hundred years ago in Varanasi, India, for use as a textbook by students of Benares Hindu University. Its original title was *Sanatana Dharma, An Advanced Text Book of Hindu Religion and Ethics.*

A Brief Sanskrit Glossary
A Spiritual Student's Guide to Essential Sanskrit Terms

This Sanskrit glossary contains full translations and explanations of hundreds of the most commonly used spiritual Sanskrit terms, and will help students of the Bhagavad Gita, the Upanishads, the Yoga Sutras of Patanjali, and other Indian scriptures and philosophical works to expand their vocabularies to include the Sanskrit terms contained in these, and gain a fuller understanding in their studies.

BOOKS ON ORIGINAL CHRISTIANITY

The Christ of India
The Story of Original Christianity

"Original Christianity" is the teaching of both Jesus and his Apostle Saint Thomas in India. Although it was new to the Mediterranean world, it was really the classical, traditional teachings of the rishis of India that even today comprise the Eternal Dharma, that goes far beyond religion into realization.

In *The Christ of India* Swami Nirmalananda presents what those ancient teachings are, as well as the growing evidence that Jesus spent much of his "Lost Years" in India and Tibet. This is also the story of how the original teachings of Jesus and Saint Thomas thrived in India for centuries before the coming of the European colonialists.

May a Christian Believe in Reincarnation?

Discover the real and surprising history of reincarnation and Christianity.

A growing number of people are open to the subject of past lives, and the belief in rebirth–reincarnation, metempsychosis, or transmigration–is commonplace. It often thought that belief in reincarnation and Christianity are incompatible. But is this really true? May a Christian believe in reincarnation? The answer may surprise you.

"Those needing evidence that a belief in reincarnation is in accordance with teachings of the Christ need look no further: Plainly laid out and explained in an intelligent manner from one who has spent his life on a Christ-like path of renunciation and prayer/meditation."—Christopher T. Cook

The Unknown Lives of Jesus and Mary
Compiled from Ancient Records and Mystical Revelations

"There are also many other things which Jesus did, the which, if they should be written every one, I suppose that even the world itself could not contain the books that should be written." (Gospel of Saint John, final verse)

You can discover much of those "many other things" in this unique compilation of ancient records and mystical revelations, which includes historical records of the lives of Jesus Christ and his Mother Mary that have been accepted and used by the Church since apostolic times. This treasury of little-known stories of Jesus' life will broaden the reader's understanding of what Christianity really was in its original form.

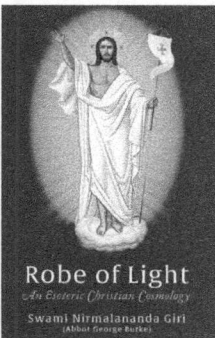

Robe of Light
An Esoteric Christian Cosmology

In *Robe of Light* Swami Nirmalananda explores the whys and wherefores of the mystery of creation. From the emanation of the worlds from the very Being of God, to the evolution of the souls to their ultimate destiny as perfected Sons of God, the ideal progression of creation is described. Since the rebellion of Lucifer and the fall of Adam and Eve from Paradise flawed the normal plan of evolution, a restoration was necessary. How this came about is the prime subject of this insightful study.

Moreover, what this means to aspirants for spiritual perfection is expounded, with a compelling knowledge of the scriptures and of the mystical traditions of East and West.

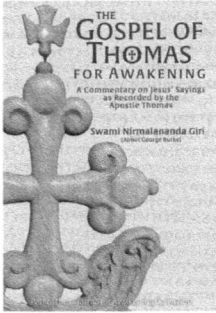

The Gospel of Thomas for Awakening
A Commentary on Jesus' Sayings as Recorded by the Apostle Thomas

When the Apostles dispersed to the various area of the world, Thomas travelled to India, where evidence shows Jesus spent his Lost Years, and which had been the source of the wisdom which he had brought to the "West."

The Christ that Saint Thomas quotes in this ancient text is quite different than the Christ presented by popular Christianity. Through his unique experience and study with both Christianity and Indian religion, Swami Nirmalananda clarifies the sometimes enigmatic sayings of Jesus in an informative and inspiring way.

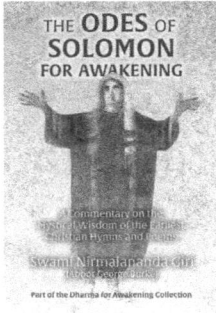

The Odes of Solomon for Awakening
A Commentary on the Mystical Wisdom of the Earliest Christian Hymns and Poems

The Odes of Solomon is the earliest Christian hymn-book, and therefore one of the most important early Christian documents. Since they are mystical and esoteric, they teach and express the classical and universal mystical truths of Christianity, revealing a Christian perspective quite different than that of "Churchianity," and present the path of Christhood that all Christians are called to.

"Fresh and soothing, these 41 poems and hymns are beyond delightful! I deeply appreciate Abbot George Burke's useful and illuminating insight and find myself spiritually re-animated." –John Lawhn

The Aquarian Gospel for Awakening (2 Volumes)
A Practical Commentary on Levi Dowling's Classic Life of Jesus Christ

Written in 1908 by the American mystic Levi Dowling, The Aquarian Gospel of Jesus the Christ answers many questions about Jesus' life that the Bible doesn't address. Dowling presents a universal message found at the heart of all valid religions, a broad vision of love and wisdom that will ring true with Christians who are attracted to Christ but put off by the narrow views of the tradition that has been given his name.

Swami Nirmalananda's commentary is a treasure-house of knowledge and insight that even further expands Dowling's vision of the true Christ and his message.

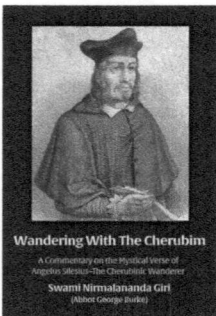

Wandering With The Cherubim
A Commentary on the Mystical Verse of Angelus Silesius–The Cherubinic Wanderer"

Johannes Scheffler, who wrote under the name Angelus Silesius, was a mystic and a poet. In his most famous book, "The Cherubinic Wanderer," he expressed his mystical vision.

Swami Nirmalananda reveals the timelessness of his mystical teachings and The Cherubinic Wanderer's practical value for spiritual seekers. He does this in an easily intelligible fashion for those wishing to put those priceless teachings into practice.

"Set yourself on the journey of this mystical poetry made accessible through this very beautifully commentated text. It is text that submerges one in the philosophical context of the Advaita notion of Non Duality. Swami Nirmalananda's commentary is indispensable in understanding higher philosophical ideas, for Swami's language, while readily approachable, is rich in deep essence of the teachings."–Savitri

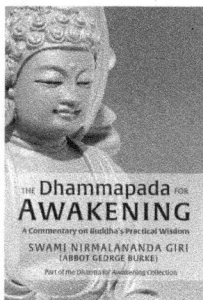

The Dhammapada for Awakening
A Commentary on Buddha's Practical Wisdom

Swami Nirmalananda's commentary on this classic Buddhist scripture explores the Buddha's answers to the urgent questions, such as "How can I find find lasting peace, happiness and fulfillment that seems so elusive?" and "What can I do to avoid many of the miseries big and small that afflict all of us?" Drawing on his personal experience, the author sheds new light on the Buddha's eternal wisdom.

"Swami Nirmalananda's commentary is well crafted and stacked with anecdotes, humor, literary references and beautiful quotes from the Buddha. I have come to consider it a guide to daily living." –Rev. Gerry Nangle

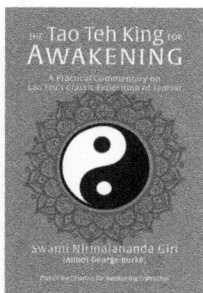

The Tao Teh King for Awakening
A Practical Commentary on Lao Tzu's Classic Exposition of Taoism

"The Tao does all things, yet our interior disposition determines our success or failure in coming to knowledge of the unknowable Tao."

Lao Tzu's classic writing, the *Tao Teh King*, has fascinated scholars and seekers for centuries. Swami Nirmalananda offers a commentary that makes the treasures of Lao Tzu's teachings accessible and applicable for the sincere seeker.

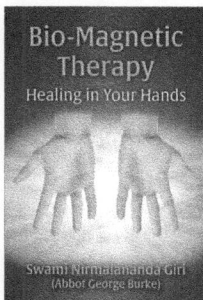

Bio-Magnetic Therapy
Healing in Your Hands

In *Bio-Magnetic Therapy* Swami Nirmalananda teaches the techniques to strengthen your vitality and improve the body's natural healing ability in yourself and in others with specific methods that anyone can use.

Bio-Magnetic Therapy is a simple and natural way to increase the flow of life-force into the body for general good health and to stimulate the supply and flow of life-force to a troubled area that has become vitality-starved through some obstruction. It does not cure; it simply aids the body to cure itself by supplying it with curative force.

How to Read the Tarot
A Practical Method Using the Rider-Waite Deck

Discover Swami Nirmalananda's unique method of reading the Tarot specifically for use with the Rider-Waite deck, with detailed instructions on how to use the cards to develop your intuition for understanding the meanings of the cards. Illustrated with color plates of each of the cards of the Rider-Waite deck with full explanations of their symbolism.

More Titles
The Four Gospels for Awakening
Light from Eternal Lamps
Vivekachudamani: The Crest Jewel of Discrimination for Awakening

www.ingramcontent.com/pod-product-compliance
Lightning Source LLC
Chambersburg PA
CBHW021043090426
42738CB00006B/156